The Rescue of Joshua Glover

Ohio University Press Series
on Law, Society, and Politics in the Midwest

SERIES EDITOR: PAUL FINKELMAN

H. ROBERT BAKER

The Rescue
of Joshua Glover

A FUGITIVE SLAVE, THE CONSTITUTION,
AND THE COMING OF THE CIVIL WAR

Ohio University Press   Athens

Ohio University Press, Athens, Ohio 45701
www.ohio.edu/oupress
© 2006 by Ohio University Press

Ohio University Press books are printed on acid-free paper ⊚ ™

HARDCOVER 14 13 12 11 10 09 08 07   5 4 3 2 1
PAPERBACK 14 13 12 11 10 09 08 07   5 4 3 2 1

First paperback printing in 2007
ISBN-10   0-8214-1813-0
ISBN-13   978-0-8214-1813-0

Library of Congress Cataloging-in-Publication Data

Baker, H. Robert.
  The rescue of Joshua Glover : a fugitive slave, the constitution, and the coming of the
civil war / H. Robert Baker.
      p. cm. — (Ohio University Press series on law, society, and politics in the midwest)
  Includes bibliographical references and index.
  ISBN-13: 978-0-8214-1690-7 (cloth : alk. paper)
  ISBN-10: 0-8214-1690-1 (cloth : alk. paper)
  1. Fugitive slaves—Legal status, laws, etc.—United States.—History—19th century. 2.
Fugitive slaves—Legal status, laws, etc.—Wisconsin—History—19th century. 3. United
States. Fugitive slave law (1850) 4. Booth, Sherman M.—Trials, litigation, etc. 5. Glover,
Joshua. I. Title.
  KF4545.S5.B35 2007
  342.7308'7—dc22

                                                                              2006022720

For Jan,

who lifts those heavy clouds . . .

you dig?

CONTENTS

ILLUSTRATIONS

PREFACE

It is doubtful that many in Wisconsin knew of Joshua Glover on March 10, 1854. He had been living and working on the outskirts of Racine, a burgeoning port city, for about two years. Glover was quiet and inconspicuous. Then, on March 10, he was arrested after nightfall as a fugitive slave, the legal property of Benammi Garland of Missouri. The following day, news of his arrest and incarceration in a Milwaukee jail was telegraphed across the state. His calamity became the abolitionist cause in Wisconsin. His rescue at the end of the day on March 11 became the stuff of legend, and these events helped propel the Republican Party into power.

Not everyone celebrated Glover's rescue. It was a black eye for federal officers charged with enforcing the Fugitive Slave Act. Slaveholding states threatened secession if their citizens' slave property was not protected when it fled northward, and many believed that execution of the law was vital to the survival of the Union. News that the first attempt to enforce the act in Wisconsin had prompted several thousand to gather outside the county jail, rescue the fugitive, and spirit him out of the country did little to reassure slaveholders that their northern brethren were upholding the law. Embarrassed, the U.S. district attorney brought charges against the principals involved in the rescue.

For the next six years, the federal government's efforts to punish Glover's rescuers met with the same kind of dogged resistance as had the attempt to return the fugitive Joshua Glover to slavery. The Wisconsin Supreme Court freed the rescuers on a writ of habeas corpus and, in the process, declared the Fugitive Slave Act unconstitutional. Nor did this resistance end in the courts. Antislavery Republicans came to power in Wisconsin and arrayed the powers of the legislature and the executive against the Fugitive Slave Act. This opposition became more stubborn over time, setting Wisconsin in defiance of the federal government through the coming of the Civil War.

This book traces the means by which Wisconsinites resisted the Fugitive Slave Act. It was a resistance imposed in the name of the Constitution against the settled judgment of the U.S. Supreme Court. To modern eyes, the sight of such resistance to the Court's constitutional pronouncements by a people to whom the rule of law was an oft-intoned mantra may appear a fundamental contradiction. Not so for antebellum Americans. Resistance to the Supreme Court sprang from a constitutional source—namely, the popular belief that the Constitution belonged in the last instance to the people. This was not an age in which the courts had a lock on constitutional interpretation. Judicial officers may have interpreted the Constitution, but so did legislators, governors, and even the people at the polls. The constant struggle to find meaning in the Constitution both fueled support for enforcement of the Fugitive Slave Act (no matter how distasteful those supporters found its content) and animated resistance against it. Here was the thread that bound all Americans into one polity—the notion that, in the last instance, the final arbiter of the Constitution was the people themselves.

This thread tied together not only the supporters and detractors of Glover's rescue but also myriad political issues, constitutional disputes, and cultural divides in Wisconsin society. It began with citizenship, for among its duties are both respect for the ordinary process of law and the defense of fundamental rights. To understand this properly, one must explain how and why these duties and privileges were denied to black Americans. This was not an issue that anyone in the 1850s could ignore. The slavery question hung on nearly every political election. Although Wisconsin's free black population was miniscule and many whites rarely came into contact with blacks, culturally they were bound together by the forms provided in sentimental literature and popular entertainment. Everywhere, the rescue of Joshua Glover was a reference point for Wisconsinites' struggle to fix meaning to these complicated questions about their constitutional order. In short, it was the central event in Wisconsin during the political scuffles and ideological battles that marked the coming of the Civil War.

Understanding the popular origins of constitutionalism and appropriate (and inappropriate) means of constitutional resistance in the 1850s means embracing a host of unsettling issues. Chief among them was the consequence of resistance to the Fugitive Slave Act. It was a contributor to the snapping of the bonds that held the Union together. Constitutional resistance had internal problems as well, problems that its proponents failed at times to resolve. This means understanding why white Wisconsinites were determined to stand up for the rights of a fugitive slave but unwilling to extend suffrage to their state's free blacks. It means addressing why the principles of popular resistance invoked by Glover's rescuers sowed the seeds of their own destruction. It also means understanding the inconsistencies of abolitionists and, sometimes, their failure to live up to the high standard they set for political and personal action.

There are many to thank for completion of this project. I owe much to Joyce Appleby, my mentor, whose critical eye and firm tone helped to discipline my somewhat eccentric and stubborn mind. DeLloyd J. Guth read and commented upon the entire manuscript, and Kristen Foster provided cogent cultural critiques for me. Important criticisms and suggestions were also provided by Gordon Wood, Larry Kramer, Greg Vanderbilt, Patricia Tilburg, Dan Hamilton, Bryan Camp, Sean Overland, Ted Porter, Joan Waugh, Karen Orren, Richard Drew, Chris Gantner, Eric Altice, Sandy Moats, Arthur Rolston, Gabe Wolfenstein, John Schmidt, and Aaron J. Stockham.

The editorial staff at Ohio University Press has been professional, creative, and a joy to work with. Many thanks to Gillian Berchowitz for her encouragement and helpful suggestions. Anonymous readers for the press forced me to sharpen my arguments and extend my research. Ricky S. Huard is a first-rate editor and has labored mightily to make this book readable. Of course, one cannot work on fugitive slaves without dealing with the prodigious scholarship of Paul Finkelman, and I have borrowed much from his research. I have also benefited from his close reading and astute criticism. I was fortunate to have him as series editor.

Several institutions provided financial and intellectual support at crucial points during the development of this project. The Institute for Constitutional Studies' 2003 summer seminar on judicial review had a strong influence on my ideas. Many thanks to the leaders and participants, particularly Maeva Marcus, whose efforts keep the institute alive. The American Historical Association supported my research with a Littleton-Griswold Grant in the summer of 2005. My colleagues in the Department of History at Marquette University provided a stimulating environment for research and writing. The department generously supplied me with two research assistants, Christopher Chan and Chrissy Jaworski, who deserve praise for their intrepid work. Many thanks go to the archivists and librarians at the Newberry Library, the Young Research Library at UCLA, the Library of Congress, the National Archives at College Park, the National Archives Regional Facility in Chicago, the State Historical Society of Wisconsin, and the Milwaukee Urban Archives. I owe much to Steve Daily and Kevin Abing, the fine archivists of the Milwaukee County Historical Society, whose hard work in the archives and enthusiasm for history helped me launch the project that eventually became this book.

My first debt, even if mentioned near last, is to my parents, who attended to my education from an early age. They introduced me to (in no particular order) Mark Twain, Beethoven, Béla Bartók, the myths of the Greeks, Dave Brubeck, Robert Frost, and other great artists, writers, and thinkers. Raising me in cattle country, they infused in me a sense of civic duty, community participation, and a healthy suspicion of centralized power. It would, I think, have made Jefferson smile.

And finally, I owe a debt of gratitude to Jan Berry Baker. I met her in 2001 at the Green Mill, a jazz club in Chicago, when she was a doctoral student in classical saxophone performance and my project was still in its infancy. She has been a steady source of comments and criticism, and she copyedited the completed manuscript. More important, her many musical performances have gotten me out from behind the computer and into the city. She has nourished my soul and sustained me throughout.

Chicago, Illinois

ONE

Rescuing Joshua Glover

Again I say, let the people abandon their state courts and consent to their being disarmed of the writ of Habeas Corpus, and their liberties are gone.—Not only the liberty of the citizen, but the sovereignty of the state require a firm resistance to this monstrous assumption of power on the part of the federal courts.

—*Milwaukee Sentinel,* March 16, 1854

IT WAS Friday night, March 10, 1854. Seven men stood outside Joshua Glover's cabin. They had departed from the port city of Racine in two wagons just before dusk to make the four-mile journey to Glover's home. The last hundred yards or so they walked, ensuring a stealthy approach. Among the men was Benammi Garland, of St. Louis, the man who claimed Joshua Glover as a fugitive slave owing him service under the laws of Missouri.

Garland had made that claim a month earlier at the court of common pleas in St. Louis. There Garland made proof of his ownership of a slave named Joshua Glover and of Glover's escape in 1852. Garland further swore that he had credible information that his slave was living close to the town of Racine in Wisconsin. How he learned this is something of a mystery. Wisconsin did not have a reputation as a state friendly to the interests of slaveholders. Some suggested later that one of Glover's friends—a mulatto named Nelson Turner with freedom papers from Natchez, Mississippi—played the turncoat. Whatever evidence Garland had was enough to satisfy the St. Louis court, which issued him a certificate of removal.

The certificate licensed the removal of a fugitive slave from one state to another. It gave Garland the authority to take hold of the fugitive and present him before a federal judge or commissioner in Wisconsin. If the proof satisfied the judicial officer—and the threshold for evidence was notoriously low—the fugitive could be removed from Wisconsin to the slave state of Missouri. This was all the legal process needed under the Fugitive Slave Act of 1850, but Garland assiduously attended to legal detail. He took the additional step of securing a warrant for Glover's arrest from Judge Andrew Miller of the U.S. District Court for the Eastern District of Wisconsin. Strictly speaking, the warrant was superfluous. But Garland now had direct authority from a federal court in a free state.[1] Armed with certificate and warrant and aided by two deputy U.S. marshals and four assistants, Garland was ready to apprehend his fugitive slave.

Glover lived in a cabin owned by Duncan Sinclair, a local businessman who employed Glover at his sawmill.[2] Glover was apparently something of a skilled carpenter, for he showed up from time to time in Racine with handcrafted goods for sale. On March 10, Glover was inside with two friends, William Alby and Nelson Turner, playing a game of cards when Garland's party knocked. Glover was suspicious. The U.S. marshals had been there the day before but, finding no one home, had left. A black woman residing there had fled, thinking the men were after her. Glover may not have known any of this, but he undoubtedly knew that slave hunters were abroad in the countryside. Glover told his friends not to answer until they knew who it was. But Turner unbolted the door.[3]

Garland and the marshals rushed in. Glover surely knew their purpose even without the formality of presenting the warrant. He did not give up his freedom willingly. One of the party pressed a pistol to Glover's head, and when Glover pushed it away, Deputy Marshal John Kearney struck him with a cudgel. The blow knocked Glover to the floor, where three men attempted to manacle him, but Glover was strong enough to ward them all off. The others in the arresting party assisted and finally succeeded in manacling Glover. If one is to believe the report of the *Racine Advocate,* he then broke these irons from his wrists. During the fray, William Alby escaped through the window and made haste for Racine, where he tipped off abolitionists about the arrest. The arresting party finally subdued Glover and put him, manacled and bleeding from the head, in one of the wagons.[4]

The other wagon, carrying Kearney and his assistant Daniel F. Houghton, made the four-mile trip back to Racine. There, at the livery stables, they met a welcoming party that included Racine's county sheriff. The cry had gone up that slave catchers were at work, and hundreds had gathered in the immediate excitement. They had sent the delegation to await the marshals and to find out what they had done with Glover. Now they questioned Kearney and his assistant. Houghton denied having taken part in the affair. Kearney curtly replied that he had arrested a man on the authority of a warrant. When interrogated as to where the prisoner had been taken, Kearney retorted that it was none of their business. Sheriff Timothy D. Morris arrested the two officers on suspicion of kidnapping and assault and battery.

Glover was in the wagon with Garland and Deputy Marshal Charles Cotton, headed due north for Milwaukee. Garland and the arresting party had sent the two wagons on different paths to disguise the whereabouts of the fugitive. That they chose to make a thirty-mile journey in the dead of night when Racine was only a few miles away indicated that they expected no hospitality in that staunchly abolitionist town. Milwaukee was larger and more anonymous, and it represented more diverse interests. It had the added benefit of being the seat of Judge Miller and of the U.S. commissioner for Wisconsin, Winfield Smith. Either was authorized by the Fugitive Slave Act to hold a summary proceeding to determine whether Garland could remove Glover from Wisconsin and carry him to Missouri. In Milwaukee, Garland could obtain a hearing and remove his fugitive to Missouri much faster than if he spent the night in Racine. There was less chance of trouble.

Federal officers had reason to be nervous. The year 1854 had not begun auspiciously for the Union, and public sentiment was much agitated on the question of slavery. For nearly two decades, it had invaded almost every political issue and election. The Compromise of 1850 had temporarily papered over the nation's fissures by opening territory gained from Mexico to the possibility of slave settlement, prohibiting it in the Oregon territory, admitting California as a free state, and passing a stringent new fugitive slave law. The law evoked conscientious rants from northerners squeamish about sending people back to slavery, and the first attempts at enforcement led to spectacular and sometimes violent rescues in Boston, Syracuse, and Christiana, Pennsylvania. Nevertheless, the outrage abated with time, and by 1853 many of the fugitives recovered under the new law had been sent back to the South.[5]

Enforcement became markedly more difficult in January 1854, when Senator Stephen Douglas, of Illinois, reported a bill out of committee to organize the Nebraska Territory. The bill contained provisions initially permitting slavery within the territory and giving the territorial legislature, when formed, the power to revisit the issue. His term "popular sovereignty" loosely described the idea that the people who moved to the territories could express their sovereign will about the inclusion or exclusion of slavery. Douglas's own motives had little to do with settlement or slavery; rather, they had to do with enterprise.[6] Like many savvy Illinois businessmen and eastern capitalists, Douglas had invested heavily in the burgeoning metropolis of Chicago and wanted to ensure that the western railroads ran from his city.[7] Because the northern territory was unorganized, however, the more likely route was through New Orleans or St. Louis in the South.[8] Douglas worked hard to get the bill onto the Senate floor quickly. To gain votes from his proslavery colleagues, he included the popular sovereignty clause in the bill.

The Kansas-Nebraska bill fell like a sledgehammer, shattering the earlier compromises. Popular sovereignty, meant by Douglas as a solution to placate all, pleased no one.[9] Southern Whigs and Democrats, with few exceptions, argued that the territories were common property and that not even a territorial legislature could keep slavery out. They defended the extension of slavery on principle. Popular sovereignty, many southerners believed, was a northern ruse to open territories to settlement faster than southerners could fill them. For northerners, popular sovereignty was an outright attempt to extend slavery north of the 36° 30' line agreed to in the Missouri Compromise of 1820. What was worse, a slave territory controlling access to the far West threatened to isolate the free states. In Wisconsin, as elsewhere across the North, outraged citizens organized in opposition to the bill. They formed Nebraska societies, sent petitions to Congress, and contemplated political coalitions to organize this opposition into a third party.

So the arrest of Joshua Glover took on a greater significance than it might otherwise have had. Emotions ran high over slavery in the territories, and the intrusion of federal officers to protect slave property in a free state now looked something like a conspiracy. If free states had to recognize slave property within their borders, then it required no great leap of imagination to reach the next proposition—that slave property was an absolute right protected by the Constitution and enforceable everywhere.[10] What would prevent slaveholders from claiming the right to bring their slaves permanently into states that prohibited slavery? However farfetched this response, it carried force. Douglas's introduction of the Kansas-Nebraska bill to the floor of the Senate still reverberated across Wisconsin in March 1854. It was reason enough for Cotton and Garland to make the nearly six-hour journey on a cold March morning and lodge Joshua Glover in Milwaukee's county jail in the hours just before dawn.

———

March 11, 1854, began as most any other Saturday morning in Milwaukee must have, as wagons from the surrounding countryside rumbled over one of the dozen plank roads that led to the city's shops and laborers contemplated the construction work that lay ahead on a cold day by Lake Michigan. Milwaukee was a city on the move in the 1850s. The bluffs that greeted Milwaukee's visitors by lake were constantly being graded to allow for easier construction and settlement. Thousands flowed into the city every year—ten thousand between 1850 and 1855 alone—and tens of thousands more spread to Wisconsin's prairies in search of farmland to buy or lease. Entrepreneurs erected hundreds of dwellings and business blocks each year: not just frame buildings of timber on "the California model" but permanent edifices in Milwaukee's trademark cream-colored brick, "unequalled," said one visitor from New York City, "in point of architectural beauty, by those of any other city in the West."[11] Nearing completion was the first leg of the Milwaukee & Mississippi Railroad, connecting the city with the state capital, Madison. More railroads were planned. These new transportation routes brought grain from the hinterland to Milwaukee en route to New York. Between 1850 and 1860, Wisconsin farmers more than quadrupled the acreage devoted to tillage and nearly doubled their yield. And all moved through Milwaukee, the city that was Wisconsin's wholesaler, marketer, supplier, and banker.[12] Saturday, March 11, 1854, was just another busy morning. Except for federal officers, no one knew that a fugitive slave lay bleeding in the county jail.

Abolitionists in Racine knew, and they rang the bells to awaken the city. Shortly after 9:00 AM, the "largest meeting of citizens ever assembled in Racine" gathered in the courthouse square. While speakers addressed the crowd, a committee worked up a set of resolutions. The preamble

Figure 1.1. Bird's-eye view of Milwaukee, 1853. *Photo courtesy of the Milwaukee County Historical Society*

decried the "kidnapping" of Glover, "a faithful laborer and honest man." The first resolution condemned the arrest as "an outrage upon the peaceful rights of this assembly," as it was made "without the exhibition of any papers" but by knocking him down with a club. The second resolution stated that "as citizens of Racine," the assembly demanded that Glover be afforded a fair and impartial trial by jury. To these resolutions defending Glover, they added a third. Blaming the Senate for repealing "all compromises heretofore adopted by the Congress of the United States," the citizens of Wisconsin "declare the Slavecatching law of 1850, disgraceful, and *also repealed*."[13] After adjourning the meeting until 1:00 PM, the committee telegraphed its proceedings and resolutions to Milwaukee's abolitionist printer, Sherman M. Booth.

Booth was a stalwart antislavery man with an established reputation as a radical, a bombast, and a hothead. He wore a long black beard, and his intense dark eyes contrasted with the gentleness of his round face. His father, a schoolteacher active in New York State's temperance reform movement, had instilled a hatred of slavery deep within him. Sherman Booth went to Yale, where he assisted in the famous *Amistad* cause by helping to teach the African slaves how to read and write English. He graduated as a member of Phi Beta Kappa and delivered the society's commencement address on the "duties of the citizen at the ballot box."[14] After Yale, Booth

Figure 1.2. Sherman Booth was the first Milwaukee abolitionist notified of the presence of Joshua Glover in the county jail. He alerted the city of Glover's incarceration by printing handbills and riding about town shouting, "A man's liberty is at stake!" Some also said that he shouted, "Freemen to the rescue!" but Booth denied uttering these specific words. He had reason enough to deny them in 1854 and 1855—they were evidence for the prosecution that he had planned a rescue from the start. Later in his life, Booth admitted that he had played a role in encouraging the rescue. But as for shouting, "Freemen to the rescue"? "I respectfully decline the honor," said Booth, "of a deed which I never performed." *Wisconsin Historical Society, image number WHi-9485*

worked for the *Christian Freeman,* an abolitionist newspaper in Connecticut, where he was active in the eastern wing of the Liberty Party. When the newspaper's editor moved to Prairieville, Wisconsin (just outside Milwaukee), Booth followed him and assisted him in publishing the *American Freeman.*

Booth's abolitionism was harsh and unrelenting. He brooked no compromise with the Slave Power and condemned out of hand any attempts to do so. But as hardheaded and moralistic an abolitionist as Booth was, he had a pragmatist's instincts. His work in Connecticut had elevated him to high ranks within the Liberty Party, and there he encountered the difficulties of party formation. It was difficult enough to attract people to an untested third party that lacked the power to dispense patronage, but he also found himself defending the party from attacks by radical abolitionists like William Lloyd Garrison. Before long, he was advocating an alliance with like-minded Democrats. After attending the convention in Buffalo, New York, that announced the emergence of the Free Soil Party, Booth joined with Barnburner Democrats in building the new party. He relocated to Milwaukee and began publishing his own paper, the *Daily Free Democrat.* He became the most vocal of Wisconsin's abolitionists.

At nine o'clock on the morning of March 11, Booth received the Racine cable announcing that the Milwaukee jail held a fugitive slave. He went immediately to see the clerk of the district court, who told Booth to talk with Judge Miller. On his way to Miller's office, Booth ran into Deputy Marshal Cotton. He asked Cotton whether he had kidnapped a man in Racine and showed him the cable he had received. Cotton denied kidnapping anyone, although he neglected to mention that he had *arrested* a fugitive slave.[15] Booth, for his part, began to wonder whether the entire dispatch had been a rumor but went to see Judge Miller anyway. Miller confirmed that he had issued a warrant a few days earlier but claimed to have no idea whether it had been executed. Befuddled, Booth left Miller's office. He then crossed paths with the prominent abolitionist lawyer James H. Paine, who told him that a fugitive slave had indeed been deposited in the Milwaukee jail. They hurried there together to see the fugitive.

Like Sherman Booth, James Paine had cut his teeth on the Liberty Party revolt and the Free Soil synthesis in the 1840s. Paine had been active in Ohio's Liberty Party, in which he and Salmon P. Chase had been among the early leaders. He left little in the way of a record, but it is clear that he led the wing that rejected reconciliation with either Whigs or Democrats.[16] In 1847, Paine left Painesville—a town named after his family—to pursue more lucrative opportunities in Milwaukee. He opened a law firm with his sons and practiced primarily commercial law.

Paine never abandoned his passion for the age's great reform issues of temperance and abolition. When a fugitive slave turned up in the county jail, his principles demanded action. He took an affidavit from Glover, obtained a copy of the warrant for his arrest, and left for the residence of Charles E. Jenkins, judge of the Milwaukee County Court. There he applied directly to the judge for a writ of habeas corpus for Joshua Glover. Habeas corpus was an ancient writ and one of the key elements of the common law's due process. It commanded an officer detaining a person to "have the body" in court and to explain by what authority the person was detained. If the detention was according to law, then the judge who had issued the writ was bound to return the prisoner to jail. If not, the prisoner could be set free. Judge Jenkins issued the writ and ordered the city marshal to serve it on the federal marshals and the county sheriff who held Glover.

While Paine busied himself obtaining Glover's writ of habeas corpus, Booth printed a handbill publicizing Glover's arrest. It made sensational claims. Slave catchers had "kidnapped" a man. They had "pressed" the county jail and local officers into service, making them hold the slave while "fetters were being riveted on his limbs." Slave catchers planned a secret trial to deny Glover the aid of counsel. Booth ended with a plea: "Citizens of Milwaukee! Shall we have Star Chamber proceedings here? and shall a Man be dragged back to Slavery from our Free Soil, *without an open trial of his right to Liberty?*"[17] Few educated Wisconsinites would have missed the historical analogy. In the great story of the triumph of liberty over absolutism, the seventeenth century had been the watershed.[18] As Americans understood it, the Stuart monarchs of England had spent much of that century employing every available means to aggrandize their own power. Star Chamber a was particularly valuable court to the absolutist Stuarts because royal judges decided cases without a jury. Booth extended the analogy when he referred to Judge Miller as Judge Jeffries, the chief justice of the most pernicious of all the Stuarts, James II. Jeffries had affirmed the right of his king to suspend habeas corpus and had engineered the "bloody assizes" in 1685 to punish rebels. Booth used these images consciously to analogize the federal government to absolutist monarchs operating under color, but not substance, of law. The analogy also implicitly invoked popular sovereignty. The victors in the seventeenth-century struggle against absolutism were the English people, who had jealously defended their right of trial by jury and recourse to habeas corpus, even removing the head of Charles I in 1649 and running James II out of England in 1688. Booth now asked whether Milwaukee's citizens were ready to surrender these hard-won freedoms. It was a powerful plea.

Booth, Paine, and other Milwaukeeans reconvened in Booth's office at one o'clock to telegraph a report of the events to Racine and decide what to do next. They understood that Judge Miller, despite the writ of habeas corpus, intended to proceed with Garland's hearing on the removal of Glover to Missouri. After a few minutes of discussion, they decided that a general meeting was in order and that they would call it by ringing the church bells and distributing handbills. The men set to work. But as time ran short, Booth abandoned the handbills and took up the reins of his horse. From his office at West Water Street and Spring, he rode north on Third Street into the heavily German Second Ward, crossed the river, rode south down East Water through the heart of Milwaukee's business district, and down to the Fifth Ward, where he returned via Main and Milwaukee through the Third Ward. It was a tremendous distance to travel in twenty minutes, particularly when stopping at street corners and shouting "A man's liberty is at stake!"[19] Booth called for all freemen who did not wish to be made slaves to meet in the courthouse square. Some later swore that he shouted "Freemen to the rescue," but Booth denied it.

Whatever he yelled, it brought people by the hundreds to the courthouse. By 2:30 PM, several thousand—including Milwaukee's acting mayor, the city marshal, newspaper publishers, and wealthy businessmen—had turned out, motivated by sympathy or curiosity.[20] Garland's hope of removing Joshua Glover quietly from Wisconsin was dashed. The fugitive slave's status was now the concern of a large crowd that gathered in the courtyard square.

———

Milwaukee's courthouse was built in 1836 on land donated by Solomon Juneau, one of the city's earliest promoters. The site was equidistant from the Milwaukee River and Lake Michigan, a little more than one-half mile

Figure 1.3. Milwaukee's courthouse square was home to the Milwaukee County Circuit Court, the U.S. District Court for the Eastern District of Wisconsin, and the county jail (located behind the courthouse). Hasty frontier-style construction created an awkward aesthetic. The courthouse in the center was a rather blockish, unimaginative two-story frame building with narrow windows. A pediment supported by four Tuscan columns gave it a Greek Revival veneer, but the building's gabled roof had merely been extended into a portico, and a bell tower stood where a dome should have been. The intent had been fashionable solemnity. The effect was, at best, an uncomfortable imbalance. Additions had been built in asymmetric wings connected to the central courthouse and spanning the entire block, more reminiscent of a commercial mall than of a public square. Still, this was the popular destination of political marches and parades in Milwaukee. It was the center and the symbol of public life for the city and the county. *Photo courtesy of the Milwaukee County Historical Society*

north of the confluence of the Milwaukee and the Menominee rivers. When the three separate settlements at Milwaukee—Juneautown, Kilbourntown, and Walker's Point—were joined by charter in 1846, the courthouse stayed there on the east side, close to Milwaukee's central business district. Because commercial paper and debt were often registered with and litigated through Milwaukee's courts—Milwaukee in the late 1830s registered one lawsuit for every eighteen residents—this proximity was key. The courthouse expanded with Milwaukee. By 1854, it was home to the U.S. District Court for the Eastern District of Wisconsin, the Milwaukee County Circuit Court, the Milwaukee County Court, and the county jail.[21]

The courthouse square had been hastily constructed and was somewhat awkward in appearance, but it served as Milwaukee's only true public forum. The courthouse steps served as a natural platform for speakers, and larger crowds could be addressed from the roof of the courthouse or from those of buildings directly adjacent. The quadrangle provided enough space for hundreds or, if they spilled over fences onto the sidewalk and into the streets, even thousands to gather. For these reasons, it was a common destination for political marches, rallies, and parades. Such was the typical scene during the city's Fourth of July celebrations. Long parades wound through every ward in the city and ended at the courthouse steps. Celebrants lounged in the quad while speakers delivered orations in English and German. Political assemblies followed the same formula. The 1847 rally in support of the proposed state constitution marched through all the wards before settling at the courthouse steps, where citizens of note delivered speeches.[22]

Not every crowd that gathered in the courthouse square followed a peaceful parade. Milwaukee saw its share of angry mobs in the 1840s and 1850s. On April 1, 1848, a riot broke out in the predominately Irish Third Ward. Particularly vexing to the English-language press were its origins in "some disturbance at the 'democratic' caucus." Irish rioters attacked a German boardinghouse, the residents returned gunfire, and many people were badly injured. Rufus King, editor of the *Milwaukee Sentinel* and a key supporter of the antislavery cause, noted with more than just a little anxiety that "a good deal of excitement got up between some of our Irish and German fellow citizens. But we trust that the matter will end here and not lead to disturbances, which would bring discredit upon our fair city."[23] On March 4, 1850, Germans rioted at a speaking engagement of Senator J. B. Smith, a temperance advocate. The English-language press expressed its outrage, and two weeks later a mass meeting of native-born Americans publicly condemned the riot. Several Germans felt the need in the days following the riots to quell fears that their countrymen did not know how to behave in a democracy.[24] One man, German-born but a naturalized citizen of the United States, protested the "imputation that the Germans by nature were disorganizers and disturbers."[25] Two more German citizens contributed to the debate in both the German- and English-language papers, revealing divisions in the German community as well as deep-seated fears that the Germans were prone to demagoguery and disturbance.[26] Less than one year later, German Catholics and Protestants clashed in the Second Ward, a riot that produced fourteen arrests but no convictions.[27]

Much of the concern expressed both within and without the German community dealt with the danger of class-based riots. Those who condemned the riots often pointed fingers at demagogues "pretending to be friends of the laborer."[28] The issue came to a head in 1853, when German railroad workers went on strike after being stiffed on wages. They organized and marched around the city, ending at the railroad company's headquarters. Despite entreaties by the mayor and by a German-born alderman, the crowd remained agitated. When officers arrested a man taking handfuls of sugar from a hogshead that had been forced open, the crowd turned angry. Officers arrested all who resisted and took them to the county jail. The Germans rallied around a man wielding a tricolor flag and marched after them. Sheriff Herman Page met them at the jailhouse steps and told them in no uncertain terms that the full weight of the law would come down on any who attempted a rescue. Meanwhile, the police and fire companies assembled across the square. The mayor attempted to defuse the situation by walking coolly into the crowd and removing the tricolor flag. This act did not have the intended effect: "he was instantly assailed by a number of men around it and a general melee at once commenced. Sticks, stones and fists were freely used; the Engines commenced playing on the mob and the latter, in turn, pelted the Firemen with brickbats. Thereupon the Firemen and Police charged upon the mob and drove them fairly off the ground."[29] As dramatic as the scene was, it ended with few injuries. The *Sentinel,* for its part, weighed in on the side of the laborers but added that "the moment they undertake to right themselves *by force,* both the community and the law will be marshalled [*sic*] against them."[30]

Riots such as these prickled the popular consciousness. Most everyone was aware of the troubling rise in urban disorder. Contemporaries fretted about this trend, which was not simply the result of random crime or growing pockets of poverty in northern cities. The frequency and lethality of urban riots escalated in the nineteenth century. By the eve of Civil War, riots had claimed nearly a thousand lives.[31] But casting this as a mere escalation in urban violence disguises much. Riots themselves had changed in character from the eighteenth to the nineteenth century, as had their relationship to the political process. In the eighteenth-century Atlantic world, riots were highly disciplined affairs that usually occurred during times of exigency.[32] These crowds derived their legitimacy from three primary factors: a purpose for gathering, a consensus among the community about the nature of the danger, and an urgency that justified extraordinary action. Remarkably, social elites often supported crowd action if it helped restore order or cured perceived disorder within the community.[33]

Even if tolerated, such crowd action was strictly extralegal. In the development of American constitutionalism, the extralegal crowd played its part. From the revolutionary committees of correspondence and the enforcement of nonimportation agreements to the Boston Tea Party, extralegal assemblies formed a vital part of the revolutionary movement. What some might have condemned as riotous violence, others defended on the principle of popular action.[34] Deeply embedded in the American Revolution was the concept that the people, properly organized, might act on their own.

This idea of direct popular action became central to American government in the first decades of the nineteenth century. As the population expanded and the Democratic-Republicans held the federal government in check, a need for basic services arose. The people responded. In the first two decades of the nineteenth century, voluntary associations organized for mutual benefit, charitable purposes, or the provision of civic services mushroomed.[35] They proved to be a particularly useful tool on the trans-Appalachian frontier, where settlement quickly outran the reach of the territorial government.[36] Voluntary associations filled the void and, by the 1850s, were well established in American law.[37] Several generations of usage had made them commonplace, and they had existed in Wisconsin since its days as a territory. Merchants, artisans, and professionals formed mutual benefit societies. Charities, orphanages, and schools were run by private associations. Milwaukee's first library, lyceum, and lecture series were established by such groups. Newspapers regularly published resolutions adopted by voluntary associations and praised their efforts.[38]

The cumulative effect was to connect popular sovereignty to democratic procedure. The fundamental right of the people to assemble was an ancient one, derived from the English constitutional tradition and confirmed by the principles of the American Revolution.[39] The 1848 Wisconsin constitution granted this right in the fourth section of its first article in simple and forceful language: "The right of the people peaceably to assemble, to consult for the common good, and to petition the government, or any department thereof, shall never be abridged." The achievement of the Democratic-Republicans was to expand this right into a governmental practice. If the Revolution had removed the need for direct crowd action in theory, Jeffersonian politics removed the need in practice by incorporating the crowd into the polity.

This was what made Jacksonian-era riots so terribly frightening. The participants did not assemble properly in the American traditions of popular action and voluntary association. They did not pretend to represent the community or to enforce its values. Instead, these riots rumbled in the crowded metropolises of the East, in neighborhoods formed from the swell of immigrants arriving in the 1840s. Riots often pitted one ethnicity against another, particularly when immigrants competed with native-born Americans for jobs during lean times or when strange cultural practices stirred nativist sentiments. Some feared that this violence was endemic in foreigners who were unable to understand and participate in democracy. Others pointed to the brutal poverty of city life, voicing fears that American cities were developing a European-style underclass. This raised the chilling specter of class warfare.[40] The overblown antiriot literature of the period continually asked the rhetorical question: how could the poor rise up against a government established in their name?[41] There seemed to be no answers to this question when urban violence was random and contemptuous of the rule of law. Beneath these questions lurked a greater fear, that democracy was too fragile to keep order.[42]

This fear intensified on the frontier. Lacking established roots and situated far from centers of power, businessmen and capitalists believed that the frontier could degenerate into violence at any time. Rather than leading to an abhorrence of violence, this belief produced an ambivalence that tolerated it on certain occasions. When respected members of the community used extralegal violence to maintain order, the community permitted and even condoned it.[43] This phenomenon on the rural frontier occurred primarily because fledgling settlements lacked formal institutions or an established elite that kept order. The same was not true on the urban frontier. Fast-growing frontier cities like Milwaukee depended on the sinews of commerce that extended directly from eastern centers to the rural hinterland. Violence disrupted commerce, in turn discouraging investment and potentially putting Milwaukee at a disadvantage in its competition with Chicago to become the premier port of the Great Lakes.

In order to compete, Milwaukee had to accept the very conditions that had seemingly destabilized cities in the East. Milwaukee required a large labor supply, and the city's promoters advertised in Europe for settlers. Immigrants had clustered together during the fast-paced growth of the 1840s and 1850s. Native-born Americans had settled the north and the east in Milwaukee's First and Fifth wards. The Irish gravitated to the Third Ward, settling close to the industry along the Milwaukee River. The Germans settled to the west, across the river in the Second Ward. Residential segregation did not deter commercial mixing, however. The vast majority of retailers, wholesalers, and professionals did business in a set of buildings totaling roughly eight city blocks, all in the First Ward.[44] As Milwaukee grew in the 1850s, business expanded slowly outward from this center, forcing manufacturing farther downriver, southward into the Third Ward.[45] Importantly, the business divisions that had pushed commission merchants and wholesalers downriver kept German and American wholesalers alike within the business district. Professionals and retailers advertised directly to Germans in Milwaukee in the city directories, offering special services (primarily legal services) designed to integrate them immediately into the city's commerce.[46]

These were the tensions that pulled in every direction during the 1850s. The need for labor encouraged the foreign immigration that many nativists feared would endanger democracy. The desire to integrate foreigners into the city's commerce went hand-in-hand with deep suspicions about the cultural habits of Germans and Irish. Frighteningly, Milwaukee's riots resembled those of eastern cities and polarized the city along ethnic and class lines. Democratic politics, instead of acting as the glue to hold these disparate groups together, proved to be the hammer and chisel that could fracture the city at any moment. The fact that democratic caucuses and political speeches served as contact points for ethnic rioting suggested that foreigners were particularly susceptible to demagoguery or simply lacked the ability to understand Anglo-American democracy.

The city elections on March 7, 1854, confirmed these fears. At the First Ward polls at Market Square, right on the edge of Milwaukee's business district, an Irishman challenged the election return of a German. As the two groups began to argue, a German vociferously challenged the Irish to fight. This continued "until the Irish blood was up," and a bloody riot ensued. The Irish won the ground, chased away the Germans, and kept a "murderous fire of stones and brickbats upon the windows of buildings in the neighborhood, and upon every one who came near."[47] The sheriff was "badly hurt," as were an alderman and the former sheriff who attempted to quell the riot. Newspaper editors uniformly recoiled in horror at this display of ethnic violence. The *Milwaukee Sentinel* lamented that "the moral injury done to the good name of our city is incalculable."[48]

———

Understandably, then, it was with some trepidation that Milwaukeeans regarded the gathering of thousands in the courthouse square only four days after the election day riots. They watched closely for signs of violence and disorder, and they measured the crowd against the standards set by the tradition of voluntary association and its parliamentary procedures. The antislavery men who called together the meeting also worked hard to ensure that its proceedings not only would conform to these standards but would gain the community's approval. When James Paine called the meeting to order—and thus gave the assembly its legal sanction—he nominated for its president Dr. Edward B. Wolcott. An antislavery man, Wolcott was also a prominent citizen of Milwaukee. He had invested heavily in real estate and was one of the directors of the Milwaukee & Mississippi Railroad Company. His presence was a firm reminder that this crowd was led by people deeply invested in the community.

Abram Henry Bielfeld was nominated secretary of the assembly, to keep its minutes and official records. Bielfeld was German by birth, originally from Bremen. He had immigrated to New York and spent several years testing his fortunes there and in Mexico before settling permanently in Milwaukee in 1845. He alternately practiced law and provided services as a translator, and invested in real estate in the city's commercial district.[49] Bielfeld had a talent for this kind of work. He had served as the city's clerk in 1847, well enough to be asked by the mayor to conduct Milwaukee's census that year. He earned praise in the English-language press for his efficient and reliable work as a public servant, and he appeared as secretary for various political meetings in the 1840s and 1850s.[50] Bielfeld also acted as a political and cultural bridge between Milwaukee's German and Native populations.[51] He was a liberal German who had joined the Barnburner wing of the Democratic Party in 1848, serving as secretary for the party and delivering orations in favor of the Adams and Van Buren ticket. The *Milwaukee Sentinel* noted that Bielfeld was "a fine speaker" and was of "no small influence among his countrymen."[52] Here was a German familiar with parliamentary proceedings, active politically in the city, and widely respected among a population that harbored strong suspicions about slavery. For the abolitionists, there could be no better choice to serve as secretary of the meeting.

In his capacity as president, Wolcott nominated a committee of five, one from each ward, to draft resolutions. Among those selected were two who had organized the meeting itself: Sherman M. Booth and James Paine. The selection of a member from each ward was intended to create a broader democratic consensus on the resolutions, or at least to give the appearance that the mass meeting represented the sentiments of the entire community. The committee set about drafting resolutions.

Out of view of the crowd, local and federal officers sparred over legal process. Deputy Marshal Cotton faced a tough situation. He had in his custody a federal prisoner, arrested on the authority of a warrant issued by a U.S. district court judge. The city marshal had served him with a writ of habeas corpus commanding him to take the prisoner before the judge of the county court and explain this detention. He turned to Judge Miller of the federal court for advice. Miller advised him to make no return on the writ—essentially to ignore it. Sheriff Page was in less of a bind. At three o'clock, he made return on the writ, explaining that the prisoner was in his jail, but not in his custody. Wisconsin law bound him to accept federal prisoners in his county jail, but he had no power to remove them. Frustrated, Glover's lawyers returned to the county court judge's residence for a new writ of habeas corpus directed solely to the U.S. marshal.

Meanwhile, the crowd milled about in the courthouse square. Questions arose about the writ of habeas corpus and the Fugitive Slave Act, and people from the crowd called loudly for Byron Paine to explain the legal technicalities. Byron was James Paine's youngest son, and possibly his brightest. He had developed a stronger taste for politics and reform than had his brothers. He began addressing political meetings as early as 1845, at the age of eighteen. He attended the Free Soil convention in Buffalo and returned to Wisconsin to address abolitionist political meetings. He continued to do this for the next several years, lecturing on free soil, on temperance, and in 1850 on resistance to Congress's new Fugitive Slave Act.[53] In 1853, he went to Madison to report on the legislature's sessions for Booth's *Daily Free Democrat*. His abilities as a reporter—both in the legislature and in the courts—attracted great praise. Rufus King, the antislavery editor of the *Milwaukee Sentinel,* engaged Paine to report on lectures and trials in 1853 and 1854. He did so despite having bristled earlier at the suggestion that Paine—"the child among us," as one editor referred to him— had taken better notes on court trials than the *Sentinel's* stenographic reporter.[54] Paine's abilities, despite his youth, marked him among abolitionists and commanded respect even from his political enemies.[55] One Democratic paper, although noting that it had little sympathy with Paine's abolitionism, denounced his slanderers: "His abilities and his unbending integrity will hardly yield to sneers and ridicule. He is one who will be a man of mark in this State, respectable and respected as he deserves to be, when those who have attacked him with low bred insolence and indecency are quite forgotten."[56]

So when people from the crowd called for speakers to provide the legal background, they called for Byron Paine. Paine explained to the crowd that the Fugitive Slave Act was unconstitutional "inasmuch as it denied the Writ of Habeas Corpus and the right of trial by jury, which were sacredly guarantied to us by the Constitution of the United States, and of this State."[57] No more than a summary of his speech was provided by the city's newspapers, but one can be sure that Paine delivered it in his usual style, a blend of forensic argument and romantic rhetoric. This was the man, after all, who later called Supreme Court justice Samuel Nelson "that arch-enemy of liberty, that traitor to the rights of the states,"[58] the same lawyer who, when addressing Milwaukee's German citizens, quoted Schiller and compared Sherman Booth to William Tell.[59] But while Paine was a fervent abolitionist and an admitted romantic, he was at heart a lawyer and a very good one. Sentimental prose supplemented rather than replaced reasonable arguments: the Fugitive Slave Act was illegitimate because it violated constitutional guarantees. Constitutions in the United States emanated from the sacred sovereign—the people—and could not be circumvented by any branch of government—executive, judicial, or legislative.

Sherman Booth also spoke, giving the crowd a history of the case to that point. Booth's short speech ended when the committee appointed to draft resolutions finished its work and came forward to present them to the assembly. The preamble recited the facts of Glover's arrest, presumably taken from Glover himself and from the Racine cable. Marshals had held a gun to Glover's head and beaten him "before any legal process was served upon him." He had been "brought by night to this city" and incarcerated. The preamble also stated that federal officers had refused to obey a writ of habeas corpus issued by the judge of the county court. Three resolutions followed. The first declared that "every person" had a right to a fair and impartial trial in all matters regarding personal liberty. Byron Paine, from his place in the crowd, moved that the resolution be amended to read that he was "entitled to a fair and impartial trial *by jury.*" The assembly adopted the motion and amended the resolution.[60] The second resolution exalted the writ of habeas corpus, noting that it was "the great defense of Freedom," and demanded "for this prisoner, as well as for our own protection, that this Sacred Writ shall be obeyed." The third resolution pledged that the assembly would stand by the prisoner and do its utmost to secure him a trial by jury.[61] The chairman put the resolutions to the crowd. According to Sherman Booth's *Daily Free Democrat* and Rufus King's *Milwaukee Sentinel,* the people adopted the resolutions without a dissenting voice.[62]

The president next called for the appointment of a vigilance committee to see that federal and state officers heeded the meeting's resolutions. The assembly affirmed the appointment of twenty-five men and delegated to them the power to call public meetings and to add to their numbers if need be. The chosen men possessed the requisite antislavery credentials, but, even more importantly, they hailed from the ranks of the professional and entrepreneurial elite of the city. Lawyers like Byron Paine and Edwin Palmer and entrepreneurs like John Furlong and John Ryecraft were among the members. Herbert Reed, a grocer and real estate owner of the First Ward, was appointed chairman of the committee.[63]

Speeches continued in the courthouse square. Bielfeld addressed the crowd in German while the assembly's leaders conversed with the editors of the city's German-language newspapers. At some point during Bielfeld's address, the clerk of the Milwaukee County Circuit Court approached the crowd and complained that the meeting was disrupting the court's proceedings. To accommodate the court, Bielfeld and the other officers moved to the northwest corner of the courthouse square and gave their speeches from the roof of the clerk's office. His speech explained the Fugitive Slave Act and the constitutional guarantees of habeas corpus and trial by jury for the benefit of those Germans unfamiliar with American legal practice. James Paine spoke next, warning the members of the crowd that Glover's fate was part of the larger national drama. The Kansas-Nebraska bill threatened the liberty of all free men, said Paine, and this was but another encroachment of the Slave Power upon the people of the North. Sherman Booth spoke last. The issue was not Joshua Glover, claimed Booth; the issue was every man. If the federal government could make laws suspending the writ of habeas corpus and trial by jury, then any man, "German, Irishman, or American," could be made a slave.[64]

This fiery rhetoric alarmed federal officers already nervous about the crowd's intentions. Deputy Marshal Cotton sent requisition orders to local militia companies to protect the prisoner. The U.S. district attorney for Wisconsin, John Sharpstein, came to Cotton's aid. Until then, the district attorney had not involved himself in what the law defined as the essentially private matter of fugitive slave reclamation. The presence of several thousand men outside the jail convinced him otherwise. Sharpstein called on a nearby U.S. military battalion to obey the marshal's requisition, going so far as to guarantee in writing that they would receive payment for their services. Although the commander of the battalion seemed satisfied with Sharpstein's promise, neither the federal battalion nor the local militia arrived to protect the prisoner.[65] Passing time did little to quell these anxieties. Although Wolcott adjourned the meeting sometime after four o'clock, several hundred people still milled about in the square.[66] The vigilance committee remained at the courthouse steps, and a committee of two stood inside the courthouse, waiting to hear how federal officers would respond to the writ of habeas corpus.

At five o'clock, the abolitionists returned with a new writ directed to Deputy Marshal Cotton. The sheriff himself served the writ on the marshal, ordering him to have Glover before the county court judge immediately. Cotton went to Judge Miller, who advised him not to respond. Obeying the writ meant marching Glover out of the jail and through the crowd gathered in the courthouse square while protected only by several deputy marshals. Miller, Cotton, and Sharpstein believed this would be tantamount to discharging the prisoner. They resolved to hold tight, remain firm, and postpone any hearing on Glover until Monday. Plenty could happen—passions could cool, the crowd could disappear, or reinforcements could arrive.

Just as Miller was informing the assembly's representatives that Glover would receive a fair hearing in his court at ten o'clock on Monday morning, the afternoon ferry arrived, carrying a delegation of one hundred from Racine's meeting. They marched "in a solid column" from the dock to the courthouse. The procession attracted attention, bringing back those who had left the meeting and others curious about the proceedings. The crowd's numbers swelled again. The committee emerged from the courthouse and informed the crowd that Deputy Marshal Cotton would not obey the writ of habeas corpus.

As dusk fell, the mood was tense. Cotton's requisition orders to the local militia and the U.S. Army were now common knowledge. Rumors spread that the fugitive would be taken away that night, after the assembly dispersed. Men argued about whether he should go back to slavery, regardless of any constitutional imperative to return fugitives to southern states. Some spoke openly of rescue. Tempers rose, and several speakers addressed the crowd. This time, however, the subject was not the proper limits of constitutionally inspired resistance. Charles Watkins, an abolitionist lawyer working with Sherman Booth, told the crowd that sometimes the people must take the law into their own hands or become slaves themselves. Whether this was such a time, Watkins coyly declined to say. Sherman Booth spoke too, saying that if the community only made its sentiments known, then the Fugitive Slave Act would never be enforced. No lawyer would aid the slave catchers, and federal officers would resign their posts before aiding in the execution of that odious law. Exactly how the people were to make their sentiments known, Booth left to the popular imagination. Booth and the rest of the vigilance committee then self-servingly counseled the crowd to break no laws and voted to retire to the America House to take tea and discuss their next course of action.

The committee never made it to tea. The crowd demanded the keys to the jail, and the jailer refused. A burly blacksmith—a recent emigrant from Cornwall, England, by the name of James Angove—borrowed a six-by-six-inch wooden beam from the lumber lying about for the construction of St. John's Cathedral. Declaring it a good enough key, the crowd rushed the jail and broke down the door with pickaxes and Angove's makeshift battering ram.[67] The men guarding the jail offered no resistance, and they were not treated violently by the crowd. William Parsons, the assistant jailer, saw the crowd break down the gate separating the jail yard from the street and enter the premises. He told the crowd there was "no communication with the jail" through the back door, which was locked, and "most of them then went back."[68] They went straight to the front door and battered it open. It was messy, but the crowd did no more damage than was necessary to free Glover.[69]

The crowd led Glover out of the jailhouse while the federal marshals stood by helplessly. They made for the bridge to Walker's Point, where local businessman John Messinger offered up his two-horse buggy. Sherman Booth rode horseback next to the buggy as the crowd cheered, and Glover doffed his cap to them, crying "Glory, Hallelujah!"[70] The buggy disappeared, bound for the Underground Railroad station at Waukesha. Glover remained there until abolitionists could make arrangements for passage to Racine and then across the lake to Canada. Garland never saw Joshua Glover again.[71]

———

In the months that followed, much was made of the breaking of the jail. For most observers, it had marked the end of the assembly's lawful behavior. Still, one can sense a collective sigh of relief over the crowd's restraint. The German-language newspaper *Der Milwaukee See-Bote* remarked that "[t]he meeting occurred without any excessive behavior."[72] The *Wisconsin Daily*, edited by the Democrat William Cramer, described the crowd as "sober" and "composed of Americans, Germans and Irishmen." The refusal of Deputy Marshal Cotton to obey the writ of habeas corpus "intensely exasperated the crowd," wrote Cramer, and led to the breaking of the jail. He reported no other violence on that day. Cramer was no friend of Booth's, nor was his paper supportive of the antislavery meetings. He called the actual breaking of the jail an "outrage upon law" and continued to denounce it for the next year. Still, he took care to note the crowd's restraint and made distinctions between violence done against the Fugitive Slave Act and violence done against the public peace.[73]

The distinction was an important one. Antebellum Americans felt no need to defend direct action by the people. Two generations of practice had cemented voluntary association and popular government into the foundations of American democracy. But these same generations also understood the difference between citizens assembled to protest and a mob gathered to riot. Milwaukee's sheriff—the same man injured while quelling a riot on March 7—made no effort to stop the rescue of Joshua Glover on March 11. When questioned, he bluntly explained that the prisoner belonged to the marshal and that the marshal could defend him. The state militia companies stood on the same ground. They refused to come to the aid of federal officers unless their requests met every technical requirement of the law. In essence, they stalled. The Fugitive Slave Act failed to command the consensus and respect of the community, a necessary element for its enforcement.

Although the distinction could be made, danger accompanied it. Sherman Booth cautioned that Glover's rescue might be used as precedent by the unscrupulous, "and the distinction may not be made between resistance in an attempt to destroy our liberties, under the color of law, and an unjust decision affecting property or individual interests."[74] It was a good standard, though one that Booth himself had trouble living up to. The leaders of the crowd had molded their own actions to it. They had made simple demands based on the principle that federal officers must observe the fundamental rights of trial by jury and recourse to habeas corpus, secured by Wisconsin's constitution for the prisoner "as well as for our own protection." They made these demands in the form of a petition submitted by an assembly of law-abiding citizens. Their protest had been, at its heart, a legal one. Milwaukee's assembly had not gone as far as Racine's, which had declared the Fugitive Slave Act repealed; but they had trenchantly asserted a position of constitutional liberty. In the face of a federal statute that purported to quash these rights, they firmly stated that the people themselves would enforce those rights. It was an unsettling doctrine that they invoked, one traceable to revolutionary origins.

The rescue also raised a number of troubling questions. Who was Joshua Glover? Few knew anything more than that he was a fugitive from slavery. Almost nowhere in America did blacks claim full republican citizenship. In the South, African features—the dark skin, the wooly hair, the flat nose—were the mark of perpetual bondage, putting the onus on blacks to prove their own freedom. But even those who could prove it did not share in freedom's benefits. North and South, blacks lived under a harsh legal regime that restricted their movement, limited their privileges and immunities, and denied them political participation. Few whites questioned these laws, either in practice or principle. In the popular imagination, blacks were a degraded race not possessed of the qualities necessary for republican citizenship. However a Frederick Douglass or a William Lloyd Garrison might labor to prove the contrary, literary and popular images of blacks cast them as buffoonish and dim-witted. The resistance in Glover's name had to consider, at some point, Joshua Glover himself.

Then there was the question of resistance. If citizens had a right—a duty, even—to resist unconstitutional encroachments on their liberty, how did this intersect with the duty of citizens to obey the law? The federal government prosecuted several participants in the rescue and returned indictments on John Ryecraft and Sherman Booth. This question took center stage at the public trials of Glover's rescuers over the next two years. Those who believed in the legitimacy of resistance had to defend it from those who charged that it would lead to disunion and eventual anarchy. Those who opposed it had to explain why the people owed fidelity to a law that suspended civil liberties arbitrarily. The rescue of Joshua Glover became a six-year struggle not only to determine whether the Fugitive Slave Act was unconstitutional but to determine the substance and meaning of the Constitution itself.

The Fugitive Slave Act

> That such a doctrine [of unlimited obedience to civil govern-
> ment] should be received and acted upon by the descendants
> of the English Puritans; that they should have so soon forgot-
> ten the disobedience of their fathers, for many long years, to
> the Act of Uniformity of Charles II, and other penal laws,
> and the fines, imprisonments, and persecutions they suffered
> for conscience' sake, is almost incredible.
>
> —J. G. Forman, *The Christian Martyrs,* 1851

A VOCAL portion of Wisconsin's citizenry, in popular assembly, had declared the Fugitive Slave Act of 1850 unconstitutional. Their actions made
the act virtually unenforceable—in practice, a nullity. But was that law
unconstitutional? The Constitution, after all, mandated the return of
fugitive slaves across state lines. There had been an act regarding the procedure for their return on the U.S. statute books since 1793, and proposals
to amend it had arisen on many occasions before 1850. The law had come
before both state and federal courts, and, more than once, lawyers had
argued that its provisions were unconstitutional and void. Yet the U.S.
Supreme Court upheld the act in 1842 in *Prigg v. Pennsylvania.* In the eyes
of the law, then, the Fugitive Slave Act was constitutional, and the people
of Wisconsin had adopted an extralegal attack on its execution.

This conclusion, while satisfyingly simple, misleads. It assumes that the
law's constitutionality was determined in the last instance by the courts
and, necessarily, by the U.S. Supreme Court. It also denigrates the role of
popular resistance, suggesting that it carries no constitutional weight. The
latter assumption is easily dispensed with. Such resistance was a variation

on the tradition of assembly and petitioning, a cherished constitutional right. The resolutions adopted by the Milwaukee assembly were echoed by countless other assemblies and in petitions to Congress asking for—and sometimes demanding—the repeal of the act on constitutional grounds. Given the composition of Congress in 1854, this was unlikely, but Wisconsinites worked to change this after Glover's rescue by making the Fugitive Slave Act a central issue in congressional elections and U.S. Senate appointments. Popular resistance was only the first stage, signaling the failure of the law to achieve the consent of the community. The next stage was to effect change through the political processes specified by the Constitution. This was part and parcel of antebellum constitutionalism.

The assumption that the courts settled the question in favor of constitutionality is also flawed. It is true that the act's supporters repeatedly cited the courts' acceptance of the statute. But they also pointed to congressional action and to the country's long acquiescence as decisive evidence of the act's constitutionality. In truth, the courts had not had much to say about the matter. Most opinions upholding the Fugitive Slave Act had not presumed to test the law against the Bill of Rights to determine whether it violated civil liberties. In fact, very few of these decisions had taken seriously the question of constitutionality.

This was due, at least in part, to judicial deference to congressional action in the early nineteenth century. In the first challenges to the Fugitive Slave Act in appellate courts, judges respected the law as a constitutional settlement by Congress, one that directed state and federal officers to provide for the reclaiming of fugitive slaves and left to the states the matter of protecting free black citizens. The business of the courts was not to pass judgment on the substance of the settlement but to work out its details by interpreting both federal and state law. It was not until the 1830s that increasing political tension over slavery split apart this constitutional settlement. Northern courts were asked, in essence, to refuse to comply with the Fugitive Slave Act as a kind of constitutional resistance. Not without trepidation, some courts did begin to refuse compliance. For the most part, however, the courts attempted to hold together the old compromise that balanced the duties of fugitive slave rendition and protection of free blacks. When Justice Joseph Story authored the opinion of the court in *Prigg v. Pennsylvania,* the weight of settled authority establishing the constitutionality of the Fugitive Slave Act was far more qualified, circumscribed, and ambivalent than he claimed. Nor did *Prigg* settle the matter. Discontent and disagreement led to congressional action and a new Fugitive Slave Act in 1850. The new law dramatically altered accepted practices and led to resistance far more ferocious than any that the 1793 law had ever occasioned.

The Fugitive Slave Act's constitutionality was more complicated than the issuance and acceptance of judicial opinions declaring it so. Its constitutionality was bound up in its history, a skein of issues stretching from compromises over slavery to the duties of states to their citizens; from the role of Congress as a mediator among sovereign states to its increasingly difficult role as balancer of the interests of free and slave states. The 1793 constitutional settlement that made the rendition of fugitive slaves both a federal and a state imperative and left the protection of free blacks to the states came under enormous pressure as slavery expanded into the trans-Appalachian southwest and as antislavery sentiments quickened in northern and border states. By the 1830s, strain on the old compromise had permanently altered its features.

The constitutionality of the Fugitive Slave Act was not based on timeless principles extracted from the nation's founding document. Instead, its constitutionality was in the process that created it, sustained it for six decades, and ultimately brought it crashing down under the weight of public opinion after 1854. In a very real way, its history was its constitutionality and, ultimately, its unconstitutionality.

———

The Fugitive Slave Act was firmly rooted in several sources of law, but the compromises that created it did not tie these sources together in a neat way. There was the common-law right of recaption, the well-recognized right of a master or a paterfamilias to pursue dependents bound to his authority, capture them, and return them to his household. There were limits to this power. It was not to be attended with violence or to breach the peace.[1] If the threat of violence existed, it was the duty of peace officers to intervene. This right of recaption had long been exercised by slaveholders in Britain's American colonies, and most presumed that it would continue after independence. The issue came up at the 1787 constitutional convention. Early on, James Madison noted that "the great division of interests among the states was over slavery, and that this, more than anything else, would strain the bonds of union over time."[2] Time bore out Madison's prescient observation; but in the midst of the convention, more immediate details needed hammering out. Representation and taxation topped the list, and delegates from South Carolina and Georgia made it clear that they wanted assurances that the slave trade would not be banned, at least until those states could replenish their supply of labor depleted by the Revolutionary War.[3] The various compromises between free and slave states engendered controversy both inside and outside the convention, especially as the antislavery cause gained powerful spokesmen like Benjamin Franklin.[4]

There was no row, however, over the addition of a fugitive slave clause to the Constitution. This may have been due, in part, to the presence of fugitive slave clauses in both Pennsylvania's 1780 gradual abolition statute and article VI of the Northwest Ordinance of 1787, which banned slavery in that territory. In at least one respect, fugitive slave clauses were nods to the doctrine laid down by Lord Mansfield, the chief justice of the Court of King's Bench in England, in the case of *Somerset v. Stewart* in 1772.[5] Mansfield ruled that a slave brought to England could not be there restrained. Slavery, said Mansfield, was against natural law and so odious that it could not exist without the positive sanction of municipal law. Once slaves were taken, or took themselves, from the jurisdictional limits of the municipal law that allowed for slavery, the condition of servitude disappeared.

Somerset influenced the thinking of both those eager to protect and those seeking to end the institution of slavery. Fugitive slave clauses in statutes meant to abolish or restrict the spread of the peculiar institution smoothed over potential conflicts and reaffirmed the belief that, with patience, slavery could be gradually abolished. Moral imperatives aside, antislavery men in the revolutionary era evinced a healthy respect for property rights.[6] So when Pierce Butler and Charles C. Pinckney, of South Carolina, proposed a clause to the Constitution that would have fugitive slaves delivered up "like criminals," the only protest from delegates north of the Mason-Dixon line was that the language suggested that states should bear the costs of locating, capturing, and extraditing fugitive slaves. As Roger Sherman, of Connecticut, put it, the better analogy was to seizing and returning a horse, not a criminal.[7] Pinckney and Butler reconsidered. They came back with language that simply specified that fugitives escaping into states that did not recognize slavery would not be freed by the laws of that state but should "be delivered up on claim of the party to whom such service or labour may be due." With no further opposition, this paragraph became a permanent part of Article IV, Section 2, of the Constitution upon ratification.[8]

The fugitive slave clause may have occasioned little controversy at the convention, but fugitive slave rendition proved more troublesome in practice. The first case of note occurred in 1791 in western Pennsylvania, along the border with Virginia. Uncertainties about the exact location of the border left people in two counties unsure of their residence and, therefore, of the jurisdiction under which they owned slaves. After commissioners appointed jointly by the legislatures of the two states agreed on the location of the border, Pennsylvania notified its residents (many of whom thought they had been living in Virginia) that, in order to comply with the 1780 gradual abolition statute, they had to register their slaves with the state or surrender their claims to them. Although many former Virginians (now Pennsylvanians) complied, a few slipped through the cracks. One slave on the northern side of the border, called "John" or "John Davis," was not registered and thus became free, but was rented by his owner to a Virginia planter all the same. John escaped to Pennsylvania, but three Virginians crossed the border, seized him, and returned him to bondage in Virginia. When the governor of Pennsylvania requested the extradition of the three men to face charges of kidnapping, the governor of Virginia objected on technical grounds provided by his attorney general.[9] The governor of Pennsylvania submitted the matter to President George Washington, praying for congressional settlement of this problem.[10]

The complexity of the issues here is revealing. The trouble had originated not over the rendition of a fugitive slave but over the rendition of three Virginians accused of kidnapping a free black. That the free black had once been the legal property of a man who thought he lived in Virginia played no small part in the determination of Virginia officers to refuse the extradition request. The impasse lay between two sovereign police powers, each faced with a constitutional duty to deliver up fugitives—whether from justice or from labor—across state lines. Congress had to balance its constitutional duties with the sovereignty of the states and with the practical consideration that federal law-enforcement administration was skeletal at best, consisting of only a few U.S. marshals, district attorneys, and customs officers. It relied consistently on state infrastructure—

jails, courthouses, horses, and wagons—to enforce its limited criminal jurisdiction. The resulting "Act respecting fugitives from justice, and persons escaping from the service of their masters," signed into law by President Washington on February 12, 1793, attempted a solution by specifying the legal process. Extradition required a copy of the indictment or a sworn affidavit certified by the state's governor. Once agents of that state presented it to the officers of another state, it became "the duty of the executive authority" of the latter state's officers to arrest the fugitive and turn him over or to allow the requesting state's agents to arrest the fugitive on their own.[11]

For fugitive slaves, the statute outlined a different procedure. It empowered slaveholders or their agents to seize fugitives without the aid or approval of either state or federal officers. To remove a fugitive slave from one state to another, a claimant needed only to go before a state or federal judge and produce "proof to the satisfaction of such judge or magistrate" that the fugitive owed labor to his owner according to the laws of his home state. That judge could then issue a certificate of removal. The statute's final section made anyone who obstructed the slaveholder or who rescued or harbored the fugitive liable to the slaveholder up to $500, recoverable by an action of debt. The statute made the arrest of a fugitive slave—unlike that of a fugitive from justice—a private affair. The slaveholder needed no warrant to seize his runaway, and the statute established no criminal penalties for interfering with recaption. In this sense, the statute simply codified a private right.[12] But the language of the act made its purpose clear—it specified the duties of both state and national officers and outlined a procedure that would restore comity within the federal union.

Absent was any protection for free blacks. The evidentiary threshold for granting the certificate of removal was low—the oral testimony of the slaveholder could be sufficient. Judges could exclude the testimony of the alleged fugitive or prevent any evidence from being offered on his behalf. In theory, the fugitive slave, like the fugitive from justice, could have his day in court in the state from which he fled. In most slave jurisdictions, the law declared African features the mark of slavery, leaving alleged fugitives to shoulder the burden of proving their own freedom.[13] This was cold comfort to free blacks.

What was worse, the Fugitive Slave Act had created a temptation to kidnapping, a temptation only sweetened by booms in sugar and cotton production in the trans-Appalachian South. In the first decades of the nineteenth century, planters relocated westward in search of the vast profits of these cash crops. Although some carried their slaves with them, the majority looked to traders and smugglers to supply the want. The African slave trade—banned by Congress in 1808—no longer sufficed, even though smugglers imported slaves through Caribbean markets. Much of the supply came from the surplus available in the upper Chesapeake, where soil exhaustion and market demands had led farmers to switch from tobacco to wheat after 1790. Wheat demanded far less intensive labor than did tobacco, and the change left many Virginia and Maryland slaves idle. Between 1810 and 1861, slave traders and planters carried one million slaves across the Appalachians into the southern interior, as far up the Mississippi as was profitable and as far west as Texas.[14] Although kidnapping could never serve as a major source for the new slave trade, the rising price of slaves made it tempting to the unscrupulous. Free blacks in the states bordering this westward migration—Pennsylvania, Maryland, Delaware, and Ohio—were most at risk. The possibility of kidnapping, however, existed everywhere and anywhere for African Americans.[15]

With its minimal safeguards for free blacks, the Fugitive Slave Act served as perfect cover for kidnappers. Congress investigated this issue several times in the 1790s. In April 1796, the House of Representatives passed a resolution instructing the Committee of Commerce and Manufactures to inquire into a law preventing "the kidnapping of negroes and mulattoes."[16] The House took up the issue in December, during its second session. A report from the committee suggested a bill for registering free blacks brought into port to prevent their kidnapping. The report was not well received. It attracted criticism from slaveholders, such as William L. Smith, of South Carolina, who did not believe "the Constitution allowed that House to act [on the matter]."[17] His reasons were clear enough. The states had adequate laws to prevent kidnapping, and the job of regulating their ports and protecting free blacks was up to them. In his words, it was "altogether a municipal regulation."[18] Northern representatives, such as Joshua Coit and Edward Livingston, concurred with Smith, stating forcefully that the greater evil was the federal government meddling in state matters.[19] The House sent the report back to committee, which reported back several weeks later its recommendation that the House pass a resolution stating that it was "not expedient for this House to interfere with any existing law of the States on this subject."[20]

Congress also entertained a petition from North Carolina slaves who claimed to have been manumitted by their owners and then illegally re-enslaved. James Madison employed the same dual federalism argument to recommend denying their petition. He thought it a judicial case. "If they are free by the laws of North Carolina," said Madison, "they ought to apply to those laws, and have their privilege established."[21] Madison's argument did not touch on the rights of free blacks residing in free states but suggested that it was up to the states to determine their residents' status. By implication, they also had the right to protect them. In any case, the House of Representatives voted against receiving the petition. The problem surfaced again in 1799, when a number of Philadelphia free blacks submitted a petition praying for protection against kidnapping. This time, the report was referred to a special committee. The report that emerged from that committee—but was never submitted to Congress, for reasons unclear—identified that "there is reason to believe that many Blacks & People of Colour entitled to their Freedom . . . are under color of the Fugitive Law entrapped, kidnapped & carried off."[22] Even before the cotton explosion or the prohibition on the international slave trade, evidence of kidnapping was abundant.

In defeating even the possibility of federal antikidnapping legislation, slaveholders evinced a ruthless efficiency in uniting against any perceived threat to their peculiar institution.[23] In the 1790s, however, northerners joined them in their concern that Congress should not overstep constitutional limits. The regulation of ports and protection of citizens, northern congressmen argued, was a police issue left by the Constitution to the states. They consistently rested on this same principle whenever proposals surfaced to strengthen the Fugitive Slave Act. A bill proposed in 1802 would have required anyone employing a black person to make certain that the worker had a certificate under county seal attesting to his or her free status. Anyone employing a fugitive slave would be liable for a $500 fine. Northern representatives opposed the bill on the grounds that it would be inconvenient to force free people of color to carry about such certificates.[24]

The situation nearly blew up in December 1817, when Congress considered amendments to the Fugitive Slave Act. The bill would have required state officers to accept certificates of removal issued by southern courts as definitive and imposed penalties on any state officers refusing to aid in fugitive slave reclamation. Southerners, theretofore concerned over the power of Congress to direct state officers, came to the bill's defense. James Pindall, of Virginia, argued that there were many cases in which the federal and the state governments had concurrent jurisdiction. Besides, he argued, the Constitution ordered that fugitives from labor shall be delivered up: "This duty of delivering up the slave is not imposed on private men or individuals, . . . [it] is imposed on the State." And the state, Pindall asserted, "acts by the intervention of its officers." Pindall was right, historically speaking. More important, he believed that early congressional action was ipso facto evidence of its constitutionality. "*Contemporaneous practice*," he argued "might be deduced from the earliest acts of this Government."[25] Although Pindall was not content to rely solely on this point, it was important evidence. His argument carried the House. Clearly, southern qualms over granting the federal government power to direct state officers could be soothed if the direction was to protect slave property.[26]

Southerners did have serious reservations about an antikidnapping amendment that Vermont Republican Charles Rich attempted to attach to the bill. The amendment would have eliminated the right of recaption by requiring anyone claiming a fugitive first to obtain a certificate of removal. New York Federalist Henry Storrs proposed a milder amendment, which would have subjected to fine or imprisonment anyone convicted of procuring a certificate "with intention, under color or pretence" of the Fugitive Slave Act to arrest or transport "any person whatsoever, not held to labor or service."[27] This substitute amendment received the assent of Pindall. Rich objected, vindicating his amendment on the grounds that the crime of kidnapping required the interposition of Congress. Nevertheless, Storrs's amendment to Rich's amendment was accepted. Rich attempted one last vote on recommitment to committee to attach a substantive antikidnapping provision, but Pindall objected as "the House had already once decided against doing so on the same ground of the want of necessary connexion of the proposed amendment with the bill."[28] Fugitive slave reclamation and protection against kidnapping, argued Pindall, were two separate issues. The House agreed and voted against recommitment.

Clifton Clagett, of New Hampshire, raised another constitutional issue in the House. Although he understood the fugitive slave clause to be imperative and congressional legislation proper, he objected to the Fugitive Slave Act's codification of recaption. "This is a great latitude," he argued, "and there is danger of an abuse of this power to the injury of the free citizen, who may never appear before such tribunal!" This, urged Clagett, was what required amendment. In pursuance of fulfilling the obligations of Article IV, Clagett urged his fellow representatives to "be cautious lest we infract another, equally important" obligation. The bill, he argued, virtually suspended the writ of habeas corpus by ordering anyone arrested under it to be remanded automatically to the arresting officer.[29]

Answering this claim was William Smith, of South Carolina. On March 6, he gave a full exposition of the proslavery response to the problem of due process. Habeas corpus, he argued, had never been intended to grant a right of trial. It was meant only to ensure that the prisoner was held by legitimate process. It would be perverse, he argued, to assert that judges issuing writs of habeas corpus could remove questions that belonged before juries and decide them in a summary hearing. This would violate rights granted by the Sixth and Seventh Amendments.[30]

Congress had become embroiled in a debate on how to balance fugitive slave rendition with the problem of kidnapping. While willing to admit that intentionally false claims made before courts of record were punishable, slaveholders would not assent to a procedure that outlawed recaption. They were unwilling to consider antikidnapping measures, which, they argued, were a different matter altogether. This clash was one of the first tests of the law's constitutionality. Several very different positions had been staked out. Pindall, for example, believed it completely constitutional for Congress to direct state officers—primarily because it had long been congressional practice—but many others now expressed doubts on this subject. Several northerners had raised concerns that the act of fugitive slave recaption was illegal, although they could not get a majority to agree on this subject. Likewise, some northerners pushed for antikidnapping measures, but many congressional representatives conceptually separated this problem from fugitive slave rendition. If nothing else, southerners demonstrated they could move in a block to secure proslavery legislation. Despite this southern solidarity, the new fugitive slave bill never became law. The House and Senate passed different versions but were unable to agree on a single bill. It was finally tabled and quietly died.[31]

These debates revealed the precarious nature of the constitutional settlement embodied in the 1793 Fugitive Slave Act. Congress had presumed to direct the states as to their constitutional duties, and by all accounts the states had acquiesced in enforcing it.[32] But the states had also taken seriously their duty to protect their free blacks. In a 1785 statute, Massachusetts extended the protection of habeas corpus to prevent slave owners from exercising the right of recaption. Pennsylvania amended its 1780 gradual abolition statute to include antikidnapping measures in 1788, and Connecticut included a section punishing kidnapping in its anti–slave trade statute. Several slave states passed similar laws. In 1787, Virginia made the kidnapping of a free Negro a felony, and Delaware made the act of exporting a free black as a slave punishable by fine.[33] The implications of revolutionary ideology certainly contributed to the extension of protections to free blacks in free states and slave states alike. Mississippi passed an antikidnapping statute in 1820, and Georgia passed an act "more effectually to protect free persons of color" in 1835. Although Georgia's law imposed on blacks the burden of proving their freedom, it did offer some means of legal protection to the state's free black population.[34]

With some difficulty, free states negotiated the differences between kidnapping and the legitimate reclamation of fugitives. Pennsylvania in 1788 and New York in 1808 passed laws that not only enforced penalties for kidnapping but also demanded that when the status of a fugitive was in question, that question would be decided in their—not the slave state's—jurisdiction. Ohio passed laws intended to establish a definite procedure for the removal of fugitive slaves, all of which were favorable to slave owners. Indiana passed an 1816 law preventing kidnapping and requiring—if either party demanded—a jury trial to determine the status of an alleged fugitive slave. In 1819, an Ohio statute required a court proceeding in accordance with the Fugitive Slave Act in order to remove a fugitive slave from the state, effectively criminalizing recaption.[35]

The conflict between state and federal law came before the federal circuit court for the district of Indiana in 1818. An 1816 Indiana statute required nonresidents making fugitive slave claims to obtain certificates of removal from a state magistrate who could, at his discretion, order a jury trial.[36] Because two different modes of reclamation, one prescribed by Congress and the other by Indiana, were now in conflict, the case ended up in the federal district court. The lawyer for Susan, the alleged fugitive, suggested that the Fugitive Slave Act was unconstitutional because the Constitution did not give Congress the authority to legislate on the matter. In a second argument, he admitted the constitutionality of the law but stated that state law overrode the federal law. The district court judge admitted that "this case has probably furnished the first occasion on which the validity of this law has been questioned." But he entertained no doubts about its constitutionality: it had been "recognized in many cases before the judges and courts of this country."[37] The New York Supreme Court, for example, had upheld the law in 1812.[38] Jurists had cited it, including the distinguished St. George Tucker. The statute in Indiana that mandated a trial by jury for the return of fugitives—in accordance with the common law—conflicted with national law and was thus void. The court did not rule out the states' power to pass legislation on the subject altogether; only in cases in which conflicting laws had the same end could one be valid and the other "useless." Congress's law superseded that of the states, and "it is unnecessary to inquire whether one or the other is best calculated to promote the ends of justice. It is sufficient that congress have prescribed the mode."[39]

It is important to consider what the judge in this case did not do. Although he affirmed the constitutionality of the Fugitive Slave Act, he did not examine the law's particulars. Instead, he took other courts' acceptance of the law as prima facie evidence of its constitutionality and deferred to Congress on the question of the substance of the law.[40] Judicial deference to congressional constitutional interpretation was a fundamental feature of the early republic's constitutionalism. Whatever tacit right to review legislation the courts claimed, the power of judicial review was circumscribed by constitutional practice.[41] State courts that exercised a muscular judicial review found themselves under attack by legislatures jealous of their powers.[42] Federal courts, particularly the Supreme Court, exercised that power solely in cases connected with federalism. When two conflicting sovereignties claimed the right to legislate on a certain matter, the courts read the Constitution to determine whether the power belonged to the states or to Congress. This was the substance of the ruling in *Susan*. The judge held that Congress had the power to legislate the mode of fugitive slave rendition. Once it did, the Indiana statute, insofar as it prescribed a different procedure for rendition, was invalid. How Indiana's laws might operate on a free black, the court declined to say.

But the state of Indiana did. When slave catchers removed Susan without complying with Indiana law, a grand jury indicted them for kidnapping, and Indiana's governor demanded their extradition. The Kentucky legislature responded with resolutions decrying Indiana's antikidnapping law as unconstitutional. Indiana's legislature referred the matter to its judiciary committee, which returned a report dissenting from the ruling in *Susan*. The lack of antikidnapping measures in the Fugitive Slave Act, read the report, left it open to abuse. The state of Indiana could not suppose that Kentucky would correct these abuses. Therefore, the federal law might direct state officers, but it was not binding, for such laws "might, in time, be altogether perverted from what our constitution intended." Because Congress had not provided a remedy for kidnapping, and because the Fugitive Slave Act relied on state officers for its execution, "it became both the right and the duty of our state to pass some law on the subject."[43] In 1824, the Indiana legislature passed a new law respecting fugitive slaves that specified a summary procedure for rendition. The law allowed evidence to be presented to establish claims of freedom and provided for an appeal by either party.[44] It was a more substantive interpretation of the summary procedure provided by the Fugitive Slave Act.

Antikidnapping laws were not the only remedies available to alleged fugitive slaves seeking to establish their claims to freedom. In addition to the writ of habeas corpus, most states recognized the common-law writ de homine replegiando, or personal replevin. Although Blackstone had considered it an ineffectual remedy in the eighteenth century, it remained a common-law writ at large.[45] It also had particular advantages for those seized as fugitive slaves. The alleged fugitive, or someone on his or her behalf, could sue out the writ, which directed the sheriff to take the person from his or her captor. In the event the alleged fugitive could not be found, the captor would be imprisoned. Importantly, the issues involved would be joined in a trial before a jury. This writ also guaranteed the alleged fugitive a jury trial in the state in which he was found rather than the state in which he was claimed.

An 1819 Pennsylvania case tested this procedure. Lawyers had sued out a writ of habeas corpus for an alleged fugitive, and the hearing ended in the grant of a certificate of removal because it appeared that the plaintiff was in fact a fugitive slave. Lawyers subsequently sued out a writ de homine replegiando, which the Pennsylvania Supreme Court quashed in *Wright v. Deacon*. Chief Justice William Tilghman held that the habeas corpus proceeding had been "in conformity" with the Fugitive Slave Act and that the certificate of removal was thus binding. The writ de homine replegiando served only to arrest the process "and thus defeat the constitution and law of the United States." Tilghman noted that the issue was of some importance and that, "whatever may be our private opinions on the subject of slavery, it is well known that our southern brethren would not have consented to become parties to a constitution under which the *United States* have enjoyed so much prosperity, unless their property in slaves had been secured."[46] Although this analysis inaccurately lumped the fugitive slave clause in with other compromises over slavery, it was not an apology for refusing arguments on the unconstitutionality of the Fugitive Slave Act. Rather, it was a response to the plaintiff's claim that the habeas corpus proceedings were irregular because the matter of a certificate of removal had been pending before another justice of the peace. For Tilghman, what mattered was that the "summary proceeding" required by the act of Congress had been satisfied. "If he had really a right to freedom," explained Tilghman, "that right was not impaired by this proceeding; he was placed just in the situation in which he stood before he fled, and might prosecute his right in the state to which he belonged."[47]

This last sentence was crucial. Tilghman firmly stated that claims to freedom had to be prosecuted in the state of residency. If the fugitive claimed freedom by the laws of Maryland, then he must press his claim there. Although Tilghman was silent about what rule might apply if a free black resident of Pennsylvania was claimed as a fugitive, his acceptance of a habeas corpus hearing as definitive suggests that he had not ruled out the interposition of state courts. In any event, Tilghman was not construing a Pennsylvania statute but ruling on a common-law writ that had been called upon to impede rendition under a federal statute. Quashing the writ did not imply that Pennsylvania could not legislate on the subject of free blacks. It meant only that fugitives from slave states could not claim rights under Pennsylvania laws.

In 1823, antislavery lawyers asked the Massachusetts Supreme Court to declare the Fugitive Slave Act unconstitutional because recaption without a warrant violated the Fourth Amendment. Chief Justice Isaac Parker, who wrote the opinion for the court in *Commonwealth v. Griffith*, disagreed. Slaves could not claim Fourth Amendment rights, explained Parker, because they were not parties to the Constitution. The summary procedure for rendition, then, was constitutional. "But it is objected that a person may in this summary manner seize a freeman," noted the chief justice. "It may be so, but this would be attended with mischievous consequences to the person making the seizure, and a habeas corpus would lie to obtain the release of the person seized."[48] Put simply, fugitives fit into a different category than free blacks, and the remedies available to an individual were determined by his or her status.

The highest courts of Massachusetts and Pennsylvania had not given an unqualified judicial endorsement of the Fugitive Slave Act. Certainly, neither explored its substance—they simply evaluated procedure in several cases and ruled as to what constituted a fair construction of the statute. They denied alleged fugitives the right to a trial by jury, on the presumption that they were not residents of the state within which they were found. In both cases, the courts maintained the right of free blacks to resort to state courts for writs of habeas corpus, essentially giving judicial recognition to the constitutional settlement reached by Congress.

Antislavery societies spent less time testing cases in court than lobbying state legislatures for more protections for free blacks. They enjoyed success in the former slave states of Pennsylvania, New Jersey, and New York. A Pennsylvania law of 1820 fixed the penalty for kidnapping at twenty-one years at hard labor and forbade state officers from aiding in fugitive slave rendition. Neighboring Maryland complained mightily, as the meager federal court infrastructure made capturing fugitive slaves almost an impossibility. Under pressure, the Pennsylvania legislature revised its law in 1826. The new law left intact the criminal penalties for kidnapping but lifted the ban on state officers' aiding in rendition. The law also set new standards for evidence. The slave owner had to produce a sworn affidavit sealed by a court in his home jurisdiction. The act also negated the slave owner's right of recaption. In order to remove a fugitive, the slave owner had to go through a court in Pennsylvania. Also in 1826, New Jersey passed a personal liberty law that largely conformed state procedure in fugitive slave rendition to that of the Fugitive Slave Act, even as it provided more protections, including a ban on recaption. New York passed a law in 1828 securing alleged fugitives' access to the writ de homine replegiando. The steps taken by New Jersey, New York, and Pennsylvania were soon replicated in other northern states in the 1830s and 1840s.[49]

These personal liberty laws ostensibly sought to balance the constitutional duties of fugitive slave rendition and the protection of free black residents. Mounting opposition to slavery in the 1830s, however, turned these solutions into new conflicts. Just as the Fugitive Slave Act had created a temptation to kidnapping, personal liberty laws provided abolitionists with the means to frustrate legitimate rendition of fugitive slaves. The increasing militancy of the antislavery movement crystallized with its turn to the doctrine of immediatism in the 1830s, and this change inaugurated a new era of resistance.[50] Slaveholders found themselves forced to appear before local judges to defend their claims and oftentimes jailed for restraining fugitives. This practice occasioned a rant by Supreme Court justice Henry Baldwin in a jury charge that he delivered while riding circuit in 1833. Members of the Pennsylvania Antislavery Society had attempted to stop a slaveholder from seizing his fugitive. This interference had brought threats of force from the arresting party. Shortly thereafter, the slave catchers were arrested under Pennsylvania's antikidnapping law. Noting that the noble intent of the personal liberty laws of Pennsylvania had been to prevent kidnapping, Baldwin complained that such a perversion of the purpose of the law was unconscionable. "Would a wise, just, or humane body of men," he asked rhetorically, "pass a law which would put on a level the man who reclaimed his own property by lawful means, and the wretch who would drag a freeman into bondage?"[51]

Although such collisions were quite real in the 1830s, there is little evidence that abolitionists were successful in using the personal liberty laws to thwart fugitive slave rendition.[52] Even antislavery judges did their duty. In 1835, evidence was admitted on behalf of an alleged fugitive named Charles Brown before the recorder of Pittsburgh in conformity with the 1826 Pennsylvania personal liberty law. Despite his personal abhorrence of slavery, the recorder granted the certificate of removal.[53] Still, the willingness of abolitionists to use the personal liberty laws to attempt to frustrate legitimate rendition contributed to sectional agitation in the heated 1830s. Abolitionists had succeeded in making the rendition process lengthier and more expensive and had brought federal and state laws into collision. The old constitutional compromise was breaking down, and the hybrid system of state and federal duties regarding fugitive slave rendition and antikidnapping protections was coming to a halt.

Responses to this situation were varied. When the issue came before Judge Samuel Nelson of the New York Supreme Court in the 1834 case of *Jack, a Negro Man v. Martin,* he took counsel's requests to entertain questions on the constitutionality of the Fugitive Slave Act seriously. Jack averred to being an escaped slave, held under the laws of Louisiana, but he claimed freedom because his owner, Mary Martin, was a citizen of the free state of New York. Because Jack's admitted status as a fugitive mooted the issue of his freedom, counsel argued that the constitutional duty of fugitive slave rendition belonged to the states, each of which had the right to determine the method by which it would deliver up fugitives. Therefore, the 1793 law was unconstitutional. Judge Nelson thought not. Once the national government had legislated on the matter, he ruled, the supremacy clause of the Constitution made the congressional law paramount. Nelson then went one step further: the states could not legislate concurrently because the power was exhausted. Nelson justified this conclusion on instrumentalist grounds: that is, on its reasonableness rather than on precedent. It was "obvious" that if each state could determine for itself how fugitives from service would be delivered up, then Congress's "solemn guaranty may be wholly disregarded, in defiance of the Government. This power seems indispensable to enable it faithfully to discharge the obligations to the States and citizens interested."[54] Nelson cherry-picked authorities to buttress his position, but his reasoning was primarily instrumentalist.[55] It was "appropriate," said Nelson, that the power belonged to the national government. The problem of fugitive slaves required that slavery briefly "be enforced within the jurisdiction of States other than those in which the citizens generally interested in them reside, and on a subject, too, known deeply to affect the public mind." This was proof enough for Nelson to come to his conclusion that a uniform rule was necessary and that such a rule "could be attained only by placing it under the action of the National Government."[56]

In many ways, this was an extraordinary opinion. It suggested that anti-kidnapping laws might be unconstitutional or at least that they must yield to federal law upon invocation of the Fugitive Slave Act. This reasoning rejected several decades of jurisprudence that had understood the congressional settlement of the matter to be a compromise between differing duties of the states and the federal government. Nelson had made no attempt to understand this. Instead of looking to Congress's constitutional position or perhaps reviewing the intent of the legislation, he applied an instrumentalist reading to the problem to justify, logically, why it was an issue that lay solely with the federal government.

Even Supreme Court justice Smith Thompson, in a ruling in the federal circuit court for New York, was not willing to go this far. The fugitive slave clause required legislation, he wrote, "and it cannot be presumed that it was intended to leave this to state legislation." Furthermore, he noted that in the act "there is no express injunction upon the states to pass any laws on the subject." Thompson was not willing to rule out concurrent state legislation. He simply noted that it would be "an extravagant construction of this provision in the constitution, to suppose it to be left discretionary in the states to comply with it or not, as they should think proper." The key word was *comply:* if the Constitution enjoined a duty, it was not within the power of the states to slough it off.[57]

Nelson's ruling in *Jack v. Martin* was appealed to New York's Court for the Correction of Errors, where the result was upheld, but not without some ambivalence. The court was an unusual one in the American judicial system. It was composed of the New York state senate and either the chancellor, if the case was appealed from the supreme court, or the justices of the supreme court, if the case was appealed from the chancery. There was no deliberation. The members of the court simply voted on the outcome. Opinions, if any, were delivered seriatim.[58] In *Jack v. Martin,* this led to a strange result. The court voted to uphold the outcome of the case, but the two opinions filed did not necessarily affirm Nelson's reasoning. Senator Isaac Bishop agreed that Congress should have power to legislate on the matter, noting that the confusion of disunified procedure (one for each state) would amount to an act of abolition.[59] Although this was instrumentalism of a kind, Bishop did not go nearly as far as Nelson in finding an exclusive congressional jurisdiction.

For Chancellor Reuben Walworth, such a position presumed too much. Largely unimpressed with Nelson's reasoning, he interpreted the fugitive slave clause as a command to the officers of the states—judicial, executive, and legislative. He could find no express grant of power in the fugitive slave clause that gave Congress the power to pass a law under which "any free citizen of this State may be seized as a slave or apprentice who has escaped from servitude, and transported to a distant part of the Union, without any trial except a summary examination before a magistrate, who is not even clothed with power to compel the attendance of witnesses upon such investigation."[60] Key in Walworth's ruling was the judicial determination of status, which was clearly an affair of the states. Although fugitives should be returned—and Walworth made clear in his opinion that Jack's avowal to being a fugitive was fatal to his defense—the Fugitive

Slave Act could not prevent free residents of New York from suing out writs of habeas corpus or availing themselves of writs de homine replegiando. Even Senator Bishop's hearty concurrence described a fugitive slave rendition process that allowed for status determination in the state of capture.

At least one state judge repudiated Nelson's reasoning. In an unreported 1836 case, the Superior Court of New Jersey rejected national law in favor of state law. Chief Justice Joseph Hornblower accepted an application for habeas corpus and during the hearing took up the problem of the conflict of New Jersey law and the Fugitive Slave Act. Hornblower admitted the supremacy of national law but denied that the fugitive slave clause contained any grant of legislative power to Congress. Noting that other clauses in Article IV contained specific grants of power, Hornblower concluded, as had Chancellor Walworth, that Congress had no warrant to legislate. He did not presume to rule the federal law null and void, but he did declare that, in the matter before him, state law took precedence.[61]

Judicial interpretation of the Fugitive Slave Act and the states' personal liberty laws had produced confusion and uneasiness, particularly in the eyes of slaveholders who resented any delay in the return of their property. Some kind of judicial resolution was needed. In 1837, agents of Marylander Margaret Ashmore—a man named Edward Prigg among them—arrested Ashmore's fugitive slave residing in Pennsylvania. They brought the fugitive and her children before the justice of the peace who had issued the initial arrest warrant, but he refused to have anything more to do with the case. Prigg and the party carried the fugitives back to Maryland without obtaining a certificate of removal. Two months later, a Pennsylvania grand jury indicted them all for kidnapping, and Pennsylvania's governor officially requested their extradition to Pennsylvania for trial. Maryland's governor refused the extradition request and instead submitted the matter to the legislature. The Maryland legislature responded with resolutions decrying state interference with fugitive slave rendition and called for a vindication of slaveholders' rights in the U.S. Supreme Court. Pennsylvania's legislature acquiesced to a judicial settlement, and the case went to the U.S. Supreme Court in 1840 with the consent of both states.[62] Their hope was a clear resolution of the conflict between laws. But the decision in *Prigg v. Pennsylvania* was anything but settling. John Quincy Adams wrote that *Prigg* consisted of "seven judges, every one of them dissenting from the reasoning of all the rest."[63] Adams overstated the case, but he put his finger on a controversy that raged for the next two decades.[64]

Joseph Story wrote the opinion of the court. Boldly, he announced his intention to settle the matter once and for all. "We do not wish to rest our present opinion upon the ground either of contemporaneous exposition, or long acquiescence, or even practical action," wrote Story, "on the contrary, our judgment would be the same if the question were entirely new, and the act of Congress were of recent enactment."[65] The notion that timeless principles of interpretation could produce a static constitutional jurisprudence was not new; but the implication that the Supreme Court might have the final—and, by logical extension, irreversible—decision in the matter rankled many in Jacksonian America. Story had not meant to offend. Rather, he hoped that his nationalist jurisprudence might prove a salve for sectional wounds. The Fugitive Slave Act presented a golden opportunity to prove to southerners that the national government was important in protecting their interests, too. In his 1833 *Commentaries on the Constitution,* Story had noted that "it cannot escape the attention of every intelligent reader, that many sacrifices of opinion and feeling are to be found made by the Eastern and Middle states to the peculiar interests of the south."[66] In *Prigg,* these "sacrifices" now became a necessity for adoption of the Constitution.[67] This was bad history. It inaccurately lumped the fugitive slave clause together with the more serious compromises over congressional representation and the slave trade. The latter were sine qua non for the southern states to enter into the compact. The former was not.[68]

Story's reasoning in *Prigg* proceeded from his idiosyncratic reading of the constitutional bargain, and he laid out the sources of law in a manner that privileged the powers of the national government. Although Story began by rooting the master's right of recaption in the common law, for which proposition he cited Blackstone, he also invoked the commonly held notion set forth in *Somerset,* that slavery had no place in natural law and could exist only by an express sovereign command. Before the ratification of the Constitution, therefore, the right of recaption had stopped at the territorial borders of the slave states. But the fugitive slave clause of the Constitution had created "a new and positive right" of recaption "independent of comity, confined to no territorial limits, and bounded by no state institutions or policy." Recaption would in practice be difficult, concluded Story, and thus required legislation.[69] "The natural inference deductible from this consideration," he continued, "is, in the absence of any positive delegation of power to the state legislatures, that it belongs to the legislative department of the national government, to which it owes its origin and establishment."[70] And, once Congress had legislated on the matter, this necessarily exhausted the power and preempted state legislation.[71]

There was much of the amazing in this opinion. It implied that the states would abrogate their constitutional duties. It neglected to take account of the legislative history of the statute, particularly the need to balance slaveholders' rights with the duty of the states to prevent the kidnapping of their residents. Most impressively, it stood the Tenth Amendment on its head, suggesting that because the Constitution had not provided positively for state action, the power belonged to the national government. It also indicated the extent to which Story's nationalist instrumentalism supplanted the need for relevant authority.[72] He claimed that the country had long acquiesced to the federal law and that all cases on point had upheld the validity of the Fugitive Slave Act.[73] This was at best disingenuous. Until the 1830s, no court had presumed to examine the substance of the act, making many of Story's citations irrelevant. Nor did the deep ambivalence on the subject expressed by Chancellor Walworth of the New York Court for the Correction of Errors or Justice Hornblower's striking down of the federal law receive any attention from Story. Even if he was unaware of Hornblower's opinion—which, given its limited circulation in the North, was unlikely—the Pennsylvania Supreme Court had laid out its own arguments against the Fugitive Slave Act.[74] Story did not even bother dismissing these opinions. Instead, he ignored them.

For Story, the matter of conflict of laws went to a single issue, one close to his heart: national supremacy. The thrust of his opinion was to demonstrate not only the national government's power to pass the Fugitive Slave Act but its sole jurisdiction in the matter. For this proposition, he went to the authority of the 1819 case of *Sturges v. Crowninshield*.[75] *Sturges* was a case concerned with New York's insolvency laws, and the issues as well as the decision were notoriously complex. The justices agreed that there was concurrent jurisdiction between the states and the national government but that national laws would necessarily preempt state legislation. This was a familiar holding in cases involving bankruptcy laws and interstate commerce, two issues for which there was a clear constitutional directive.[76] Even Marshall admitted in *Sturges* that the question was not entirely one of preemption but also one of distribution of powers between the states and Congress.[77] There was no easy answer, and certainly no easy analogy to the problem of fugitive slaves. Story smoothed over these problems by ignoring them.

Story's nationalism had one antislavery qualification. He had long argued that officers derived their authority from the sovereignty that established them, and this postulate led him logically to conclude that no other power could direct them. This meant that the United States could not direct officers of the state, and vice versa. Although this conclusion ran afoul of constitutional practice concerning fugitive slaves—the Fugitive Slave Act of 1793 had been intended to do just that—it did provide Story with an opportunity to relieve northerners of the undesirable task of sending men, women, and children back to slavery. States could, by statute, prohibit their officers from aiding in fugitive slave rendition and not be in defiance of the article.[78] Chief Justice Roger B. Taney dissented forcefully from this position. In his reading, the Constitution imposed a duty on the states to aid in reclamation. States prohibiting their officers from acting were in dereliction of that duty. What was more, the states retained the right to pass legislation aiding rendition. The Constitution, wrote Taney, "contains no words prohibiting the several states from passing laws to enforce this right. They are in express terms forbidden to make any regulation that shall impair it. But there the prohibition stops."[79] Taney then repudiated the theoretical apparatus Story had constructed concerning the master's right of recaption, which Taney argued, was a matter of common law rather than constitutional law. It was absurd, in Taney's estimation, to assume that the mere mention of fugitive slaves in the Constitution necessarily entailed a surrender of power to the national government. He analogized the fugitive slave clause to the contract clause. The Constitution prohibited any state from passing laws to abrogate contracts, but this did not remove the right of states to pass laws enforcing contracts. Congressional law did not preempt this right of the states, whether the issue was enforcing contracts, bankruptcy, or returning fugitive slaves.[80] As he would state in *Moore v. Illinois* in 1852, the states' power was limited only in that they could not set fugitives free by virtue of their own laws.[81]

As the constitutional disagreement between Story and Taney made clear, *Prigg* was not the final word on the matter of fugitive slave rendition. Story was aware that the power of his opinion depended primarily on the willingness of many to defer. Praying for this end, Story wrote that he trusted "the judgment of this Court in this cause shall meet with the same patriotic acquiescence which the tribunals of the states and the people of the states have heretofore accorded to its decisions."[82] And many states did signal such an acquiescence to Story's constitutional interpretation. Although most laws making writs of habeas corpus and de homine replegiando available to fugitives stayed on the books, Ohio repealed its law, and several New England states repealed their laws requiring a jury trial for fugitives.[83] Massachusetts, Pennsylvania, and Rhode Island responded by forbidding state officers to aid in fugitive slave rendition, thereby bowing to Story's interpretation of the Constitution and putting it to good antislavery use.[84] Justice Levi Woodbury upheld the principle of *Prigg* in the case of *Jones v. Van Zandt* in 1847.[85]

But abolitionists, white and black, were not discouraged. They interpreted the decision as further evidence that a "Slave Power conspiracy" had bent the federal government to its own purposes, an argument that brought more people into line, or at least into sympathy, with the antislavery cause.[86] People continued to subvert the law by helping fugitives escape to Canada along the Underground Railroad. By the 1850s, southern states complained that nearly a thousand slaves a year were escaping with the help of complicit northerners. Although this claim was fueled by bluster and anecdote, few would deny that white abolitionists and free black communities were organizing more effectively to help fugitives escape to Canada.[87]

This strain of resistance ran through Wisconsin as well, where antislavery sentiments arrived with the early settlers. Waukesha and Milwaukee were the northernmost stations in the state's Underground Railroad. The first recorded fugitive to escape via this route was Caroline Quarlles, an escaped slave from St. Louis who arrived in Milwaukee in the summer of 1842. She took refuge with a black Milwaukeean named Titball, himself an ex-slave, who betrayed her the moment lawyers sent by her owner arrived from St. Louis. With the help of a black boy, Caroline evaded capture. The slaveholder's lawyers, sensing trouble from the abolitionist community, attempted to secure legal help in finding and returning Caroline but were turned down by a number of prominent Democrats, including Horatio Nelson Wells (later to be a county judge) and the office of Asahel Finch and William Pitt Lynde (later to be a congressman).

They eventually retained Jonathan E. Arnold, the lawyer who later represented Benammi Garland in the Booth affair. Arnold and his party pursued Caroline, but were frustrated by the conductors of the Underground Railroad—well-known abolitionists all—who led them on a wild goose chase while Caroline slipped away to Canada. Caroline was the first, but not the last, passenger to travel the clandestine path to freedom. Lyman Goodnow, one such conductor on the line, remembered that the "underground railroad had an abundance of business in those days" and that, of all those who traveled through the Milwaukee station, "*every one* arrived safely in the land of freedom."[88]

Nor did northerners abandon the use of state courts and laws to frustrate the claims of slaveholders who captured fugitives on free soil. When a Kentucky slave owner passed through South Bend, Indiana, in September 1849 carrying fugitives he had retrieved in Michigan, a number of South Bend residents confronted him with writs of habeas corpus. A local judge heard the case and released the fugitives, who promptly disappeared northward, presumably to Canada. Abolitionists in Iowa forced slave catchers in June 1848 to submit to a local hearing before removing fugitives from the state. When the slave catchers could not produce any evidence that they were the lawful agents of the slaveholder, the fugitives were released.[89] Such incidents were proof enough to slave owners that resistance to the Fugitive Slave Act, both under color of law and in defiance of it, was endemic in the North. None too few involved the threat of violence. In the South Bend case, hundreds of free blacks from Michigan and Indiana showed up for the alleged fugitives' hearing with firearms and other weapons, demonstrating to slaveholders' satisfaction that the Fugitive Slave Act needed teeth. A concerted campaign began in the 1840s, as southern legislatures passed resolutions and submitted to Congress requests for a new Fugitive Slave Act. Their complaints targeted all forms of resistance, whether it was extralegal violence, the imprisoning of slave catchers on bogus charges of kidnapping, or the frustration of legitimate fugitive reclamation on legal technicalities.[90] It was not an uncommon thing in the antebellum era for Supreme Court rulings to engender official and popular protest—the Supreme Court endured it almost annually in the first half of the nineteenth century.[91] As with other major constitutional controversies in American history, this one required congressional action to find a resolution.

When the Thirty-first Congress met for its first session in December 1849, the debate over a new Fugitive Slave Act differed substantially from the one that had taken place in the first decades of the century. It was for the first time inextricably linked with the question of disposition of the territories. The old compromises across sections and parties had fallen apart after the Free Soil revolt of 1848. California and New Mexico had submitted antislavery constitutions, a convention of delegates from southern states was scheduled to meet in Nashville to discuss the prospect of secession, and abolitionists were promising to revive the Wilmot Proviso: the fabric of the federal union never seemed more brittle. And in all of this, the question of fugitive slave rendition was not even of prime importance. Certainly it paled in comparison to the issues of slavery in the territories and California statehood.[92] But it impinged upon southern honor that northerners would not respect their property and behave courteously, and although fugitive slave rendition never topped their list of concerns, it always made that list. For abolitionists, the matter represented the unwarranted intrusion of slavery onto free soil and offensively asked them to subjugate conscience to political expediency. The fugitive slave problem was one that always loomed larger in perception than in reality, inflamed by unceasing rhetoric about the importance of "conscience," "constitution," "honor," "sacred compromises," "God's law," and the wounding of "tender feelings" on both sides of the Mason-Dixon line.

In January 1850, Senator James Mason, of Virginia, reintroduced a fugitive slave bill that Andrew Butler, of South Carolina, had reported out of the judicial committee during the previous session. Its timing ensured that no one could extricate the bill from other compromise measures of 1850 and may have been the only guarantee for its passage. Debate over the bill engaged constitutional issues different from those that had occupied Congress in the first few decades of its existence. Every congressman had to respond in one way or another to the Supreme Court's decision in *Prigg*. Daniel Webster cited it as evidence that the responsibility for legislation on the matter lay with the federal government. For his own part, he believed the Constitution laid the duty on the states. But, while allowing that *Prigg* "may not have been a fortunate decision," Webster accepted it as authoritative.[93]

Debate on the bill picked up again in August, when the senators quarreled over its constitutionality. William L. Dayton, of New Jersey, argued that *Prigg* had relieved the individual states of any responsibility whatsoever, making the federal government liable—in somewhat idiosyncratic language—as "endorsers" for the defaulting states. This argument to replace rendition with some sort of monetary settlement angered Thomas G. Pratt, of Maryland, who accused Dayton, among other things, of investing the Supreme Court with too much constitutional authority. He challenged Dayton, who, he said, "believes that the Supreme Court is a tribunal appointed by the Constitution for the purpose of deciding constitutional questions, and that its decision in regard to constitutional questions is final and conclusive," to reject the bill on any such grounds.[94] Although carefully distancing himself from this constitutional position, Pratt had set a rhetorical trap for northerners purporting to believe in rule by law. Andrew P. Butler, of South Carolina, made it clear that he rejected any attempt by the Court to determine constitutional duties for the states. He said he would follow *Prigg* "so far as regards the only question adjudicated, but not beyond that."[95] For Butler, this meant ignoring that part of Story's opinion declaring that the states were under no obligation to assist in fugitive rendition.

The most telling, and perhaps nuanced, speech about *Prigg* came from James Mason during debate in January 1850 when he first introduced the fugitive slave bill. The dereliction of duty by northern legislatures had made such legislation a necessity, but Mason warned that the law's success would still depend on the goodwill of northerners, for "no law can be carried into effect, unless it is sustained and supported by the loyalty of the people to whom it is directed." Mason bristled at the suggestion, put forth by a Vermont congressman, that Story's opinion in *Prigg* meant that the northern states were not obliged to pass legislation for the return of fugitive slaves. "I do not so understand that decision," said Mason. He understood *Prigg* to mean that the states could not be *coerced* into passing such legislation, even though it was their duty to provide for it. But Supreme Court justices could not absolve states of constitutional duties, explained Mason, "because they have not the power."[96]

On September 18, 1850, the new fugitive slave bill was signed into law by President Millard Fillmore. Like its predecessor, the statute attempted to settle a sectional dispute. This time, it did so by making fugitive slave rendition entirely a federal matter. It authorized U.S. district courts to appoint U.S. commissioners and gave them concurrent jurisdiction to issue certificates of removal for alleged fugitives in a summary hearing. It reaffirmed the right of recaption for slaveholders or their agents but also specified a procedure by which they could obtain arrest warrants. To obtain the certificate of removal, the slaveholder had to produce an affidavit or a deposition certified by a magistrate in the slaveholder's home state that proved the identity of the fugitive slave. This amounted to proof of ownership, proof of escape, and a description of the fugitive. Once the evidence was presented, the duty of federal judges and commissioners in free states was clear: the statute compelled the return of the fugitive. William Seward, of New York, had attempted to introduce an amendment to the bill providing for trial by jury, a move that provoked the outrage of southern senators. Moving in a bloc, they defeated even Henry Clay's compromise measure that would have afforded fugitives a jury trial in their state of origin.[97]

The result was a summary procedure that forbade the testimony of the alleged fugitive or the introduction of any evidence on his behalf. It also prevented "all molestation . . . by any process issued by any court, judge, magistrate, or other person whomsoever."[98] It went further. The statute increased the civil liability for anyone preventing reclamation of fugitives to $1,000 and added criminal penalties of up to six months in prison and an additional fine of up to $1,000. The statute directed U.S. officers to assist the slaveholder in confining and transporting the fugitive across state lines. To this end, they were given authority—and in essence were required by the statute—to enlist as many persons as necessary to aid in rendition. Lest there should be any doubt about the ability of the marshal's requisitions, the act provided that "all good citizens are hereby commanded to aid and assist in the prompt and efficient execution of this law, whenever their services may be required."[99] Short of forgoing a judicial hearing altogether for alleged fugitives, it was as one-sided an act as it could have been.

The new Fugitive Slave Act elicited outrage in the North. It united diehard abolitionists with more moderate antislavery men, resulting in a growing call for disobedience. For radicals like William Lloyd Garrison, this was simply more proof that the U.S. Constitution was a "slave document," itself an obstacle to reform and abolition.[100] What offended most moderates was the provision admonishing people to come to the aid of slave catchers if so requested. This had in essence removed the possibility of neutrality through noncooperation. A new pamphlet debate erupted after 1850 that condemned the Fugitive Slave Act for its incompatibility with God's law rather than its compatibility with the Constitution.[101] One minister even went so far as to claim that excessive debate about the constitutional legality of slavery was irreligious. By calling the Constitution the "higher law," he claimed, people had made it into a false idol.[102] Whatever abolitionists' fidelity to the Constitution, their assault proceeded largely from the religious imagination and was built on moral and personal foundations.[103] Still, much of the anger over the law coursed through constitutional channels. Not four months after the law's passage, Congress had received eleven petitions calling for its repeal. Each tabled.[104]

Quiet petitioning went alongside more active resistance. Antislavery societies formed vigilance committees—voluntary associations that published their intentions to stand by any fugitives arrested under the law. On February 12, 1851, a fugitive named Shadrach Minkins was arrested in Boston. Antislavery lawyers swung into action. A previously appointed vigilance committee prepared a defense for Shadrach and went to obtain a writ of habeas corpus. The U.S. commissioner in the case, George T. Curtis, gave Shadrach's counsel time to prepare and delayed proceedings for three days. In the meantime, U.S. marshals found it exceedingly difficult to protect their prisoner. City officers invoked the Massachusetts personal liberty law to prevent the federal officers from using Boston's jails, nor did the marshals find many able-bodied men willing to come to their aid. Outnumbered by the huge crowd that gathered outside, they were easily overwhelmed by a cadre of Boston's black residents, who stormed the commissioner's courtroom, removed Shadrach, and spirited him away to Montreal.[105]

The fallout from the rescue was spectacular. Henry Clay demanded an investigation. Secretary of State Daniel Webster accused the rescuers of treason and zealously pursued their prosecution.[106] President Fillmore requested clarifying legislation allowing him to use the army, navy, and militia to help execute the law. At the same time, he issued a proclamation calling on all citizens to support the laws of the country. That occasion would come soon, in April 1851, when a slave named Thomas Sims from Georgia was arrested and brought before the U.S. commissioner's court in Boston. Eager to avoid a repetition of the Shadrach affair, the marshal enlisted more than three hundred men to guard Sims. Mass meetings gathered thousands outside the jail, and lawyers tried desperately to use the old strategy of interposing the state courts by filing a writ of habeas corpus with the state supreme court. Chief Justice Lemuel Shaw denied the petition flatly, first refusing to grant it without convening the court and then rejecting it during a formal hearing a few days later. Quite mechanically, Shaw stated that the Fugitive Slave Act was constitutional and that this prevented him from issuing the writ. Sims was carried back to Georgia under heavy guard, at a cost of nearly $20,000.[107] The successful rendition of Thomas Sims was soon overshadowed by violence not half a year later in Christiana, Pennsylvania. When a slave owner and his son attempted to arrest a fugitive, the fugitive and local whites who came to his aid attacked them, leaving the slave owner dead and the son seriously wounded. Shortly thereafter, police in Syracuse, New York, proved no match for an organized crowd that rescued a fugitive slave named Jerry.[108]

The reports of thousands gathering in opposition to the law, of courthouses rushed and peace officers overwhelmed, and of slaveholders killed attempting to exercise their rights overshadowed the more numerous instances of the Fugitive Slave Act's successful execution. Popular resistance waned between 1852 and 1854, as many seemed willing to accept the Compromise of 1850 as necessary for the survival of the Union.[109] Attempts to raise the issue in Congress went nowhere. On August 26, 1852, Charles Sumner, of Massachusetts, held up an appropriation bill in the Senate while attempting to attach an amendment to forbid the use of federal monies to enforce the Fugitive Slave Act. Responding to the argument that the endorsement of the Second Congress and President Washington gave the law special constitutional sanction, he reasoned that "the wise fathers did not treat the country as a Chinese foot, never to grow after infancy; but, anticipating progress, they declared expressly that their Great Act is not final."[110] He urged Congress to rethink its position and repeal the law on constitutional grounds.[111] He encountered staunch resistance from Democrats—many of whom were northerners—who elevated the compromise measures and the Fugitive Slave Act to near permanency. They repeatedly asserted that the Constitution demanded that fugitives be delivered up and that this directive gave Congress authority, although their reasoning varied. Jesse Bright, of Indiana, argued that the enforcement of a constitutional directive was a political issue, one that Congress had decided belonged to the national power. Isaac Toucey, of Connecticut, argued that the Supreme Court had adjudged the Fugitive Slave Act of 1793 constitutional, and he had no doubt that others thought it legal too. Charles T. James, of Rhode Island, said that no state could be bound in the Union "politically or morally, longer than the constitutional guarantee for the protection of life and property shall be continued and faithfully carried out. And, sir, what is the Fugitive Slave Act, but a law to execute this guarantee?"[112] Sumner's amendment was soundly defeated.

In 1852, the Democrat Franklin Pierce triumphed in the presidential race. Lest there should be any doubt about the way he interpreted his victory at the polls, he announced in his March 4, 1853, inaugural address that the compromise measures of 1850 were "strictly constitutional" and that they would "be unhesitatingly carried into effect."[113] His attorney general, the decidedly antiabolitionist New Englander Caleb Cushing, developed a strong plan for executive enforcement of the Fugitive Slave Act. Cushing's legal opinions claimed that it was the duty of the U.S. government to pay all expenses involved in rendition, including the salaries of any people whom the marshal pressed into service with his power of posse comitatus. He advised marshals that they had the right to compel the state militia as well as the U.S. Army to act.[114] Still, state officers continued to serve writs on federal officers who attempted to execute the law. Cushing instructed the solicitor of the Treasury that it was the duty of the government to pick up the tab for any legal defense, as these "notorious plans of resistance . . . concocted by fanatical and dispersed persons" could be defeated only by swift and steadfast resolve.[115]

Attorney General Cushing's push for vigorous enforcement came in the face of the most ferocious resistance yet to the Fugitive Slave Act. There was little doubt as to its cause. One conservative Whig predicted that the passage of the Kansas-Nebraska bill would mean "the complete nullification of the Fugitive Slave Law."[116] History bore out this observation.[117] The first fruits of the Kansas-Nebraska bill appeared in Wisconsin with the rescue of Joshua Glover. Not two months later, the arrest of Anthony Burns in Boston led to a botched rescue attempt in which one of Burns's federal guards was shot dead.[118] Violence had now claimed the life of a peace officer, and this troubled many. It ossified positions both for and against the act and led many to equate any kind of resistance with lawless disorder. Cushing himself noted that even resistance under color of law— the obtaining of writs of habeas corpus and the harassment of federal officers—"had sufficed to produce violence and bloodshed."[119] His solution was strict and more vigorous enforcement. But after the Glover and Burns affairs, no fugitive would be removed from Wisconsin or Boston.

—

As the Senate debates of the 1850s reveal, the context of the Fugitive Slave Act's constitutionality had changed dramatically since 1793. What began as an attempt to restore comity over the question of fugitive rendition—fugitives from labor and fugitives from justice—had been transformed into a brokered compromise to save the Union. What began as a congressional clarification of the duties of state officers ended in complete arrogation of the power to federal officers. In the 1790s, the debate about congressional responsibility regarding fugitive slaves had referred to the necessity of protecting free blacks from kidnapping. Although Congress never claimed this duty, the underlying assumption was that the states possessed ample power to protect their residents. By the 1850s, this was in doubt. The Supreme Court had ruled that the states' personal liberty laws were unconstitutional, and Congress had insulated fugitive slave rendition from state interference.

The Fugitive Slave Act of 1850 was a forceful step by Congress, and its most decisively proslavery statute. Was it constitutional? The Supreme Court had indicated that it was ready to defer to congressional constitutional interpretation in the matter. The only issue that the Court had confidently settled was that Congress held constitutional warrant to legislate on the subject. The failure of Story's opinion to quell state and popular opposition to fugitive slave rendition indicated at the very least that the matter would not rest easy upon only a Supreme Court decision. Congressional action, however, fared no better. Resistance only increased after Congress enacted the Compromise of 1850. The long acquiescence cited to justify the constitutionality of the Fugitive Slave Act was decidedly over. People who petitioned for its repeal in Congress asserted their own interpretations of the Constitution, often at odds with Story's understanding expressed in *Prigg*. Some who spoke in defense of its constitutionality expressed a difference of opinion with Story as well.

There was also the question of the act's abrogation of the right of jury trial and the halting of potential state habeas corpus proceedings. Although many believed that the 1793 law accomplished the same thing, there was a distinct difference in the 1850 act. At least until *Prigg*, states had considered habeas corpus proceedings to be within the scope of the act, and the federal courts had acquiesced. Even if the procedure was onerous and problematic, states had the right to defend their free blacks from being reduced to slavery. Story's opinion in *Prigg* had removed this possibility, and the 1850 law gave statutory force to this portion of the decision. Did this unconstitutionally violate the reserved powers of the states to protect their residents? Very likely. In the 1790s, congressional refusal to enact a statute protecting free blacks from kidnapping had hinged on the understanding that states had the appropriate power to obstruct the practice. True, the Supreme Court had since decided otherwise, and Congress had agreed when it passed the Fugitive Slave Act of 1850. The question that lingered was whether the federal government had the ability to declare in the final instance whether this decision itself was constitutional.

THREE

The Disappearance of Joshua Glover

FUN WITHOUT VULGARITY
YOUNG'S HALL
FOR ONE WEEK ONLY, COMMENCING
MONDAY EVENING, MARCH 26TH, 1855,
THE ORIGINAL
AMERICAN HARMONEON ETHIOPIAN
OPERA TROUPE . . .
COST OF ADMISSION, 25 CENTS.

—Advertisement in *Milwaukee Sentinel*, week of March 19

JOSHUA GLOVER disappeared on March 11, 1854, just as quickly as he had appeared to most Wisconsinites. Most who argued about the merits of his arrest and rescue, in fact, had never laid eyes on him. Milwaukeeans who had vowed in their resolutions to protect him did not see Glover until his actual rescue. Even those who visited him in jail before the rescue did not know him. He was to them a fugitive, one of many such victims in a much larger political saga. He appeared only briefly, and then was gone—disappeared on the Underground Railroad to Canada.

The constitutional resistance to the Fugitive Slave Act carried out by Wisconsin's abolitionists made Joshua Glover important. It also raised a number of cogent questions. What rights did free blacks have in Wisconsin? What duties did the state have toward them? What separated them from free whites? In Wisconsin, as elsewhere in the North and South, free blacks lived under different laws than whites. These laws diminished their privileges and immunities, restricted their duties, and for the most part denied them political voice. They lived under a different legal regime, even as they walked the same streets and subsisted in the same economy as white Wisconsinites.

In Wisconsin, as in the rest of America, blacks and whites were intensely bound together by culture. The most popular entertainment of the antebellum era was the minstrel show, a gaggle of traveling troupes that crisscrossed the country taking their variety acts to every city, town, and village. The minstrel shows featured as their stars "plantation darkies," who were whites made up as blacks. But the music, the humor, and the acting were advertised as an authentic representation of plantation life and its exotic inhabitants. The 1850s were also the age of the sentimental novel, and none was more sentimental or successful than Harriet Beecher Stowe's *Uncle Tom's Cabin*. The sentimental novel and minstrelsy touched different emotive keys in Americans, and they did not necessarily play in harmony. By treating blacks as both alien and human, by portraying the vagaries of plantation life as both humorous and frightening, these cultural forces convinced whites of their natural superiority over blacks, but only by inextricably binding blacks to white consciousness.

When Joshua Glover disappeared on March 11, 1854, the vast majority of white Wisconsinites had no idea who he really was. Most tried to piece together his character from the images and representations gleaned from sentimental literature, abolitionist rhetoric, and minstrelsy. Such was the case for most blacks in Wisconsin, who had no independent churches or schools in the 1850s and only a tenuous presence within the state. Glover's arrest and rescue had both a liberating and a chilling effect on Wisconsin's blacks. Although a few began speaking publicly, they did not develop a political voice as in other abolitionist strongholds. And fewer reported for the census takers, literally diminishing their visibility. At the same time, abolitionists in Wisconsin confronted the question of race seriously and forced others to think about the place of free blacks within Wisconsin's society and polity. Still, abolitionists were unable to convince the state's voters to admit free blacks to full citizenship. Such was the mixed legacy of Joshua Glover's arrest and rescue.

———

On March 2, 1854—more than a week before Glover's arrest—the *Milwaukee Sentinel* announced the imminent arrival of the Marsh acting troupe. The all-white company had been touring the western states, performing a dramatic rendition of Stowe's *Uncle Tom's Cabin*.[1] The *Sentinel* reprinted for its readers a review from an Iowa paper that ranked the play as the number one topic of conversation in the city, the Nebraska bill not excepted. The Iowa paper gave a tantalizing glimpse of the play's popularity when it noted that "as many of our denizens as could possibly be 'stowed' in Weaver's Melodeon have witnessed the personifications of Mrs. Stowe's great work, and numberless others are anxiously waiting an opportunity."[2] Fortuitously, they landed in Milwaukee just two days after Joshua Glover had left. The flesh-and-blood illustration of the Fugitive Slave Act's application was followed by a detailed, entertaining, sentimental representation of its effects. No modern public relations agent could have planned better publicity.

Uncle Tom's Cabin was a cultural force in the 1850s, but its beginnings were inauspicious enough. It had attracted fair attention as a magazine serial, but Harriet Beecher Stowe had difficulty locating a publisher willing to put up the money to produce it as an independent novel. Typically, antislavery fiction had been unprofitable. John P. Jewett, a small Boston publisher, took the risk and offered her 10 percent royalties, which she and her husband were happy to accept. *Uncle Tom's Cabin* appeared in print in March 1852 and quickly disappeared from booksellers' shelves. The novel sold thousands of copies within weeks and three hundred thousand copies within its first year. Its immense popularity heralded a new age for American literature, that of the bestseller and the sentimental novel.[3] But not even its status as the best-selling book of the nineteenth century—aside from the Bible—can describe the impact that this novel had on American culture. Lending libraries had to keep multiple copies, Sunday schools used the novel as a textbook, and enterprising manufacturers turned out souvenirs, games, and toys to profit from the book's popularity.[4]

Doubtless, part of the popularity of the novel was due to its timing. It was published on the heels of the Compromise of 1850, the Shadrach rescue in Boston, and the president's mustering of the U.S. Army and Navy to return Thomas Sims to Georgia. Stowe's novel gave northerners a glimpse of slavery through the eyes of typecast characters—the coarse slave trader Haley, the kind Kentucky slave master Shelby, the innocent child Eva, the savage Yankee-turned-plantation-lord Legree. The reader also experienced slavery through the slaves themselves, in characters Stowe designed to elicit sympathy and perhaps empathy. The title character, Uncle Tom, was an idealized Christian martyr. He never veered from his humility and meekness. He refused to condemn those who wronged him and willingly accepted his unjust fate. Although Tom's nobility surpassed human limits,

Stowe made explicit her belief that "the negro race is confessedly more simple, docile, childlike, and affectionate, than other races." Christianity came more easily to them, said Stowe, because they were racially inclined to its teachings.[5] Not all Stowe's black characters evinced such leanings. Some slaves in the novel proved themselves self-interested rather than self-effacing, saucy rather than deferential; others were thieves, liars, and sadists rather than honest and meek Christians.[6] But for Stowe, it was not any predisposition to wickedness but an inherent weakness of character in blacks that made them susceptible to vice. However subtle the distinction, the inference was that blacks lacked independent will and strength of character.[7] Uncle Tom elicited enormous sympathy from northerners, but he was never himself an object of true empathetic identification. No reader could possibly live up to his willingness to bear the sins of slavery, Christlike, on his broad shoulders.

Stowe contrasted Tom's passive acceptance of his fate with the story of two runaways, George and Eliza. Their flight northward to Canada bespoke pride and daring that seemingly belied Stowe's characterization of blacks as "simple, docile, childlike, and affectionate." But Eliza and George were mulattoes, George with "fine European features" and Eliza with skin fair enough to allow her to blush. As mulattoes, their very existence alluded to the crime of rape that inevitably accompanied slavery, though Stowe did not address this point explicitly. Their racially mixed backgrounds also brought them steps closer to a white audience seeking to identify with the characters, a rhetorical strategy Stowe employed throughout the novel. Their ability to mix with whites aided their escape and indicated to the reader that they leaned more toward their European than toward their African ancestry. Their indomitable will came, at least in part, from their inherited white spirit.[8] Stowe's representation reveals something of her own conflicted conscience. Education might turn blacks into good or even noble creatures, but in terms of intelligence and will they were clearly inferior. That so many readers sympathized and empathized with Stowe's characters indicates just how powerfully she tapped into the dominant understanding of race in antebellum America.

Few critics have missed this problem in *Uncle Tom's Cabin.* James Baldwin famously dismissed it as a very bad book because of its cardboard characters. It was not really about blacks, Baldwin complained, but about how whites wanted them to be.[9] It did nothing to bring to the world a better understanding of the minds and hearts of those oppressed by slavery. Such was the sentimental novel. Such, too, was its power. Whatever its literary merits, sentimental prose elicited the emotional, intellectual, and moral responses of almost every reader who came across it in the 1850s.[10] The book played a part in arousing antislavery feeling in the North and hardening proslavery convictions in the South. But it did so by making the *subjects* of slavery—the slaves themselves—the *objects* of sympathy.

Theater companies wasted no time in producing a version of Stowe's novel for the stage. It was common practice for companies to keep a dramatist on hand to adapt successful novels into plays.[11] The earliest renditions of *Uncle Tom's Cabin* were written by the troupes that performed them, and most of their scripts, unfortunately, do not survive. Those few that do reveal the difficulty of adapting the play for stage. The book's multitude of characters, plots, and subplots necessitated a significant paring down of the original text. Some adaptations retained only the flight of George and Eliza from Kentucky to Canada. One version stopped the play with the death of Eva rather than the death of Uncle Tom.[12] P. T. Barnum promised that his adaptation would not "foolishly and unjustly elevate the negro above the white man in intellect or morals."[13] The specifics of the Marsh troupe's adaptation are unknown, but they told both the story of Uncle Tom's sale down the river and that of George and Eliza's flight to freedom. To do so required twenty-four actors, including a new Yankee character, Deacon Perry. This character, present largely for comic relief, can be traced to a New York adaptation written by George L. Aiken, and the *Milwaukee Sentinel* noted in its review that the deacon "seems to take very well with the audience."[14]

The exigencies of the stage shrank Stowe's already two-dimensional characters all the more. The conventions of the nineteenth-century theater downplayed implied sexuality and explicit violence, oftentimes taking the edge out of Stowe's more vivid moments. In Aiken's adaptation, the beating administered to Tom becomes three blows with the whip, and all that is required for the death blow is one stroke from the whip's butt-end. Stowe's vivid portrayal of the slaveholder Legree's groping of a pretty mulatto's neck and bust becomes in the stage direction a mere grabbing of the arm.[15] Certainly the Marsh troupe had smoothed some of the novel's brutality, for the *Milwaukee Sentinel* reassured its readers that the performance was "without slightest immoral feature" and that children who attended "might learn profitable lessons from the childlike, pretty and devoted affection of little Eva." As for Uncle Tom, he exhibited "the affection of the kindly-hearted negro domestic, with a perfection we had not expected to see at this distance from sea-board." George and Eliza were hardly mentioned by the reviewer. The approval of largely didactic characters suggests that their truncated dialogue and adapted personalities were even less conflicted than Stowe's already idealized depictions.

Uncle Tom's Cabin ran a week and a half at Young's Hall in Milwaukee, showing several afternoon matinees to accommodate families.[16] Without doubt, Joshua Glover's rescue and Uncle Tom's arrival afforded African Americans a kind of visibility they rarely enjoyed. In the 1850 census, the state registered a total population of 305,391 people, only 635 of whom were free blacks. This was the smallest number of African Americans of any state carved out of the Northwest Territory. It paled next to Ohio's free black population of 25,279 and even Michigan's, the next smallest, at 2,583.[17] There were reasons for the small numbers. Wisconsin was not nearly the established route to Canada for fugitive slaves that the better-known Underground Railroad stations in Ohio and Michigan had become. It also lacked a direct connection with the southern states from which the formerly enslaved blacks were fleeing. The Ohio River, for example, was both a border between the free and slave states and the waterway that kept them in close contact. It was no small wonder that in Ohio, the single largest free black population had settled in Cincinnati, directly across the river from Covington, Kentucky. No such conduits existed in Wisconsin. Its natural aquatic highway was Lake Michigan, and its most direct trade with the East rather than the South.

Blacks had come to Wisconsin before statehood.[18] French fur traders had brought black slaves in the eighteenth century, and American lead miners had brought some slaves in the 1830s and 1840s.[19] Wisconsin's Indian population had experienced a good deal of admixture with blacks before statehood.[20] Wisconsin's free black population was dispersed throughout the state, although individuals tended to cluster either in agricultural communes or in cities where they could form protective and supportive communities. Cities were attractive because the service sector provided ample economic opportunity.[21] In 1850, Milwaukee County registered the state's second-largest aggregate population of free blacks at 111. Of these, 98 lived in the city among its 19,963 other residents. Free blacks settled primarily in the First Ward, close to their jobs as household servants to wealthy whites and in other parts of the service sector economy.[22] Employment opportunities attracted free blacks to Milwaukee, not white sympathy for their trials and tribulations. Milwaukee was no bastion of abolitionism. In fact, slaveholders always turned to Milwaukee law firms to aid in the rendition of their fugitives. The large number of European immigrants in the city made it a Democratic stronghold not receptive to abolitionists. Free blacks and fugitives who chose to settle in Milwaukee did not do so for the enlightened principles of its populace, but for its economic opportunities.

Joshua Glover and Uncle Tom brought the plight of African Americans to the attention of the general public, but Wisconsin's fugitive slaves and free blacks had reason to fear the spotlight. The state census of 1855 revealed a drop in Milwaukee's free black population to only sixty-nine men and women.[23] The decline may have been due to an exodus or to an unwillingness to appear for census takers. Either suggests their vulnerability and invisibility. They formed no recognizable constituency in Milwaukee, a city made up of immigrant neighborhoods.[24] As late as the 1850s, they had no church of their own in Milwaukee or elsewhere in Wisconsin.[25] These were only the most general contours of a complex and diverse community. But what was most obvious was the absence of attention from the white community. There were scant references to blacks in the 1840s and 1850s. Chauncey C. Olin, an ally of Booth's who ran the Waukesha abolitionist paper *American Freeman,* received an escaped slave named Lewis Washington in 1847. Washington had run first to New Jersey, where he had taken lessons in reading and writing from an abolitionist. Olin traveled with Washington, who spoke to Wisconsin crowds about the experience of slavery. When the two were refused a room in a hotel in Racine County, Washington began his speech the next day with a righteous rant against the meanness of the hotel owner.[26] As impressive as such an event must have been, it stands as a rarity. I have found no other mention of black public speakers touring Wisconsin before 1854.

It was small wonder then, that Joshua Glover elicited such interest. The Nebraska issue had heightened public awareness of slavery, but only in the abstract. Glover was flesh and blood. Remarkably, though, no one really knows what he looked like. The most commonly quoted description of

Figure 3.1. This line drawing of Joshua Glover was completed in the 1880s. The artist is unknown. Glover fled via the Underground Railroad to Canada in 1854. He appeared in the 1861 census as a resident of York County in the modern-day province of Ontario. The census taker reported Glover's occupation as laborer, his religion as Methodist, and his age as forty-seven. The 1871 census listed his age as sixty. He died in 1888, a free resident of Canada. *Photo courtesy of the Milwaukee County Historical Society*

him was provided by Garland in his arrest warrant. Glover was "forty-four or forty-five years of age, about five feet six or eight inches high, spare built, with rather long legs, very prominent knuckles, has large feet and hands, has a full head of wool, eyes small and inflamed, is of dissipated habits, is of rather an ashy black color."[27] Witnesses whom Garland later called upon to establish his ownership of Glover described his height as closer to five feet ten than to five feet six, his age as anywhere between thirty and forty-five, and his complexion as dark brown rather than ashy. All remembered his long legs, big hands, and spare build, and one described his eyes as inflamed, most likely from hard drinking.[28] His only portrait, however, hardly resembles such a character. Drawn in the 1880s, this characterization looks more like a mulatto than a Negro and exhibits features more European than African. That this contravened every known description of Glover suggests that Stowe's fugitive slave George—a mulatto who could pass for white—still exerted a powerful influence well after slavery had disappeared.[29]

The abolitionists who sought to save Glover from slavery never described him as mulatto, but they did have difficulties discerning his identity and status. Sherman Booth alternately called him a "Negro," a "fugitive," and later a "peaceable citizen of a neighboring town."[30] The *Racine Advocate,* Wisconsin's most radical abolitionist paper, subtitled its report on Glover's arrest as an "attempt to kidnap a citizen of Racine by slave-catchers." Most people sympathetic to the federal government referred to Glover only as "the fugitive" or the "Negro." Was he a fugitive slave? A citizen? A free colored resident of Wisconsin? Each of these designations signaled differences not only in popular opinion but also in legal status. This status determined the rights, privileges, and protections afforded him.

In the 1850s, determining status was a complicated affair. Glover derived his status from state law, rather than from any notion of universal citizenship in the United States. There was little consensus on the definition of citizenship or what it meant to be a U.S. citizen. The 1850 edition of Webster's dictionary defined a citizen as a person, native or naturalized, "who has the privilege of exercising the elective franchise."[31] This association of the franchise with citizenship was powerful. Burrill's *New Law Dictionary and Glossary* (1860) and Bouvier's *Law Dictionary* (1868) both defined citizenship as the right to vote for representatives in government. But Edward Bates, Abraham Lincoln's attorney general, wrote an extended opinion arguing that citizenship and suffrage had traditionally been separated at law.[32] Few could even agree on what conferred citizenship. In a telling moment, the editor of *Harper's* chided a U.S. diplomat in France for his pretentious use of the title *Citizen* Daniel. "*Mr.* Daniel seems to us a simpler and more democratic title, inasmuch as every American is a citizen by the fact of birth."[33] This bit of wit revealed complexities and contradictions in the concept of citizenship. Birthright citizenship, a hallmark of the English common-law inheritance, did not apply to the millions of enslaved Americans born on United States soil. Nor did birthright admit women to the full privileges of citizenship. The several states announced a liberally progressive citizenship in the early nineteenth century by removing property qualifications for suffrage, but the elimination of property qualifications for voting was often accompanied by the disfranchisement of women and blacks.[34] Congress expanded women's citizenship in 1855 by naturalizing alien women who had married American citizens but denied women the franchise on the basis of their dependent status. As the argument went, women contracted into marriage and exchanged their service and obedience for support and protection. This reasoning excluded propertied, unmarried women, but such inconsistencies rarely attracted attention in antebellum America.[35]

Although this trend toward liberal suffrage—with illiberal exceptions—was nationwide, it was not the product of the national government. Congress busied itself with regulating immigration but not with defining the substantive rights of its citizens. The U.S. Constitution offered no guidance on this point. The early treatise writers of American common law dealt with the subject ambiguously, at best. Joseph Story, in his monumental attempt to provide a working national commentary on American common law, evaded a definition of citizenship. He focused instead on naturalization procedures, which the Constitution had given exclusively to the national government.[36] The power to naturalize aliens did nothing to define citizenship; naturalization conferred only "a general citizenship" that communicated "all the privileges and immunities, which the citizens of the same state would be entitled to under the like circumstances."[37] Story's editor left this portion unchanged in the 1851 revision of the *Commentaries*. James Kent ignored it altogether in his treatise on the common law, preferring to talk vaguely about the rights of persons and about the rights of citizens only intermittently and not at great length.[38]

What early jurists had made clear was that the power to define citizenship belonged to the states. The ability of a person to exercise the rights of citizenship—to own property, to appear in the courts, to appeal to the protection of the law, and to exercise the franchise—was the province of the state legislatures and not of Congress.[39] In terms of rights and privileges, the operative factor in antebellum America was status. A resident of Virginia, for example, might be a slave, a citizen, a free black, an alien white, a pauper, or an Indian. In Massachusetts, a resident might be a citizen, an alien, a fugitive slave, an Indian, or a pauper. Nor were these the only categories into which people might fall.

The states also bore the responsibility of deciding what legal process would determine the status of an individual. In Massachusetts, summary proceedings by a justice of the peace could reduce a man to a "vagabond" or "idler" and commit him to the house of correction.[40] Massachusetts was the norm rather than the exception regarding the use of summary procedure. For example, quarantine laws in the maritime states asserted the right of the state summarily to expel immigrants who threatened public welfare, health, or morals.[41] It was the states' sovereignty that gave them the police power to expel undesirables, take away someone's liberty, or restrict the rights of whole classes of people. This doctrine of state sovereignty understood "privileges," "immunities," "rights," and "duties" to be determined by one's membership in the community. Although this understanding conflicted with the rise of the liberal idea of universal birthright citizenship, the police powers of the states to regulate such matters remained a powerful force, and few questioned the proposition that the substance of one's rights derived from state laws and regulations.[42]

In Wisconsin, privileges flowed liberally to many classes of residents from the beginning. Although only the U.S. government could naturalize aliens, Wisconsin made it exceedingly easy for aliens to own property, access the courts, and establish the residency required to qualify for naturalization. Territorial legislation had enabled aliens—male and female—to purchase property and to dispose of it "as fully to all intents and purposes as any natural born citizen of the United States can." The Wisconsin legislature affirmed these rights shortly after statehood. The franchise opened political participation to white male citizens over the age of twenty-one, and to white males of foreign birth who had resided in the state for one year. This liberal access to political participation meant that many aliens enjoyed the privileges of Wisconsin citizenship without being U.S. citizens.[43]

The same was not true for Wisconsin's small community of free blacks. The legal status of free blacks differed from that of whites all across the United States. By 1860, only six states had extended suffrage to free blacks (Maine, Vermont, New Hampshire, Massachusetts, Rhode Island, and, formally, New York).[44] Many localities segregated their schools, and states passed strict laws that regulated blacks' immigration and participation in public culture. The federal Militia Act of 1792 commanded "each and every free able-bodied white male citizen" to be enrolled for service. Although this language did not necessarily forbid free blacks from serving, all the states passed their own militia laws exempting blacks from duty.[45] In Connecticut, a state law prevented Prudence Crandall from operating a school for out-of-state blacks. The Connecticut courts upheld the law, noting that free blacks were not necessarily citizens.[46] Nearly all the states of the Old Northwest retained restrictive Black Laws aimed at subjugating their black populations.[47] Illinois and Indiana prevented blacks from testifying against whites, leaving them powerless in legal disputes. Illinois, Indiana, Ohio, and Michigan all made miscegenation illegal.[48]

The laws themselves were not static, and a prominent feature of the rising antislavery movement was its demand for the repeal of racial laws that denied equal legal rights. Abolitionists enjoyed success in the 1840s and 1850s. Ohio repealed its Black Laws in 1849, Massachusetts and New York localities integrated schools, and free states strengthened their personal liberty laws in the face of perceived aggression by the Slave Power.[49] Whatever political motives guided these reforms, there was no question that the power to determine status—as well as the specific privileges and duties each status would entail—lay with the states.

Wisconsin itself had no Black Laws. Its constitution did not extend suffrage to blacks and required that any such law be submitted to a popular referendum. Black suffrage came before Wisconsin voters in 1849 and passed by a vote of about 6,800 to 5,200. But the board of canvassers rejected the result because more than 34,000 voters had participated in the elections and the 6,800 votes in favor of the referendum did not amount to a majority of *all* votes cast, as required by the Wisconsin constitution.[50] This interpretation of the constitution by the board sufficed to end the issue. Abolitionists complained, but little came of it.

Although suffrage was denied to free blacks, legal protections were not. Wisconsin's charter of liberties extended to all persons. The most basic privileges were the legal protections afforded their civil liberties, such as the rights of trial by jury and habeas corpus. These were rights granted not just to citizens, but to all people within Wisconsin's borders. Justice Samuel Crawford of the Wisconsin Supreme Court, when he considered this question, acknowledged that the highly esteemed right of trial by jury was protected by the state constitution and extended "to all *persons* within the state, regardless of color, and to the fugitive from labor or slavery as to the freeman."[51] Citizens, aliens, and, in fact, anybody arrested on Wisconsin soil could appeal to these protections. But fugitive slaves presented a particular problem. Their status as slaves was defined by the laws of another state, and the U.S. Constitution demanded their delivery to their home state as a matter of comity.

So Glover's status was important. If he was a resident of Wisconsin, he was owed all its protections and privileges. His color disabled him from the full privileges of citizenship, but even as an alien or free resident, he was owed the protection of the state's laws. If he was a fugitive, however, his right to protection came into conflict with the 1850 amendments to the Fugitive Slave Act, and he belonged to the federal courts and the state of Missouri. Abolitionists, therefore, immediately tried to claim him as a resident of Wisconsin. The *Racine Advocate* called Glover "one of our most industrious and worthy colored citizens. He has been frequently in the city with articles, the product of his labor, for sale, and is well known and esteemed by most of our business men."[52] When the Racine assembly of March 11 passed its resolutions regarding the arrest of Glover, they referred to him then as "a colored man" working for one of Racine's citizens. This kind of slippage was normal. The term "citizen" in popular discourse did not carry with it the baggage that burdened the word at law. Abolitionists across the North used it almost unconsciously to create sympathetic identification with fugitive slaves.[53]

In the process of creating this identification, abolitionists gave an indication of what Wisconsinites considered to constitute membership in the community. The *Milwaukee Sentinel*'s brief description of Glover defined him as a two-year resident of the state and self-supporting. He was in the employ of Rice and Sinclair's sawmill and was owed more than $50 for his labor there.[54] The resolutions adopted by the Milwaukee assembly at the courthouse steps referred to Glover as "an honest man and a faithful laborer." This description stuck. John Gregory, in his early history of Milwaukee, characterized Glover as an "orderly, industrious member of the community" on no evidence other than the reports furnished by abolitionists.[55] Community membership entailed hard work and industry as well as the ability to maintain a level of rugged independence.

The Democratic papers countered this depiction by assailing Glover's moral character. The *Milwaukee News* led the charge, complaining that Glover was a drunkard who lived with another man's wife. They reprinted Benammi Garland's sworn affidavit that described Glover as having "dissipated habits." William Cramer, editor of the moderate *Daily Wisconsin,* felt obliged to point out in 1855 that "the character of GLOVER was notoriously bad. He had run away with another man's wife, and was living in adultery at the time another colored man had handed him up, and informed the U.S. officers where he could be found."[56] Abolitionists returned this characterization in kind, running with the literary tropes of betrayal and corruption. The perfidious Garland had "got hold of a miserable colored man, named Turner, liquored him up, supplied him with liquor and cards, and sent him up to get Glover drunk." Turner may have been corrupted and degenerate, wrote Booth, "but Glover drank sparingly."[57] As for the charge of adultery, Glover was a victim: "slavery reduces a man to the condition of a brute, and takes away all inducement to be virtuous. It annuls marriage and licenses and compels general concubinage."[58]

These descriptions and characterizations were common devices and props. Abolitionists had long complained about the degenerating effects of slavery, particularly on moral character. In sentimentally charged antislavery literature, slave catchers often swigged from whiskey jugs and fed off the betrayal of turncoats.[59] The standard by which both friend and foe measured Glover relied on an evaluation of stereotypes derived from popular culture. Abolitionists were predisposed to believe in his essentially good character, corrupted as it may have been by slavery. Their opponents were more likely to believe rumors that emphasized Glover's perfidy and base savagery. The arrival of Stowe's *Uncle Tom's Cabin* did not illuminate Glover's character; it merely provided a new stereotype against which to judge him. This was unfortunate for Glover, for living up to Uncle Tom's standard was impossible for almost anyone. Nothing illustrated this point more than the lament that "had Glover been an 'Uncle Tom' in his moral character," no jury would ever convict a man for his rescue.[60] That the abolitionists were on the defensive against these sinister insinuations about Glover's moral character indicated the willingness of the population to accept certain traits as natural to blacks, among them the inability to control sexual urges, dim-wittedness, and an inclination to theft and deceit.

Such was the popular perception of blacks among many northerners. Although these perceptions had deep historical roots, both intellectual and popular, their wide dissemination in post-Jacksonian America flowed from the minstrel show.[61] Minstrelsy was America's first unabashedly popular theater. In an age in which morally superior Protestants regarded the stage with suspicion and acting troupes had to import most of their plays from England, the minstrel show gave Americans a native entertainment that spoke their language and made them laugh.[62] By the mid-1840s, it was a national entertainment, and minstrel troupes toured the country, playing theaters in every city and town. The core of the minstrel show was the black slave and plantation life, put on display by white performers in blackface for northern white audiences. It was exotic and folk all at once. Few, if any, northern workers had seen a plantation or even a slave, and many minstrel performers had not either. Minstrel troupes like the Ethiopian Serenaders played "authentic" Negro plantation songs derived from Irish folk melodies, and although they adopted the popularly stylized "Negro dialect," their dialogue and jokes were easily recognizable in the North.[63] Minstrelsy's appropriation of black culture never veered far from the audiences it served, favoring comedy and music that blended the exotic and the familiar in tantalizing ways.

The contours of the minstrel show were quite complex. On the whole, plantations in minstrel shows were happy places, where "childlike" slaves frolicked and displayed appropriate deference to their white masters. But they stepped out of these passive roles as well. Plantation slaves sometimes played tricks on their masters, suggesting natural wit and a small measure of identification between the white audience and the actors in blackface, allied mutually if briefly against the aristocratic pretensions of planters. Depictions of the plantation "Mammy" or the "Darky Uncle" evoked tenderness and love. Minstrel shows sometimes depicted the sale of children from their mothers and wives from their husbands, drawing forth sympathy, and even empathy, from northern audiences in increasingly ambiguous ways.[64] The appropriation of black culture for the minstrel show was not merely a means for reinforcing racist perceptions. It was a dialogue between cultures, a comic yet somewhat terrifying look at the crimes one race perpetrated against another in America. Even as it ridiculed and demeaned blacks, it drew them further into white consciousness.[65] But in the 1850s, as the public paid more attention to the issue of slavery, the minstrel show degenerated into a cathartic means of alleviating sectional tensions. Gone were the conflicted characters and grieving slaves. Left behind were only the happy slave and the buffoonish free black of the North. Audiences increasingly left minstrel shows not only thoroughly entertained but secure in their feelings of racial superiority.[66]

The racial stereotypes promulgated by minstrelsy played their part in shaping the argument over the Fugitive Slave Act in Wisconsin. *Uncle Tom's Cabin* may have come through Wisconsin once, but the minstrel shows came frequently. In 1855, Wisconsin was treated to a tour by the Original American Harmoneon Ethiopian Opera Troupe.[67] Their frequent performances drew great praise from the press as quality entertainment. Not only were they excellent singers, but comedic performances in between songs provided "witty sketches of the Negro character well told."[68] Such depictions made it difficult for abolitionists to convince their fellow citizens to take blacks seriously. Few whites did, as evidenced by the *Daily Wisconsin*'s coverage of the Anti-Slave-Catchers' Mass Convention held at Young's Hall in Milwaukee on April 13, 1854. The paper had been unable to report on the majority of Charles Watkins's speech "on account of the excitement got up by a little negro occupying the front seat. He seemed to be so much interested in the speech, that he commenced applauding until he had worked himself into a regular 'break down,' and was going it on the toe and heel."[69] The absurdity of the report—a "little negro" bursting into song and dance to everyone's amusement *at a political meeting*—spoke strongly to the expectations of both the *Wisconsin*'s editor and its readership.

Minstrelsy framed the expectations, and there is ample evidence of the ridicule heaped on blacks. Under the caption "NEGRO-HEADED," the *Daily Wisconsin* published a story of how a southerner claimed his Negro servant Sam was so strong that no one at a party he was hosting could knock him down. One particularly burly man took the challenge and delivered a "sockdologer" (heavy blow) to the back of Sam's head when he walked into the room with the candles. "The candles flickered a little, but Sam passed quietly on, merely exclaiming—'gentlemen, be careful of de elbows or the lights will be distinguished [sic].'"[70] The *Morning News* refused to answer an anonymous critic published by the *Milwaukee Sentinel*, noting that "if he will make that statement over his own signature we will give our opinion of him . . . if he does not, we shall consider him a coward as well as a calumniator." If anyone needed help spotting a coward and calumniator, the *News* added, "[W]e have no time to waste on 'a nigger on the fence.'"[71] Even the abolitionist *Milwaukee Sentinel* latched onto these familiar images for humor. Covering the police court, the newspaper told the story of a black man named Pleasant Crawford who was defending his arrest for resisting an officer. He was accused of stabbing the officer, but claimed that the officer stabbed himself—for if he had really intended to stab the officer, the officer would have been more seriously hurt. Crawford's answers to the magistrate's questions, printed in the black dialect made famous by minstrelsy, were a string of more and more unbelievable lies. In case there was any doubt as to the comedy of it all, the *Sentinel* provided an audience: Crawford's wife, seated in the court and laughing heartily at each of her husband's ludicrous statements.[72]

Depictions of blacks as hard-headed and dim-witted, as cowards and wafflers, as objects of amusement rather than subjects to be taken seriously, permeated Wisconsin as much as any other place in the United States.[73] Such representations reinforced comfortable feelings of white superiority and aided those who wanted to believe the worst about Glover. But even this admission—that Glover was *not* worth fighting over—revealed an uncomfortable ambivalence toward slavery. Were some fugitives worth fighting over? What protection did the state owe to those who could not protect themselves? Abolitionists forced these implicit questions on the public when they dwelled on Glover's physical wounds. Rufus King wrote that when he visited Glover in the jail on the morning of March 11, he was quite a sight, his head cut open in two places and "his shirt and vest . . . soaking and stiff in his own blood."[74] Sherman Booth mentioned that the Racine authorities had kept the club the federal marshals used on Glover, sticky with blood and hair, as evidence of the brutality of the federal marshals.[75] The German-language paper *Der See-Bote* quipped that the *Slavenhäscher* would have them all learn a better lesson, that they could come into Wisconsin and cut open any freeman's head. The paper condemned this "horrible brutality."[76] Over and over again, abolitionists depicted Glover's heroic resistance to Garland and the arresting party. The more radical abolitionist press credited him with fierce resistance: "three men were unable to put irons upon Glover, and even when, with the help of the others, they had succeeded, he broke the manacles from his wrists."[77]

The heroic man struggling against his oppressors was a popular trope, but it ran into the immediate problem of the abolitionists' own admission that slavery debased its victims. How could a degenerate and immoral man resist so nobly? Byron Paine, one year later, characterized this contradiction in natural terms. Slavery degraded men, and it had degraded Glover. "Nevertheless," Paine continued, "in obedience to that divine instinct planted in every human being which tells it that it is free, [he] escaped from servitude and tasted for a time of the sweets of liberty."[78] The instinct to liberty was primal. It was such a spirit that motivated Glover to resist his captors the night of March 10. Naturalist metaphors were common in romantic-era discourse, and Paine proved himself adept at deploying them. His argument allowed readers—regardless of prior racist beliefs—to identify with Glover on a primal level. Glover did not need to be a hero to escape bondage; he needed only to be human. The German press was certainly sympathetic. "The Poor Negro Slave Is Freed," ran one headline. *Der See-Bote* asked why Glover had been treated so brutally when, "after all, he is still a man!"[79]

Glover's humanity had been staked not on his own terms but on those that culled sympathy from whites. This tactic followed similar tropes in antebellum antislavery literature that portrayed the physical violence endured by slaves with increasing realism.[80] But sympathetic identification was only one rhetorical goal. Another was to posit the argument that rights, all rights, deserved defending.[81] Glover's inability to defend himself before the law brought with it the implication that others needed to provide that defense, both because society ought to protect the weak and because it had implications for the rights of all. The resolutions adopted by the assembly on March 11 put these principles in stark language. They would stand by the prisoner to secure his fair trial. They identified the writ of habeas corpus as the great writ of freedom, and demanded "for this prisoner, *as well as for our own protection,* that this Sacred Writ shall be obeyed." In his speech before the mass meeting, Sherman Booth made the import of the events clear: "The great Writ of *Habeas corpus,* old as English Freedom and sacred as our American liberties, is to be upheld or stricken down in the person of this imprisoned Negro." In a final flourish, he warned the crowd that the Fugitive Slave Act drew no color line. "Germans, Irishmen, Americans, all, no matter what our birth or condition, may be dragged into Slavery at the beck of a Federal Judge or U.S. Commissioner, on the oath of any scoundrel who chooses to swear that we owe service to a Slaveholder."[82]

Hyperbole was Booth's specialty and a common feature of abolitionist rhetoric. It infuriated Democrats, who complained of the dangers of demagoguery. But Booth had not intended to fool anyone. The "Germans, Americans, Irishmen, all" who had gathered there knew that the Fugitive Slave Act would not suddenly be used to enslave whites, even if they were German or Irish. But they well understood threats to liberty posed by powerful governments and the implications of remaining silent in the face of such threats. *As well as for our own protection,* the assembly had said. Byron Paine and Sherman Booth had posited the jealous defense of fundamental rights as common ground for the diverse crowd. Henry Bielfeld communicated these sentiments to the German press, which translated the assembly's resolutions into German, and noted that the real question was whether the population would allow the government to conduct trials in secret.[83] The sentimental argument had managed to permeate the constitutional and legal arguments against the Fugitive Slave Act. It created a measure of sympathetic identification with the fugitive that made his defense—however stymied by racist perceptions abroad in American culture—all the more possible. Even those who sought to denigrate Glover conceded the cultural and political point to their opponents—that even the weakest members of society were owed its protection. That this relationship was complicated by the layering of statuses with differing privileges and duties only highlighted the fundamental nature of habeas corpus and trial by jury. These rights were owed to all Wisconsin residents, whether citizens or not. Regardless of U.S. law, abolitionist lawyers said, they were owed to alleged fugitive slaves as well.

But even as abolitionists sought to humanize Glover and to draw others into empathy with him, this attention further marginalized the fugitive in jail. He was no longer just a person, but an issue worth defending. Moreover, he required the protection of others because he lacked the strength and the ability to protect himself. This reinforced Glover's—and all blacks'—status in the penumbra of citizenship.

The essential paradox of the situation lay in the simultaneous visibility and invisibility of free blacks in Wisconsin. A group that had very little in the way of political voice did not gain a loud one during the rescue. At the antislavery meeting held in Milwaukee only a month later, a "quick head count" by the *Daily Wisconsin* reporter revealed 235 people in attendance, of whom 19 were of African descent.[84] None spoke or participated in the meeting in any meaningful way. Wisconsin may have placed fewer restrictions on free blacks than did other states, but only 0.21 percent of the state's population in 1850 was African American. Although the 1860 census showed that the African American population had almost doubled since the previous census, it still trailed the growth of the overall population of the state: free blacks made up only 0.15 percent of the state's population. And, as mentioned above, the 1855 state census showed that their numbers in Milwaukee had declined since the last national count. In many ways, they were becoming less visible as a community.

The rescue, however, had shone the spotlight on blacks, and from then on the issue of race was fused into politics. Abolitionists insisted that political rights for free blacks be a central part of the Republican platform, and the press stood up and took note when blacks did speak out. They reported on Frederick Douglass's speeches, including those made during an 1854 October visit to Madison and an 1856 visit to Milwaukee.[85] And at least one black man registered his feelings about the Glover affair: William H. Noland, a versatile resident of Madison who, at various times during his career, managed an ice cream saloon, worked as a bookkeeper, ran his own hominy manufactory, and eventually held a government appointment under the Republican Party. In July 1854, Noland had a barbershop in the capital. Not four months after Glover's rescue, one of the men who had assisted in his arrest arrived in Noland's shop, threw off his coat, and took his place in the barber's chair to await his shave and haircut. Noland "very politely informed him that he did not shave kidnappers, or their underlings."[86] It was a small bit of protest, but protest nonetheless.

—

At the center of the storm around Joshua Glover was the question of his status. It was a key question because it determined the privileges and immunities due him and the corresponding rights and duties of the officers who held him. Behind the applications for a writ of habeas corpus, there lay the supposition that Glover, as a two-year resident of Wisconsin, was entitled to the protections afforded by the state constitution. When Deputy Marshal Charles Cotton refused to obey the writ of habeas corpus, he in effect decided the issue of Glover's status for the state. Around this question of status swirled popular outrage over the Kansas-Nebraska Act, obstreperous abolitionists, fears about the collapse of the Union, conflicted racial attitudes, and the cultural forces of minstrelsy and *Uncle Tom's Cabin.* All of this obscured Joshua Glover almost completely, leaving the historian with fragments of second-hand descriptions and contradictory judgments of his character. These hints cannot illuminate Glover, but they do give the historian an idea of what constituted membership in Wisconsin: the values of economic independence, thrift, and hard work. When abolitionists claimed these traits for Glover, they did so not really for his sake, but to rally support for a cause. Almost all the sentimental arguments had played on tropes familiar to antebellum Americans, whether they relied on Stowe's sentimental characters or minstrelsy's stereotypes.

This was a battle that the abolitionists won. Sympathy for Glover and his plight energized resistance to the Fugitive Slave Act and brought Wisconsin's free black community into politics. Still, it was not a watershed moment. Whether Glover was a fugitive slave or a free black of Wisconsin, he lacked the franchise and was largely excluded from community political participation. Glover's rescue did not change this, even though it began a dialogue about proscription based on color. Even if not a watershed, the rescue of Joshua Glover indicated a willingness in Wisconsin to stand up for the rights of the weak. However much can be ascribed to the negative feelings of Milwaukeeans toward slavery, this essential point must not be forgotten.

Glover disappeared several days after his rescue, most likely bound by ferry for Michigan and then Canada, where he was reported safe "under the protection of a Monarchy."[87] This barb at proslavery citizens of a *republican* country also marked the entrance of an entirely new set of issues. Now that the fugitive slave was safely out of the reach of Garland and the U.S. marshals, attention turned to the abolitionists who had been making arguments in the abstract about the rights of Wisconsin's free blacks. Those who had argued for Glover's rights had, of course, done more than just argue. By invoking the right to act on Glover's behalf in defense of his rights, they had put themselves now in opposition to the federal government. They had called attention to the dangers that the Fugitive Slave Act posed to liberty and to the necessity of defending fundamental law. Glover, once again, faded into the background. The subject of debate became the people who were "alarmed at this invasion of their rights, and assembled by thousands on the spot."[88] The rights and duties of active citizens took center stage.

FOUR

Citizenship and the Duty to Resist

Mr. President, I feel proud of Milwaukee, and of Wisconsin.
Citizenship here will henceforth be an honorable passport
among the liberty-loving in all the Earth.

—Sherman Booth, at the Anti-Slave Catchers' Mass Convention
in Milwaukee, April 13, 1854

JOSHUA GLOVER had gone to Canada, leaving the federal government unable to fulfill its duty to return the fugitive slave to his owner, Benammi Garland. Its role, however, was far from over. The Fugitive Slave Act provided criminal penalties for those who interfered with its enforcement, and federal officers intended to prosecute the rescuers. None was more important than Sherman Booth, Milwaukee's outspoken abolitionist printer, and the government focused its efforts on him. State officers also sprang into action. The Racine County district attorney claimed that Glover's arrest had violated the peace of his county, and he sought the arrest of Garland. The Milwaukee sheriff served U.S. marshal Stephen Ableman with a writ of habeas corpus commanding him to take Sherman Booth before a Wisconsin judge and to explain the reason for his detention. More legal actions followed. Garland sued Booth for the value of his escaped slave, a federal grand jury indicted Booth and Ryecraft for the rescue, Garland sued Marshal Ableman, and Booth sought further intervention by state courts. On more than one occasion, federal and state officers found themselves facing contradictory orders from different sovereignties. Conflict and confusion became the order of the day, but all within the rule-by-law world of the courtroom and its processes.

More was at stake than the legal question of who was obliged to obey which writs. Wisconsin buzzed in the months between Glover's rescue and Booth's trial. Meetings held all across the state called for the formation of a new political party to oppose the Kansas-Nebraska Act and the extension of slavery into free territory. As Wisconsinites pondered political realignment, they also paid attention to the dramatic criminal trials of John Ryecraft and Sherman Booth. Attorneys arguing the cases had to keep multiple audiences in mind. Their first task, always, was to mold arguments to persuade the judge and jury of the justness of their causes. Within the courtroom, measures of proof, rules of evidence, and criminal procedure dictated much of the form of the drama. But the public audiences that followed the trials in newspaper reports and vigorously debated the case were not bound by such rules. They listened to the arguments of counsel for their political messages and their broader implications. At the flash points provided by the trials, law and popular political culture intersected.

This intersection produced a vibrant discourse on the meanings of citizenship and its relation to governance. The federal government had a difficult task from the start. Beginning with a statute that an overwhelming proportion of Wisconsinites believed was immoral, government advocates had to preach a law-and-order argument. It ran thus: citizens had to respect laws constitutionally enacted, and to resist laws on the basis of the dictates of personal conscience invited disorder. If taken to its extreme— every man his own judge of what laws to obey—disorder would degenerate into anarchy. The logic was sound, but it implicated thousands of Milwaukeeans who had participated in the rescue and a growing number of Wisconsinites sympathetic to their cause. The government countered this by selecting only the visible leaders of the crowd for prosecution and by smearing them as demagogues. The abolitionists, claimed the government, bore more responsibility because they had incited others to action. They had duped peaceable citizens into breaking the law by lying, inflaming passions, and seeking to fulfill their own selfish and specious motives. More than once, the rhetoric of federal officers swept all progressive reform into this category.

Abolitionists defended their political resistance by explaining it in terms of the rights and duties of citizenship, an argument complicated by the double allegiance owed by all citizens to state and nation. Abolitionists privileged allegiance to the states largely because the state was favorable to their cause, whereas the federal government was not. In doing so, they also tapped into a legal regime that defined community membership locally, one that allowed for slavery in one state and not in the next and for a multiplicity of statuses defined by state laws and determined by state courts. In Wisconsin, abolitionists translated this into a plea for the state courts to defend citizens' constitutional liberties against the encroachments of the federal government.

Although citizens asked the courts to intercede, the protection of constitutional rights did not fall solely to the judiciary. As the rescue of Joshua Glover had demonstrated, many Wisconsinites believed that it was the first duty of citizens to defend their own liberties. If the federal government impinged on fundamental rights, then citizens should assemble and inquire why. If federal officers enforced these unconstitutional laws, then judges and juries had a right to refuse to enforce them. These were appropriate avenues of constitutional resistance, so the argument went, and abolitionists repeatedly asked judges, juries, and the people to declare the Fugitive Slave Act unconstitutional.

Invoking the duty of resistance exposed deep anxieties about the survival of a constitutional republic in a largely monarchical world. How could liberty be balanced with authority? How could vigilance be balanced with acquiescence? These were not easy questions, and neither abolitionists nor the federal government's defenders offered any explicit answers. Instead, the answers were bound up in their assumptions and their rhetoric. It is there that one must look to find clues to their substantive understanding of citizenship. Working alternately with the tropes of suffering and heroism, abolitionists defined resistance not only as a duty but as the necessary course to preserve freedom. To this end, they deployed a series of contrasting images to separate the citizenry from federal officers: democratic voice versus silence and secrecy; peaceful due process versus violence; liberty versus tyranny. This was not merely rhetorical color for a legal concept of citizenship. It was an articulation of the idea of the active citizen, argued before juries to convince them that Glover's rescuers had done nothing wrong. As they were well aware, more than just jurors were listening.

The first officer to act in the aftermath of Glover's rescue was the sheriff of Racine County, Timothy D. Morris. He arrived in Milwaukee on March 11 with a warrant for Garland's arrest on charges of kidnapping and assault and battery.[1] Garland was safely holed up in his attorney's office and made clear that he had no intention of coming out. Jonathan Arnold accepted service for his client and immediately sued out a writ of habeas corpus from Judge Andrew Miller of the U.S. district court. On Monday, March 13, the parties appeared before Miller. The presence of the city's press and curious onlookers made the judge nervous, and he ordered any who could not find seats out of the courtroom. Addressing the attendees more than the parties, Miller rehearsed the sections of the Fugitive Slave Act of 1850 that spelled out the duties of both state and federal officers. The lawyers also kept the larger audience in mind. Charles Watkins, appearing for Racine County, asked Judge Miller whether U.S. marshals were bound to make returns on writs of habeas corpus, which Deputy Marshal Cotton had not done in Glover's case. Jonathan Arnold tried to introduce evidence from Milwaukee's deputy sheriff that Glover had admitted his status as a fugitive slave. The judge sternly reminded both lawyers that he was not trying Glover's case.

The issue was whether the county of Racine held Garland on a legitimate arrest warrant and could continue in its prosecution. Arnold's defense sought to show that the charges of assault and kidnapping were actually performed under authority of a warrant obtained under the Fugitive Slave Act of 1850. To this end, he planned to call Deputy Marshal Cotton to confirm the process that Garland had obtained. Watkins objected. He argued that Garland was not a federal officer and thus could not be protected by color of federal process. His guilt or innocence was for the Racine court to assess. Miller overruled the objection. James Paine, assisting Watkins, rose to object. Releasing Garland simply because he claimed to be the owner of a fugitive slave left the people of the state at risk. What if Garland had killed Joshua Glover? The state, said Paine, could not prosecute him for murder. To this, Garland's attorney Arnold rose and assented. The Fugitive Slave Act, Arnold told the court, permitted the use of force in its execution, even to the point of taking life.[2]

These words caused a stir. Miller quieted the courtroom and repeated that the evidence establishing federal process was admitted. He did exclude Cotton's testimony, however, after Watkins objected that evidence that

Figure 4.1. Andrew Galbraith Miller was born in Pennsylvania in 1801. President Martin Van Buren appointed him a territorial judge of Wisconsin in 1838, and Miller moved to Milwaukee in that year. In 1848, President James K. Polk appointed Miller U.S. district judge of Wisconsin. He presided over the criminal trials of John Ryecraft and Sherman Booth in 1854 and 1855 and over Benammi Garland's civil suit against Sherman Booth in 1855. He served on the federal bench until 1873, when he resigned his office. He died the following year.
Photo courtesy of the Milwaukee County Historical Society

went toward guilt or innocence was not admissible in habeas corpus proceedings. It made no difference. Miller concluded that Garland had acted under authority of federal law and discharged him from the custody of the Racine sheriff.[3]

Although there was nothing extraordinary about Miller's reading of the Fugitive Slave Act, he made it clear in private that he had released Garland out of fear of what might happen if he were taken to Racine for trial. He had justified interposition by stretching the 1833 Force Act and released Garland even though the process served by Racine's sheriff seemed valid. His position was defensible at law, but his insistence that the Fugitive Slave Act gave a U.S. marshal or a slave owner in pursuit of a fugitive the right to employ violence, even to the point of taking life, did not serve him well in the court of public opinion.[4]

James Paine objected that Miller's decision infringed on the power of the state to protect its citizens. Miller tersely replied that "when the State complains, we will do the State justice." Paine retorted that the state appeared by virtue of the warrant, but to no avail. If Racine's district attorney desired, said Miller, he could amend the charges and rearrest Garland. Of course, Miller could then intercede again and release Garland. Most believed he would. No further charges were sought in Racine, and thus ended the first volley between Wisconsin and the U.S. government over the rights of citizens and the duties of officers.

But it was only the first. The Pierce administration took note of the events in Wisconsin, and federal officers moved to act. The U.S. commissioner for Wisconsin, Winfield Smith, issued warrants for a number of people suspected of violating U.S. law, among them the attorneys Charles Watkins and James H. Paine.[5] The real prize was Sherman Booth. U.S. marshal Stephen Ableman arrested Booth on Wednesday, March 15, on the charge that he did "unlawfully aid and abet a person named Joshua Glover . . . to escape from the lawful custody of Charles C. Cotton, a deputy of the Marshal of the United States for the District of Wisconsin."[6] He was commanded to appear before the commissioner's court and answer the charge. The stakes in this action were not particularly high. Commissioner Smith had the authority to order Booth held on bail, but only a federal grand jury could hand down an indictment that might lead to fine or incarceration.

However low the stakes, it was still a high-profile legal action that drew a number of spectators. When the court convened at half past two on

Tuesday, March 21, Smith asked for dignified proceedings and recommended that the testimony in a preliminary hearing such as this not be recorded and printed. The press and people rejected both his pleas. Smith's court was about to become political theater in which witnesses were unrestrained in testimony, Booth was to make long-winded political speeches, and two sides squared off in ideological rather than legal battle.

Federal authorities charged Booth with rescue under the seventh section of the Fugitive Slave Act of 1850. Booth had not, however, physically participated in the rescue of Glover. What was more, he had counseled against violence at the meeting, making a conspiracy charge difficult to prove. For District Attorney John R. Sharpstein to prove that Sherman Booth was guilty of rescue, he had to argue that the rescue of Glover was committed by a riotous mob and that Booth, as a member of that mob, was guilty by association. The evidentiary key was to make the crowd's actions of March 11 fit the legal definition of riot. Wisconsin law defined riot as the unlawful assembly of at least twelve armed or thirty unarmed men who gathered for the purpose of achieving a private end. Importantly, the unlawful assembly had to commit an act of violence. This went beyond the common-law legal fiction of "force and arms" (vi et armis) and constituted an essential element in the prosecution.[7]

Sharpstein did not dwell on the violence of the mob, but assumed that the act of breaking down the door to the jail would qualify in and of itself as violence. From there, he drew a logical line to Sherman Booth. The law had been broken by a mob. Those who had participated in it were guilty, and those who did not act positively to stop the act were just as guilty as those who had committed the illegal act. This was an accepted part of the law governing riot. Francis Wharton had recorded in his oft-cited treatise on criminal law that "in riotous and tumultuous assemblies, all who are present and not actually assistant in their suppression, in the first instance, are, in presumption of law, participants."[8] To prove that Booth had "aided and abetted" in the rescue of Glover, Sharpstein had to prove that an unlawful assembly had gathered with the object of removing Glover from the jail, that Booth had been part of that crowd, and that Booth had done nothing to prevent the illegal act from occurring.

This set of facts implicated far more people than just Sherman Booth, a point Booth never tired of making in his newspaper. James Paine asked rhetorically in his opening statement before the court, "[W]ill the prosecution brand four or five thousand citizens of this place with assembling to break the laws?"[9] Sharpstein was aware of the political passions that the Nebraska Act had unleashed, the general unpopularity of the Fugitive Slave Act in Wisconsin, and the tenor of public opinion on the Glover rescue. In a letter to the solicitor of the Treasury, Sharpstein acknowledged that "public prejudice has become much excited on the subject of the habeas corpus." This was not just a case of riot by the unruly rabble of the city. The presence of Milwaukee's prominent citizens at the rescue and the acquiescence of city officers seemed to indicate a community consensus against the federal law.[10] Sharpstein, therefore, went to great lengths to exonerate the crowd. He declared that he did not think that five thousand of Milwaukee's citizens would have gathered with the intention of breaking the law. That intent belonged to the rabble-rouser Booth, whose mendacious speeches and handbills had incited a riot. Even worse, he had asked the crowd to do what he would not. Too important to break the law himself, Sharpstein said of Booth, he entreated the crowd to do so.[11] The actions of the citizenry could be excused, argued Sharpstein, if the demagogues who deceived them were punished.

Booth had retained his ally James Paine to defend him. Before Paine began his defense, Booth gave a short speech to the court, declaring his innocence. He had helped to gather citizens in defense of liberty with no illegal act in mind, he stated. That the meeting had been peaceful and the federal government intractable no one denied, or so Booth claimed, and, while he was not sorry that the alleged fugitive had been rescued, it had never been his intention to break the jail or to subvert legal process. For the record, and to ensure that John Sharpstein had no doubts about his words, Booth reiterated his assertion that "rather than see the great writ of habeas corpus and trial by jury guarantied [sic] by the state of Wisconsin trampled under foot," he would sooner have every federal officer "hanged fifty cubits higher than Haman."[12] His position thus staked out, he left the particulars of his defense in the hands of James Paine.

Sharpstein called witnesses to prove that Booth had distributed handbills, had called the meeting, and had ridden about town shouting "Freemen to the rescue." He called one witness who said that he had seen Booth riding beside the wagon carrying the rescued fugitive and that he "did not look sorry for it." Booth answered from the defendant's table that, indeed, he was not sorry. Sharpstein admitted into evidence Sherman Booth's own account of his actions, published in the *Daily Free Democrat,* and let the prosecution's evidence rest on that account. James Paine countered with witnesses who emphasized that Booth had counseled the crowd not to break any laws. He called men who claimed that Booth never used the words "freemen to the rescue," but had simply called all freemen to the courthouse square, informing them that a "man's liberty was at stake."

Paine largely ignored the Fugitive Slave Act. Instead, he aimed to show that Booth's actions were protected by Wisconsin's constitution. Fusing his legal argument with religious rhetoric, Paine contended that the people had "assembled in the fear of God and in the love of man. And when the brother that was lost was found again, when the man that was dead became alive, a great shout went up from that vast multitude, which made the heavens ring; a shout for liberty and justice that bore testimony to the divine origin of human nature." Paine argued that the government's evidence against Booth—the distribution of handbills, riding about on a white horse to call the meeting, his speeches before the crowd—proved only that he had called a meeting. Was the right of assembly protected by fundamental law? Of course. Paine pushed the point further. He maintained that the people had a right to assemble to inquire into the conduct of officers "from the President down to the Deputy Marshal" and into every law from the Constitution down to the Fugitive Slave Act. "There is no doubt about that, sir," replied the commissioner. "Then," continued Paine, "it is not criminal to condemn that law."[13]

Commissioner Smith tried to remove that question from consideration. He interrupted Paine and reminded him that, as an officer of the court, he was "bound by precedent" to recognize the Fugitive Slave Act's constitutionality. "I am not arguing the Fugitive Law," snapped Paine, "I am arguing to show that Mr. Booth's resolution is constitutional, and that is perfectly legitimate." For good measure, Paine then remarked, "I am sorry, sir, that the Constitution meets with so little favor here." This was captious rhetoric, but it did expose the rift between the two positions. Paine implied that the federal government wished to stifle criticism and secure passive acceptance from its citizens. Against this position, Paine vigorously dissented: "It is the duty of all men to set their faces against cruelty and barbarity of all kinds, and especially against cruelty in the exercise of legal power."[14] Citizens in a republic were not passive recipients of the law, but active defenders of their liberties and guardians against oppression. They submitted to the rule of law, which was necessary for a republic to maintain order. The law, though, required the consent of the governed. Assembly of the people to inquire into the law as well as the conduct of officers was a crucial part of the democratic process, guarded not by institutions but by citizens at the most basic level.

This principle of voice and assent underlay "our theory of government," wherein "the confidence and respect of the people lie at the bottom of judicial power." Without it, the judiciary "becomes as impotent as was the giant of old, when he rose, shorn of his locks, from the lap of the harlot." Paine then launched a deliberate attack on the federal officers who had carried out the law, a "Praetorian Guard" sent "among us acting not for our liberties, but against them."[15] This joined abolitionists' myriad other allusions to the federal government's mendacity. Both Cotton and Miller had initially concealed Glover's arrest and then lied about it to keep it quiet.[16] Even worse, they had planned a secret trial to keep the public ignorant of the affair. Their silence may have had a practical explanation—fear of retaliation or even embarrassment over participating in the return of a fugitive to slavery—but Booth and Paine now wielded it rhetorically to call attention to the danger that power, when not scrutinized by the citizenry, posed to democracy. This was a widely held view. Even William Cramer, one of Booth's enemies, editorialized that "there is no doubt that the passage of the Fugitive Slave law of 1850, has done more to consolidate and monarchize the general government, than any law that has ever passed."[17] The charge against the national government of aggrandizing power cut across partisan divisions and was well understood by Milwaukee's foreign born.[18]

Paine also objected to the implication that speaking out against an unjust law constituted a crime, turning the government's attempt to isolate the leaders of the assembly into a universal attack on freedom of assembly and freedom of speech. Was denouncing the Fugitive Slave Act illegal? If so, Paine offered himself up for prosecution. If Sharpstein wanted evidence that he had condemned the Fugitive Slave Act, then "he need not be at the trouble of getting witnesses. I will come into Court and declare my abhorrence of it. I will declare that its provisions are devilish; a contradiction of all the commands of God, and a mock of all that deserves the name of law among men." Paine escalated his rhetoric. A man may condemn the Bible, the Constitution, "may condemn everything but the Fugitive Law.

That only is so sacred that padlocks must be put on our mouths to prevent us from speaking of it—The man who cannot swear fealty to that, is to receive no favor from the officers of the United States." Therein lay the great contrast of the Fugitive Slave Act to the process of democracy: the act could not command the consent of the governed, so the government was reduced to silencing opposition to it. This was tyranny. Paine's repeated answer to the commissioner's interruptions of his closing argument— "You may silence me if you wish, sir"—gave the imagery immediate force in the courtroom.[19]

One of the times Commissioner Smith "silenced" Paine concerned the facts surrounding Glover's arrest. James Paine repeatedly tried to claim that federal marshals had violated Glover's due process rights. The commissioner believed such facts to be irrelevant to Booth's case, although it had been a major issue of public concern during the mass meeting of March 11. The resolutions passed by the Milwaukee assembly had specifically stated that Glover was arrested "without the exhibition of any papers."[20] Sherman Booth had glibly referred to Deputy Marshal Kearney's striking of Glover with the club as "the first *service* of *process*."[21] This point was difficult to sustain because the only evidence to support it was the word of the now absent Glover. Jonathan E. Arnold, Garland's attorney, refuted this claim in a letter printed in the *Sentinel,* although he claimed only that Cotton and Kearney had arrested Glover after Garland obtained the proper warrant, without mentioning whether they had showed this warrant to Glover.[22] Arnold's point was easily substantiated: Garland had obtained the proper process under the Fugitive Slave Act, and no one disputed that.

This led to Paine's second attack on the procedure of the arrest. Whether legitimate process under the Fugitive Slave Act had been obtained or not, violence had accompanied its service. Paine pushed this point in vain before Commissioner Smith—who repeatedly refused to hear it— partly to embarrass the federal officers but also to call attention to the need for violence in enforcing the law. The symbols of violence were everywhere, even beyond Glover's arrest. Before the assembly had been called, Benammi Garland stood on the courthouse steps, "flourished his weapons, and boasted of the terrible things he would do if an attempt was made at a rescue."[23] Garland was nowhere to be found when the crowd of several thousand did attempt such a rescue later that day, but Booth reported that

Garland's attorney had gone about looking to rent guns for Garland's protection. Whether Garland did these things cannot be determined for sure; that antislavery activists wrote these symbols into their narratives of the event, is true.[24]

Federal officers also feared violence, but of a different kind. Sharpstein began his closing arguments by appealing to every citizen's duty to uphold law and order by confessing "the weakness of having a love for the laws of his country." This love for the law led to a hatred for Booth, whom he likened to Benedict Arnold. Booth had issued handbills "calculated to create excitement" and spread the falsehood that Glover had been arrested without process. Sharpstein angrily impugned Booth's righteous principles as a shield for his craven design "that men might break the law with impunity." The defense's attempt to muddle the facts by calling testimony into question and producing countertestimony was a cheap ruse. Worse, claimed Sharpstein, it was an indication of the defendant's—and all abolitionists'—hypocrisy. He called Booth a coward. He accused James Paine, an avowed teetotaler, of brandy drinking. He referred to Charles Durkee, a Free Soiler who had just served two terms as a representative in Congress, as a hypocrite, having "cheated a negro out of Seventeen Dollars." This charge of hypocrisy revealed Sharpstein's implicit assumptions—whatever the abolitionists' rhetoric, he could not believe that they truly regarded blacks as their equals. The commissioner interrupted Sharpstein and told him that such ad hominem had no place in his court. Sharpstein continued unabated: "the whole matter of abolitionism, women's rights, Fourierism, etc., is intended only to enable men to violate and trample on the laws. I despise the whole of it. I despise any man who preaches it, and I despise any man who defends him." James Paine ruffled at the insult. He rose and noted that, during the trial, he had referred to the district attorney as a gentleman who had comported himself well. "I now wish to retract entirely those admissions," he said.[25]

Sharpstein prevailed in the commissioner's court, to no one's surprise. The commissioner ordered Booth held on bail on suspicion of violating U.S. law. On the heels of the hearing, Garland filed a civil suit against Booth, notice of which Stephen Ableman served personally on March 25. On April 18, Garland's attorneys filed a declaration of facts that stated Glover's value to be $1,800. Adding the expenses and penalties allowed by the Fugitive Slave Act, he sued Booth for a total of $4,000.[26] The hammer was hanging over Sherman Booth's head. A criminal action threatened his personal liberty, and a civil action his property. It would not silence the printer. Strong reactions to the Kansas-Nebraska bill and the Glover rescue had already led some to call for meetings to consider a new antislavery party. Milwaukee's abolitionists wasted no time. Booth, Rufus King, and Edward Wolcott called for an antislavery meeting in Milwaukee, which took place on Thursday, April 13, at Young's Hall in Milwaukee.

As with the other meetings, there was much in the way of politics to negotiate. It was a question of what vision might guide the party. This meeting also evinced a slightly different leadership. A Massachusetts abolitionist minister opened the session. He was followed by an itinerant abolitionist lecturer, recently settled in Fond du Lac, Wisconsin. The two men outlined a moral position against slavery that submerged concerns about Wisconsin's, or any other, constitution. One went so far as to object to the assembly's adopted preamble, which read that "an attempt has lately been made by the officers of the United States to reduce an inhabitant of this state to slavery without a trial by jury," because he believed that no man could be made a slave by any jury.[27] Slavery, in the words of these abolitionists, had no place in God's world or God's law and, by extension, no place in Wisconsin law. One report said that he called the federal officers "lineal descendants of the Devil" and tools used by a corrupt government.[28]

The invocation of such a radical argument—one that turned on absolute morality and rejected any compromise with slavery—had not yet been broached concerning Joshua Glover. Its introduction did not sit well with the core of speakers at the meeting. The leaders in rebuffing this new argument were the lawyers James Paine, Charles Watkins, and Byron Paine and, of course, the printer Sherman Booth, out on bail. Although they denounced the Fugitive Slave Act on moral grounds, they justified resistance to it on constitutional grounds. It was not that juries could make slaves, argued Byron Paine in defense of the meeting's preamble and resolutions, but that only juries could determine whether an alleged fugitive owed service in another state. There was, he reminded the convention, a clause in the U.S. Constitution that demanded the return of fugitives from labor to their state of origin. Paine could not bring himself to agree with the radical constitutional argument that the clause did not apply to slaves.[29] The Constitution prescribed the duties of the states. If a slave owner claimed a fugitive on Wisconsin's soil, the fugitive deserved "all the defences which

ANTI-SLAVE-CATCHERS'
MASS
CONVENTION!

All the People of this State, who are opposed to being made SLAVES or SLAVE-CATCHERS, and to having the Free Soil of Wisconsin made the hunting-ground for *Human Kidnappers*, and all who are willing to unite in a

☞ STATE LEAGUE, ☜

to defend our State Sovereignty, our State Courts, and our State and National Constitutions, against the flagrant usurpations of U. S. Judges, Commissioners, and Marshals, and their Attorneys; and to maintain inviolate those great Constitutional Safeguards of Freedom—the WRIT OF HABEAS CORPUS, and the RIGHT OF TRIAL BY JURY—as old and sacred as Constitutional Liberty itself; and all who are willing to sustain the cause of those who are prosecuted, and to be prosecuted in Wisconsin, by the agents and executors of the Kidnapping Act of 1850, for the alleged crime of rescuing a human being from the hands of kidnappers, and restoring him to himself and to Freedom, are invited to meet at

YOUNGS' HALL,
IN THIS CITY,

THURSDAY, APRIL 13th,

At 11 o'clock A. M., to counsel together, and take such action as the exigencies of the times, and the cause of imperilled Liberty demand.

FREEMEN OF WISCONSIN! In the spirit of our Revolutionary Fathers, come up to this gathering of the Free, resolved to speak and act as men worthy of a Free Heritage. Let the plough stand still in the furrow, and the door of the workshop be closed, while you hasten to the rescue of your country. Let the Merchant forsake his Counting Room, the Lawyer his Brief, and the Minister of God his Study, and come up to discuss with us the broad principles of Liberty. Let Old Age throw aside its crutch, and Youth put on the strength of manhood, and the young men gird themselves anew for the conflict; and faith shall make us valiant in fight, and hope lead us onward to victory; "for they that be for us, are more than they that be against us." Come, then, one and all, from every town and village, come, and unite with us in the sacred cause of Liberty. *Now* is the time to strike for Freedom. *Come*, while the *free* spirit still *burns* in your bosom. *Come!* ere the fires of Liberty are extinguished on the nation's altars, and it be too late to re-kindle the dying embers.

BY ORDER OF COMMITTEE OF ARRANGEMENTS.
MILWAUKEE, April 7, 1854.

Figure 4.2. This handbill announced the "Anti-Slave-Catchers' Mass Convention" held in Milwaukee on April 13, 1854. The meeting featured speeches from Sherman Booth, Byron Paine, James Paine, Charles Watkins, and other prominent abolitionists within the state. It was a forerunner to the conventions that established the Wisconsin Republican Party. *Wisconsin Historical Society, image number WHi-1928*

the law could furnish"; but if a jury deemed him a fugitive, "hard as it might be, monstrous as we might regard it," that fugitive must be delivered up.[30]

Such statements may not have sat well with Watkins and Booth, but they accepted them as justification for resistance. "The writ of *Habeas corpus*," said Watkins, "the lawful key to the jail, was lost in Judge Miller's pocket." What choice did the people have but to open the jail themselves? Byron Paine noted that "good and noble men" broke the jail in defense of both the higher law and the Constitution. Booth delivered a lengthy harangue. The reasons he listed for the Fugitive Slave Act's unconstitutionality were undoubtedly cribbed from Byron Paine. He ended by urging disobedience because an "Unconstitutional Act of Congress imposes no obligations on a State, or the people of a State, and may be resisted by an individual or a community."[31] If Booth's trial before the commissioner had established the abolitionists' creed of the rights and duties of citizenship, the Anti-Slave-Catchers' Mass Convention of April 13 served as a call to action. If the provisions of the Fugitive Slave Act were unconstitutional, if they impeded fundamental rights, it became the duty of citizens to resist it in any way.

Booth had his own plans for defeating the Fugitive Slave Act as well as the criminal charges against him. In May, he sued out a writ of habeas corpus from Abram Smith, justice of the Wisconsin Supreme Court, and won his freedom. What was more, Justice Smith ruled the Fugitive Slave Act of 1850 unconstitutional. The story and substance of this monumental habeas corpus hearing is reserved for the next chapter, but it had the immediate effect of frightening the U.S. district attorney. He had been caught unprepared and faced a team of lawyers who had clearly outmaneuvered him. Although few expected the full bench of the Wisconsin Supreme Court to uphold the maverick Smith's ruling, Sharpstein did not want to risk further embarrassment over the inability of federal officers to enforce the law. He requested assistance from Attorney General Caleb Cushing, who granted Sharpstein permission to seek special counsel at U.S. expense.[32] Sharpstein retained Edward G. Ryan, one of Milwaukee's best-known attorneys.

Edward G. Ryan had drawn from the public purse before. Most notably, he had presented the case for impeachment and removal of circuit court judge Levi Hubbell before the Wisconsin legislature in 1853. He had pursued that case zealously, too zealously for some people. Animosity between Hubbell and Ryan led to charges that Ryan's prosecution was

Figure 4.3. Born in 1810 in Ireland, Edward G. Ryan immigrated to the United States in 1830 and came to Milwaukee in 1848. He was known for his eloquence in legal argument and presented the case for the impeachment of Judge Levi Hubbell before the Wisconsin state senate in 1853. The U.S. attorney in Wisconsin hired Ryan to assist in the Ryecraft and Booth prosecutions in 1854 and 1855. Ryan was appointed chief justice of the Wisconsin Supreme Court in 1874 and was elected to a full term in 1875. He died in 1880. *Photo courtesy of the Milwaukee County Historical Society*

personal rather than professional.[33] Whatever his motives, few would dispute Ryan's oratorical abilities, understanding of the law, and intellectual acumen. He wrote frequently for public consumption, delivered lectures before large crowds at Young's Hall in Milwaukee, and occasionally published his poetry in the local papers. He was also an excitable fellow, deeply sensitive to perceived insults and steadfast in his pursuit of what was right. Deeply conservative, Ryan described himself as a proslavery Democrat and was contemptuous of abolitionism, women's rights, and other reform movements. He believed the enforcement of the Fugitive Slave Act to be a constitutional duty and with relish took up the reins of the prosecution of Glover's rescuers.[34]

The new term of the U.S. District Court for the District of Eastern Wisconsin began, as required by statute, on the first Monday in July. Judge Miller issued writs of venire to empanel a grand jury to investigate crimes against the federal government. There weren't many to consider. The grand jury indicted one man for stealing the U.S. mail, another for embezzlement, and a third for counterfeiting U.S. coin. It also considered indictments against Sherman Booth, John Ryecraft, John Messinger, and Frank Raymond for aiding and abetting the escape of a fugitive slave in the U.S. marshal's custody. The grand jury dismissed the indictment against Raymond, but returned true bills for the other three men on Saturday, July 8. The next Tuesday, Miller issued arrest warrants for the three men for violation of the Fugitive Slave Act.[35] The federal courtroom was not the only one busy about these issues. The Wisconsin Supreme Court had accepted Sharpstein's appeal of Justice Smith's ruling. On July 19, the court surprised nearly everyone by upholding Smith's decision and freeing Booth from the U.S. commissioner's warrant. Booth immediately petitioned the Wisconsin Supreme Court for another writ of habeas corpus to free him from the U.S. district court judge's warrant. The Wisconsin Supreme Court denied it. Because the federal court had obtained jurisdiction, the court explained, the doctrine of comity of courts prevented interference.[36] Miller, meanwhile, set a November trial date for Ryecraft and Booth. Booth asked for and received a continuance due to illness.[37]

All the ingredients were on the table. The U.S. commissioner had exercised his powers, the Wisconsin Supreme Court had claimed the right of review, and the U.S. district court had forged ahead with its own proceedings, ignoring the Wisconsin court's judgment concerning the unconstitutionality of the Fugitive Slave Act of 1850. There were deeper rumblings as well. The Fugitive Slave Act had been declared unconstitutional at political assemblies around the state, most notably the one that had freed Glover. The trials of Ryecraft and Booth would be even more public and have more at stake than any event so far. Judge Miller worked to ensure that it went as smoothly as possible. He established firm guidelines for court procedure to maintain the dignity of his courtroom. Citing a desire not to prejudice the jury—but more likely hoping to limit public discussion of the trial until it was completed—he requested that the press forestall publication of testimony until after the trial. Although the press complained that their record would be of better quality than the jury's "fallible" memory, Milwaukee's newspaper editors honored the request.[38]

Ryecraft was tried for unlawfully obstructing legal process and for rescue under the seventh section of the Fugitive Slave Act of 1850, facing three criminal counts in all.[39] Ryecraft's direct role in the rescue made it an easy case. The prosecution called multiple witnesses who had seen Ryecraft break down the jail gate with a piece of timber borrowed from the construction site of St. John's Cathedral. Ryecraft's attorneys, George Lakin and Mitchell Steever, called witnesses to rebut the prosecution's claim, but they spent most of their time putting the government on trial. Their defense was thorough and capable, although Ryan later remarked in a private letter that they had depended on the "higher law" and raised almost no other legal defense.[40] Ryan's observation overlooked Judge Miller's refusal to hear many of Lakin's arguments, including the Wisconsin Supreme Court's constitutional objections to the Fugitive Slave Act and the question of whether the jury was in criminal trials the judge of both fact and law.

What Lakin and Steever did effectively was to juxtapose the orderly mass meeting with the violence of Glover's arrest. One witness testified that he had been at the meeting since eleven o'clock, but had left for dinner and returned before Glover was rescued. "The meeting was orderly," he said under both direct and cross-examination. Pressured by Ryan, he admitted that "I suppose that breaking open the jail would be considered disorderly."[41] But even witnesses for the prosecution recalled the meeting as peaceful. James S. Buck, one of the marshals deputized by Charles Cotton, referred to Glover's rescue in negative terms: "He was taken but forcibly by what I suppose would be called a mob; they broke open the doors." Buck also testified that the crowd had been assembled for hours without incident. The prosecution called George S. Mallory, alderman of the First Ward, to testify that he saw Ryecraft taking part in the rescue. He testified that he had, but he also said on cross-examination that he had been at the meeting for several hours "as a looker-on." He had made no attempt to interfere, as "it was an excitable crowd." Yet he had remained safely with this "excitable crowd" for several hours, gone home for dinner, and returned in time to see Joshua Glover broken from the jail and carried off in a wagon. "There was great rejoicing," he recalled.[42] The defense asked both Mallory and Parsons whether they had asked the mob to disperse. Both were, after all, sworn peace officers and bound by law to command the peace in times of disorder.[43] Neither had done anything, nor did either testify that the "mob" had threatened the general public order. Lakin and Steever went further. After returning to the subject of Glover's wounds and alleged ill-treatment, Ryecraft's counsel asked Deputy Marshal Cotton whether he had looked after Glover in jail or whether he knew whether the jailer had attended to him. Cotton replied: "There was no special provision made for his care more than ordinary."[44]

By making violence a central theme of the case, Ryecraft's attorneys implicitly invoked the ideas of consent and consensus as necessary to sustain law. The Fugitive Slave Act could not claim either in Wisconsin; therefore its execution depended on naked force. The prosecution could not dismiss this tactic of the defense out of hand in the courtroom, but instead addressed it directly. Judge Miller sided with the prosecution by taking a stand on officers' rights. Quoting Russell's treatise on crimes, Miller defended the right of a peace officer to use whatever violence was necessary, including justifiable homicide. Russell's treatise declared that because fugitives rarely submit peacefully to capture, such a rule was founded in reason and public utility. Miller added his own assurance: "it is no doubt the anxious desire and prayer of every good citizen that these laws may be faithfully administered; and the dreadful alternative of force be avoided."[45]

Miller's defense of the federal officers' use of violence indicated just how differently he understood and deployed that word. For Miller, the act of violence had been the courthouse meeting and the crowd's intimidation of officers doing their duty. As he stated in his charge to the jurors, had he obeyed the writ of habeas corpus and sent Glover before the county judge, "surely" the fugitive would have been rescued. To support this proposition,

Miller focused on the language used by the organizers of the meeting. The leaders had referred to the federal marshal and to Miller himself as "kidnappers." Here Miller rested on strong evidence. Throughout the trial, the prosecution prodded witnesses about whether the defendants had used inflammatory language. Henry Hutchins, a key defense witness who testified that Ryecraft was standing with him when others broke the jail, found himself interrogated on cross-examination about inflammatory statements he was alleged to have made. He denied them. The defense called Herbert Reed, the chairman of the vigilance committee, to testify that it was John Ryecraft himself who had proposed resolutions stating that nothing should be done in violation of the laws. On cross-examination, the prosecution asked about the committee. "One of the objects of the committee," said Reed, "was to prevent the kidnappers from taking him out of town without a trial." The prosecution pounced: "Who do you mean by the kidnappers?" Reed answered: "I mean Mr. Cotton, and his owner, and some others."[46]

This admission became crucial evidence for the prosecution's claims that abolitionists incited the crowd to action. The prosecution pushed Reed further. Had he heard Booth say that the fugitive "must not be taken away?" Reed said no. Had Reed said anything about a rescue at all? Reed declined to answer, whereupon the judge instructed him to do so. "It's possible I might have said something," he admitted, but he denied having said that it was impossible to convict someone of rescue.[47] The following day, the prosecution called to the stand William Perry, who testified that Reed had told him that "they were going to have a rescue—there was a negro taken and he was in jail—I told him he must be cautious, such things were expensive—he said they had never made anything out of the Jerry rescue [in Syracuse, New York] and they couldn't out of this—the negro should not go back to slavery."[48] Here was evidence, albeit admissible hearsay testimony, that a rescue had been the design of the meeting's organizers from the start.

Miller considered this evidence definitive in his charge to the jury. Kidnapping, explained Miller, was the heinous crime of taking a free man off to slavery. Federal officers executing warrants were not kidnappers, and "if this committee organized, in whole or in part, to control the action or the time of the action of the judge, or for treating the officers of the law and of the court as kidnappers, they are responsible for this rebellion."[49] If the jurors found the evidence credible, said Miller, then they must vote to convict. He was aware, however, of the dangerous ground upon which he tread. "In this matter," he said, "we have not arrayed ourselves against our fellow-citizens."[50] The fact that this federal law did not command the consent of the community mattered not. It was still the duty of federal officers to enforce the law. To prevent them from doing their duty, explained Miller, by "attacks upon officers of government, so as to render its laws and authority ineffective, is the first step towards insurrection, and their defence is the protection of the stability and integrity of the government." Federal officials had only executed the law and thus had "a right to expect that confidence and protection which are due to us as citizens."[51] To obey the law, said Miller, was also a duty of citizenship. The republic itself depended on the courts' enforcement of the strict rule of law, and "upon no other principle can this government exist as a government of written constitutions and laws." If jurors, or courts, or the people at large annulled one act because they found it unjust, then "every public act would be annulled in portions of the United States."[52]

Miller's jury charge revisited the accusations of hypocrisy raised during the trial. Prosecutors had hammered home the point that the assembly's organizers had stood on their righteousness, while in truth they were dissemblers. One witness recalled that Ryecraft "was as wide awake as ever—what an excitable fellow he was" and that "he was engaged in a similar case before."[53] As for Sherman Booth's intentions, who could believe his claim that he wanted only to see the writ of habeas corpus obeyed? One witness testified that a man asked Booth what habeas corpus meant. Booth "said he thought it meant body and soul. Several laughed around him; there it ended."[54] The prosecution wanted more than to embarrass Booth with this testimony. They wanted to strip away the thin veneer of legality and to expose the abolitionists' criminal intentions. In the process, the prosecution could exonerate the crowd, whose honest concerns had been inflamed with false words.

Exposing such hypocrisy was a much wider goal of the Democratic press. Levi Hubbell, judge of the circuit court in Milwaukee and a loyal Democrat, indirectly chided the abolitionists when he sent a "law and order" toast on the occasion of the St. Patrick's Day parade, reminding those present that "all good citizens" of "all lands" respected the need for orderly conduct.[55] Although Booth chose to interpret this as a rebuke for the role the Irish played in the "election-day row" on March 7, its applicability to the Glover rescue could not be missed by many.[56] The *Milwaukee News* sardonically referred to Booth as a martyr almost immediately. After Booth published a letter from a Boston abolitionist who was planning to go to jail for his efforts in a fugitive slave rescue, the *News* pounced on the perceived hypocrisy: "[Booth] covets the martyr's crown but has not the courage to pass through the fire to obtain it. If the charlatan had a manly sentiment left, or the shadow of one in his breast, he should blush to publish such sentiments as the following from an honest Abolitionist."[57] Sharpstein and the unionist Democrats made these claims far too often for to dismiss them as mere rhetoric. They revealed the core of their anxiety: progressive reform substituted license for order. The *Milwaukee News* reported the violence surrounding the attempted rescue of a fugitive slave in Boston and the death of a peace officer in similar terms: "If these disunionists had been successful in their designs and their pernicious example were followed by the cities of the north generally, the Union would be speedily dissolved . . . . [T]heir design was clearly treasonable."[58] Disorder and disunion flowed, at least in Milwaukee, from the lips of hypocrites exciting the populace.

The two-day trial of John Ryecraft ended on November 18, and the jury was out for less than a day. On November 19, the jurors returned and found Ryecraft guilty on two of the three counts, a verdict that slightly surprised even Sharpstein.[59] A jubilant Ryan telegraphed Attorney General Cushing to report the verdict.[60] Ryan was doubtlessly excited that he had proven himself worth his rather large fee—if he ever received it. The U.S. Treasury was somewhat tardy in its payment. Ryan complained loudly, both to Cushing and to other party men. Leading Democrats in the state wrote Cushing to inform him that "our friend Ryan [has] procured a conviction" and reminded him that Ryan could have pursued the easier and more popular course of defending the rescuers.[61] Another wrote a three-page letter, included Ryan's bill, and noted that "probably no other one man in the Northwest could have obtained such a vindication of the law and such an endorsement of the Government, as is this conviction, in the face of popular feeling in Wisconsin."[62] However partisan, the zeal of Ryan's advocacy was beyond question. Even Rufus King credited Ryan's prosecution as able and strong.[63] Ryan's advocates had other motives, though. The Treasury's tardiness in payment, they worried, might prompt him to resign from the case.[64] Few believed the prosecution of Booth could succeed without Ryan. Even with him, cautioned one, "I have great doubts of the possibility of a conviction."[65]

The prosecution did have a more difficult task at hand. Unlike Ryecraft, Booth had not broken open the jail. Just as Sharpstein had argued before the U.S. commissioner's court in March 1854, the government would have to show that Booth had participated in a riot that led to the rescue. The prosecutors also would have to convince a jury that Booth had intended all along to rescue Glover. Suddenly, Booth's exact words on March 11 became crucial. If he had uttered the words "freemen to the rescue," the prosecution maintained, he had intended a rescue. If he intended a rescue, it did not matter whether he acted or not. He had duped others into performing his deed and was as responsible as Ryecraft. But there was a silver lining to Ryecraft's conviction that boded well for Booth. Ryecraft had been convicted only of interfering with federal process and of removing Joshua Glover from Cotton's custody. He had not been convicted of rescue. For what it was worth, the jury had refused to return a conviction under the provisions specifically authorized by the Fugitive Slave Act of 1850. Was it because of an unwillingness within the jury to enforce that federal law? If so, it might be more difficult to convince another jury that Booth's speaking out against the Fugitive Slave Act was a criminal act.

While Ryan and Sharpstein prepared for trial, Booth's lawyers had to respond to motions in the civil case filed by Garland's attorneys. They already had received a continuance on November 14. On December 27, Judge Miller granted commissions for interrogatories to be answered under oath by Garland and two of his associates in St. Louis. Garland's attorneys simply wanted to establish an evidentiary backing for their monetary claim. Their questions to these witnesses established their relationship with Garland, whether they knew Joshua Glover, and whether he was a slave of Garland's. A final question asked them to estimate Glover's value based on the slave market in St. Louis. The cross-interrogatories submitted by Booth's counsel were more pointed. They openly asked the witnesses whether they hunted fugitive slaves for a living, and if so, whether they kept bloodhounds for the purpose. If they had answered to the plaintiff's interrogatories that Glover was Garland's slave, then the defense demanded to know by what law Glover was held, and further, "the cause why such a law was enacted placing one man of full age, without crime, in the possession of another." The next interrogatory demanded proof that Garland held Glover legally and firsthand knowledge that Garland "did not steal Glover and reduce him to slavery by brute force." A final interrogatory required them, if they testified to Glover's value, to relate their experiences with the slave trade. How many men and women had they sold? How many children had they "weighed off by the pound" and separated from their mothers? "Your experience in these matters is required to enable us to judge of the worth of your testimony," explained the lawyers, "should you fix the value of a human being in the market at St. Louis."[66]

At the same time, Garland's attorneys filed a civil plea of debt against Marshal Ableman and others who had been charged with keeping the fugitive.[67] The Fugitive Slave Act made the officers liable for Glover's escape regardless of whether the plaintiff collected from other parties. But the timing of the filing—December 2, 1854—suggested that Garland's attorneys were concerned that penalties might not be exacted from Glover's rescuers. Ryecraft's attorneys were planning an appeal, but had stayed the entire matter until after Booth's trial so that the two issues would be joined. Antislavery lawyers had boasted publicly that the indictments upon which the jury had convicted Ryecraft were defective because they had not named Glover a fugitive slave. Whether this technicality would prove fatal the U.S. district attorney seemed unwilling to leave to chance. He made new presentments before a grand jury convened by the U.S. district court in January, this time adding a charge of resisting federal officers. The grand jury handed down eight indictments, including one against Edward B. Wolcott, the chairman of the mass meeting, and one against Herbert Reed, the chairman of the vigilance committee. Also included were Booth's attorneys, Charles Watkins, James Paine, and Byron Paine. The grand jury was not content with returning only the bills submitted by the district attorney. The jurors made their own presentment against the *Milwaukee Sentinel* and the *Daily Free Democrat*, complaining that the papers had supported lawless behavior by Milwaukee's inhabitants. Although the grand jurors professed no desire "to interfere with the liberty of the press which is prized by all freemen," they respectfully suggested that the district attorney institute proceedings against those papers anyway.[68]

The district attorney already had enough on his hands with the Booth trial ahead.[69] By all accounts, spectators packed the courtroom for the four-day trial. Booth's defense team, led by James Paine and his son Byron

Paine, drew upon the mass meeting of March 11 to defend Booth's actions. They assembled evidence that hinged on public concepts of violence, the peacefulness of the assembly, the validity of its largely democratic proceedings, and the obstinacy of federal officers. The crowning moment was Byron Paine's summation. Lasting four hours on Friday afternoon, January 12, it drew together the various themes invoked over the previous ten months and unified them for an audience that extended much further than judge and jury. Paine spoke to the audience in the courthouse, and his speech was reprinted verbatim in the *Milwaukee Sentinel,* which distributed copies to sympathetic newspapers across the North.[70] It was a public statement of Paine's understanding of legitimacy and the limits of resistance.

Paine began his summation with the story of another rescue, that of the angel delivering Peter from Herod's prison.[71] "Men are now indicted," said Paine to the jury, "for imitating Angels of God." If anyone was in doubt, Paine identified the "Slave Power" firmly in control of the federal government as Herod. This not-so-subtle analogy did not admit the guilt of Booth in performing the rescue. Rather, it denied the federal government the moral authority to prosecute him for his actions. He invoked the same images—violence and secrecy—that abolitionists had used for the last ten months. Violence, claimed Paine, had been the hallmark of the slave catchers. They had arrested Glover at night, "under cover of darkness." They were armed, said Paine, and "that violence which seems to be so inseparable from the execution of this law that its record has been written in the blood of its victims" was attended on him. He was then spirited away to the Milwaukee County jail, all at night, noted Paine, a time when "sleep falls upon the lids of peaceful men, and *guilt* and *crime* are stealing abroad to do those deeds that hurt the light."[72]

This rhetoric had more than just a literary motive. The common law had defined certain crimes, such as burglary, as taking place at night. At common law, as William Blackstone noted, "an attack by night" was regarded as "much more heinous" than an attack by day. Blackstone rooted this in nature: "the malignity of the offence does not so properly arise from its being done in the dark, as at the dead of night; when all the creation, excepts beasts of prey, are at rest; when sleep has disarmed the owner, and rendered his castle defenceless."[73] Wharton's treatise on the criminal law espoused this common-law definition and noted its presence in New York, Massachusetts, and Virginia statutes.[74] Still, the intended effect of Byron

Figure 4.4. Born in 1827, Byron Paine achieved national recognition with his arguments against the Fugitive Slave Act before the Wisconsin Supreme Court in 1854. He was elected judge of the Milwaukee County Court in 1857 and associate justice of the Wisconsin Supreme Court in 1859. He resigned his seat in 1864 to fight in the Civil War but returned to the bench by appointment in 1867 and was elected again in 1868. He died in 1871. *Photo courtesy of the Milwaukee County Historical Society*

Paine's argument was rhetorical rather than legal. A government that acted at night had something to hide, and an arrest in secret belied the public nature of democracy. Paine did not deny that the slave catchers were sanctioned in their acts by color of law. A federal judge had given them a writ, a federal marshal served it upon Glover, and the accused was taken to jail to be examined at a later time. "The process—hard process though it was—was served." In a case in which resistance and violence were primary issues, Paine sought to put the prosecution on the moral defensive. Nighttime was when nature prescribed sleep. Those who committed deeds at night did so to hide their identity, a practice that was clearly unacceptable to the enforcement of public law.

Paine intended his colorful language to illustrate the principles of consent and consensus in the practice of democracy. No one could dispute that the Fugitive Slave Act lacked the community's support in Wisconsin. Paine had argued in his review of the Ryecraft trial that jurors had the right to be judges of both fact and law in criminal cases. During his summation, he repeated this argument before the jury and then turned to Judge Miller and remarked, "I know that this Court has already instructed that the jury has no right to judge of the law in a criminal case and that the court would not hear an argument on the question." But Paine contended that it was a point of the utmost importance, "one on which the safety of the citizen intimately depends."[75] Paine had resurrected the old idea of community law and consensus enforcement, a key component of the early republic's constitutional defense of rights.[76] Miller replied that there were some dicta that mentioned it but that settled practice excluded juries from determining the law.

There were authorities to support Paine's position. In criminal cases, some state legislatures and courts recognized the law-finding function of juries in the antebellum era, although there had been a steady attack on this position from several quarters.[77] In the realm of U.S. criminal law, the authorities were, at best, contradictory. In a case involving robbery of the mail in 1830, the circuit court justice instructed the jurors that they could decide the law for themselves, although he asked them to "bear in mind, that it is a very old, sound and valuable maxim in law that the court answers to questions of law and the jury to facts." That said, if the jurors were to "indulge the feelings of humanity, in construing acts of Congress," the judge asked that they do so with the ends of justice in mind.[78] The same justice qualified this decision two years later by stressing that juries could not make pronouncements on the constitutionality of laws—that was reserved for processes spelled out by the U.S. Constitution.[79] The case most clearly on point for Miller, though, came from the indictment of a black attorney charged with aiding and abetting the rescue of Shadrach in Boston. Justice Benjamin Curtis had completely rejected the defense's argument to allow the jury to decide the law. He then turned on its head the claim that it was the jury's duty to safeguard the rights of citizens: "this power and corresponding duty of the court, authoritatively to declare the law, is one of the highest safeguards of the citizen."[80]

Paine argued that this practice inverted the Constitution's purpose. Among that document's numerous bulwarks against repression was the requirement that matters of liberty be submitted to a jury. What safeguard could a jury be, asked Paine, when judges instructed them that they must find guilty verdicts?[81] Paine exploited this contradiction in his closing statement: "I charge upon this prosecution that they have come into court before you and confessed that they are engaged in the execution of an infamous law." He reminded jurors that the prosecution had asked each one of them during jury selection whether he had any conscientious scruples against the Fugitive Slave Act of 1850. Paine asked the jurors rhetorically: would the government have asked the same question if it were prosecuting someone for stealing the mail, or counterfeiting U.S. coin? Certainly not. "But when that government lays its ban on humanity, and loudly and barbarously violates the rights of the people, then the prosecution may well ask the question, which shows that they know the law they are trying to enforce, is one against which the consciences of men rebel."[82] Paine anticipated (or perhaps responded to) the prosecution's argument that the same question would be put to jurors asked to enforce the death penalty in capital cases. Paine pointed out the essential difference: in capital cases, there was no disagreement regarding the act that warranted punishment, only the form of the punishment.[83]

This was the crucial distinction in Paine's rhetoric. On the one hand, he offered his listeners the analogy of the federal government as Herod. The government passed laws to aggrandize its own power at the expense of its citizens; it silenced its citizens and demanded that they behave like passive subjects; it sneaked around at night to enforce laws secretly; it imposed its will through violence. Against the tyrannical Herod, he put the fugitive slave Glover who, responding to "instinct," had escaped bondage and sought freedom. Just as Glover's instinct to liberty was natural, so was the response of the free citizens of Racine and Milwaukee. They had awakened swiftly as news of Glover's arrest spread like wildfire among them. Then, like a "lightning track" it traveled across "the electric cords that bind all human beings in that great bond which lies at the foundation of the Christian's love and bond of human brotherhood." Paine backed this up with yet another analogy to nature. Beasts, gathering where the blood of one of their kind had been spilled, "rush together with wild looks and wild bellowings that testify to their anxiety for the fate of their murdered comrade."[84] So too with Wisconsinites, who naturally feared that Glover's plight portended something ominous. Concerned about their own rights, the people proceeded to act: "A meeting was organized. Speeches were made expressive of the sentiments of the speakers, and resolutions adopted expressive of the sentiments of the meeting." Paine then made the now familiar abolitionist argument that the crowd had freed Glover because the people were frustrated with the unresponsiveness of the federal officers. And when they freed Glover, imitating the angel who saved Peter from Herod, "a shout for freedom that shook the heavens went up from that vast multitude,—a shout that startled tyranny in its dreams of power—a shout whose echoes are still ringing, like a triumphal song of liberty chanted by the mighty voice of the people."[85]

The alchemy of Paine's speech lay in its power to transform the charge of treason made by unionist Democrats into the very stuff of civic duty. This was not mere rhetorical window dressing, but a potent description of democratic citizenship. It demanded vigilance in the face of power and direct participation in matters of fundamental importance. There were, of course, limits. Citizens had to question their government peacefully and pursue the proper political and legal remedies. Liberty required discipline; it was not merely license. But dutiful citizens could require government officials to explain themselves openly and publicly. When the government could no longer do this—when it had to enforce its laws at night through violence, shuttle prisoners around in secret, and then demand that its citizens sacrifice constitutionally guaranteed civic rights—the government had become a tyranny. That citizenship's privileges and duties were defined locally enhanced the conflict. Congress had passed a law that deprived Wisconsin of its right to define and protect the rights of its citizens. Miller's belief in the "one sovereignty" theory could not work without a distinct national understanding about status and rights, one that could not exist when determination of status remained the province of the states.

Paine finished his closing after dark on Friday night. On Saturday morning, Ryan commenced his own summation. Unfortunately, no record of it survives. The jury retired for deliberation shortly after two o'clock in the afternoon. Eight hours passed before the jurors returned to the courtroom. The verdict was "guilty." Byron Paine demanded that the court poll the jury, requiring each juror to state his verdict in open court. This last-minute appeal to the conscience of the jurors, however, was to no avail. In less than one day, they had come to the unanimous conclusion that Booth was guilty of removing Glover from the custody of Deputy Marshal Cotton. That a northern jury, in a state as progressive as Wisconsin, came to that conclusion defied most expectations. Booth's allies blamed Judge Miller, alleging that his one-sided charge to the jury, as in the Ryecraft trial, had compelled a verdict of guilty. Rumors circulated that two of the jurors had been predisposed to convict. Byron Paine filed a motion for a new trial on this point, producing a number of affidavits to back up his allegation of bias. Miller denied the motion and let the jury verdict stand.

Even the triumphant Democratic press seemed surprised. The *Daily Wisconsin* was happy to declare the matter over and suggested that if Booth had spent less time complaining about the jurors in print and more time standing on his principles, then he might have prevailed. The editor even suggested an alternate closing statement: "Had he gone into the U.S. Court and said manfully to the JURY: 'I did violate the Fugitive Slave Law—because I deem it an unjust, anti-republican, and unconstitutional law, which strikes at the very foundation of our free institutions. I appeal to you as men and as Americans whether I did any wrong in trying to release the fugitive from bonds,'" the jury might have set him free.[86] This was hardly likely. The defense had failed in its attempt to convince the jury that it held the power to judge the law, and juries were reluctant to assume the worst of their government's officers, even when they enforced a law no one liked. And lingering in everyone's minds during the trials was the possibility that Booth had dissembled and that his motives were impure.

—

The trials of Sherman Booth and John Ryecraft opened public debate about the limits of resistance and gave both unionist Democrats and their antislavery opponents the opportunity to argue their politics to the people. The trial raised more issues than the question of rescue or even of the Fugitive Slave Act. It touched on the duties and privileges of citizenship and the limits of political resistance. For the antislavery party, resistance was only one subject in a lengthy dialogue between citizen and governor. Deliberately drawing on old republican ideas, abolitionists urged citizens to be vigilant in the face of aggrandizing power. When a government threatened the civil liberties of one citizen, it was the duty of his fellows to assemble and to inquire into the conduct of the officers as well as into the laws themselves. There were limits. Only encroachments on fundamental rights, such as trial by jury and recourse to habeas corpus, could justify such extraordinary resistance. Abolitionists' rhetoric also emphasized that the duty of assembly was characterized by open speech, reasoned argument, and community consent. They made their point most tellingly, though, when differentiating the actions of the assembly from those of the national government. Federal officers had arrested Glover in secret, without showing proper warrant or process. They had lied about their involvement. They had sought to stifle debate and discussion about the law. In short, they had demanded submission, not democratic acceptance.

The lawyers defending federal law responded ferociously. They saw law in an explicitly positivist framework, although still under the republican mantle. One of the first duties of citizens was to be ruled as well as to rule—that is, to follow the laws as the legislature decided them. Personal disagreement with the law was no excuse for breaking it. Obedience was owed to the law's agents. If everyone followed his or her own ethical conscience, then no law could function. Anarchy would result. Miller, Sharpstein, and Ryan viewed radical reformers—those who led the crowd into action—as particularly bad because they put their own personal beliefs above a respect for the rule of law. Abolitionism and other progressive movements existed "only to trample on laws" because the reformers who espoused them lacked a proper understanding of what made society work. Without respect for laws, all political order would crumble, as would the union of the states—and with it "the best chance for free government in the world." Worse still—as Sharpstein charged—these radical reformers were base hypocrites. Their self-righteous rhetoric masked only perfidy and the pursuit of power. The hypocrisy charge meant more than just calling abolitionists liars. It meant identifying them as the corrupters of democratic society, foolishly and egotistically putting themselves before the republic.

January 14, 1855, was another cold, winter Sunday in Milwaukee. The brisk morning air carried the ringing of bells from the city's more than fifteen churches. The Booth and Ryecraft trials were over. Two different juries had found them guilty, a vindication of the federal government's determination to enforce its laws. A satisfied Edward G. Ryan set about writing a letter to Caleb Cushing, celebrating the "great triumph of the law over the spirit of misrule" and asking once again for his fee. Byron Paine and James Paine most likely spent a portion of their Sunday preparing an appeal. It was not, however, a writ of error from the U.S. Supreme Court, which was the only appellate court above the federal district courts. Instead, they once again asked the Wisconsin Supreme Court to intervene with a writ of habeas corpus.

FIVE

The Wisconsin Supreme Court and the Fugitive Slave Act

> With the [Wisconsin] Supreme Court to sustain them these wild and frantic fanatics will now resist the execution of [Sherman Booth's] sentence even to the taking of life and nothing short of an overpowering force will awe them into submission.
>
> —John Sharpstein, February 6, 1855

ON JANUARY 30, 1855, Sherman Booth, John Ryecraft, the county sheriff, and about two thousand well-wishers marched to the train station along a path that, not coincidentally, took them past Judge Miller's residence. As they passed his home, they sang "Jordan is a hard road to travel."[1] Booth and Ryecraft boarded the train to Madison for a hearing before the supreme court. Four days earlier, the sheriff had served U.S. marshal Stephen Ableman with a writ of habeas corpus. Federal officers wrung their hands, fully expecting the state supreme court to interpose itself in the U.S. district court's proceedings, free the prisoners, and repeat its declaration that the Fugitive Slave Act of 1850 was unconstitutional. Marshal Ableman complied with the writ, but noted on his return that he did not recognize the authority of the state court.

It was, of course, not the first time that Booth had called upon the Wisconsin Supreme Court to intercede. In all, he had sued for three writs of habeas corpus by January 30, 1855. The court had sided with him on two occasions and had refused to intercede in one. This was a legal battle different from the criminal trials argued before juries, although it ran in parallel with them. In the criminal trials, antislavery lawyers had attempted to counter charges of riot and rescue while deploying a rhetoric that sought to legitimate the spontaneous assembly against a tyrannical government. Such arguments, though they might persuade a jury of laymen, carried little weight before the bench, where the issues were primarily legal and where the facts of Glover's rescue and Booth's actions ceased to be of major importance. Rhetorical crossover definitely occurred. Just as people justified popular resistance with claims that the law was unconstitutional, so lawyers colored their arguments with sentiment and imagery. Lawyers appealed to the rights and duties of citizens in similar language before both the bench and the jury.

Still, this was a highly technical legal argument made before judges. Although the Wisconsin Supreme Court would not make a claim to be the sole—or even the highest—expositor of the Constitution, it had already on one occasion presumed to declare a federal statute void. To justify this momentous act and its later intervention in federal court proceedings, the Wisconsin court needed to deploy a strong theory of law. Byron Paine suggested one when he argued a moderate antislavery jurisprudence indebted to Salmon P. Chase and Robert Rantoul. Paine's argument put more weight on the duty of states—particularly the state judiciary—to intervene on the basis of the plenary police power reserved by the Tenth Amendment to the states. Against this, federal officers pleaded that the doctrine of comity of courts and settled practice forbade the states from interfering with federal process. They countered the arguments against the constitutionality of the Fugitive Slave Act by resorting to the convention that fugitive slave rendition was a constitutional duty mediated by Congress, accepted by the country, and upheld in the courts. The U.S. attorney argued that Wisconsin's intercession amounted to a repudiation of the Constitution. Both arguments were, in their own ways, reasonable interpretations of the Constitution. They were also incompatible, and this incompatibility inaugurated a new phase in Wisconsin's constitutional resistance to the Fugitive Slave Act.

The decision to test the Fugitive Slave Act's constitutionality came shortly after the rescue. On May 26, 1854, Booth had his bailsman surrender him to federal authorities. He immediately sued out a writ of habeas corpus before Wisconsin Supreme Court justice Abram Smith, "chiefly on the ground of the unconstitutionality of the Act."[2] Booth and his legal team of James Paine, Byron Paine, and Charles Watkins had selected the timing of their application carefully. The supreme court was in vacation, and Smith—resident in Milwaukee—was an avowed abolitionist. John Sharpstein, after some hesitation, complied with the writ. On May 29, Booth and his counsel appeared in court, and, after weathering some fairly minor objections by Sharpstein, Byron Paine began a two-day oral argument in support of Booth's right to a writ of habeas corpus.

Paine made clear from the start that he was not making a "natural law" argument: "I do not stand here to oppose that law because it is a monstrous moral deformity—detestable in its purpose and detestable in its details, sinking to the depths of depravity to punish mercy as a crime."[3] Such a disavowal could only be captious, intended to embarrass those who would defend the Fugitive Slave Act. But it also signaled his acceptance of a moderate antislavery constitutionalism.[4] Radical abolitionists, William Lloyd Garrison chief among them, rejected the Constitution as a slaveholder's document and objected to Paine's constitutionalism as a compromise with slavery. They stressed a militant abolitionism that rested on resistance to the Fugitive Slave Act on moral principle. No law could obligate man to commit a "monstrous moral deformity," that is, the sending of men to slavery. Paine had rejected this position publicly, and now he did so before the bench.

Byron Paine came by his views honestly. His father had been an early leader of the Liberty Party in Ohio, where he had worked with Salmon P. Chase and had become much taken with his constitutional theories. Chase first articulated his arguments in the case of the alleged fugitive slave Matilda, claimed by a Missourian named Larkin Lawrence. Lawrence had taken Matilda with him on a trip from Missouri to Kentucky in 1836. Matilda escaped during a stop in Cincinnati and hid among the city's free blacks. Lawrence continued on to Missouri, and Matilda took a job in abolitionist James Birney's household as a maid. Lawrence hired a slave catcher, who located Matilda, obtained a warrant from a local justice of the peace, and arrested her. Birney sued out a writ of habeas corpus and enlisted Chase to defend her claim.[5]

Chase's arguments wove together objections to the sufficiency of Matilda's arrest warrant and demands that the reviewing court construe fugitive slave statutes narrowly and scrutinize lower court proceedings stringently. But the passion and gravity of his argument centered on the Fugitive Slave Act's unconstitutionality. He made five primary arguments: the fugitive slave clause did not authorize a congressional statute because it was a matter of compact among the states; Congress could not confer federal judicial authority on state officers; the statute violated due process guaranteed by the Fifth and Sixth Amendments; it was repugnant to the Northwest Ordinance of 1787; it violated the sacred right of trial by jury.

His arguments were unsuccessful. Matilda was remanded to the slave catcher's custody, and the state prosecuted James Birney for harboring a fugitive slave, an act made illegal by an 1804 Ohio statute. A jury convicted Birney, and Chase appealed, alleging a defect in the indictment.[6] Chase made a similar argument, but this time laid out more fully his theory of an "antislavery Constitution." He fully admitted the constitutional duty of returning fugitive slaves to their masters. Matilda, however, was not a fugitive slave: her owner had brought her voluntarily to a free state, whereupon she escaped. Because the Northwest Ordinance and the Ohio constitution had prohibited slavery within the state, Matilda was presumptively free. Relying on the foundation provided by Lord Mansfield in *Somerset,* Chase argued that slavery could be established only by municipal law. As a creature of municipal law, it could not command any authority outside its jurisdiction. Chase here cited decisions from the courts of Louisiana and Mississippi in defense of his position. Nor could the owner of a slave expect the laws of his municipality to be extended to Ohio courts. Citing Justice Joseph Story's treatise on conflict of laws, Chase declared that a sovereign jurisdiction was not bound to admit laws that were prejudicial to its citizens.[7]

The court did not accept Chase's reasoning. Birney was released, but only because an omitted word of substance turned out to be fatal to the indictment: the prosecution had not averred that Birney was aware that Matilda was a fugitive slave. The judge overruled the prosecutor's objections that the 1804 statute had required no such averment. Birney's act of hiring a black woman as a maid did not impute any crime. Because slavery did not exist in Ohio, the presumption of the law was in favor of Matilda's freedom. Intent, therefore, became essential to prove that Birney's act—blameless on its face—was criminal.[8] It was a technicality, but an enormously important one, at least for Birney.

Chase extrapolated from this moderate antislavery constitutionalism in *Birney* when he wrote the Ohio Liberty Party platform. Slavery, being a creature of municipal law, could find no sanction in the law of nations, natural law, or reason. The Constitution's preamble stated that the people instituted the government to "secure the blessings of liberty," not to further the ends of slavery. Chase also noted that the founders had scrupulously avoided using the word slavery so as not to admit that one person could have property in another. Clearly they had meant to limit slavery and spread freedom. Because the Constitution indirectly referenced slavery, Chase turned to the debates of the Convention and other acts passed in the revolutionary period—arguably a legislative program—that clarified intent. Thomas Jefferson had consciously organized the Northwest Territory to introduce five free states into the Union, whereas the extension of slavery into the Kentucky country and the Tennessee River valley would have produced, at best, two slave states. Jefferson, argued Chase, was well aware that the balance of the Union would have been tipped toward the free states. "The framers of the Constitution did not design that slavery should extend beyond the limits of the then slave states," declared Chase.[9] Instead, the framers and the founding generation "endeavoured to establish the national Government and Policy upon such principles as would bring about, at length, the desired result of Universal Freedom."[10] Chase's constitutionalism constrained Congress in two ways. It demonstrated that the national government had no authority to extend slavery into the territories or pass legislation aiding masters in reclaiming their fugitives. The converse was that Congress also had no authority to alter the municipal law that created slavery within sovereign states.[11]

Chase had sketched a credible, if one-sided, antislavery constitutionalism. So convinced was he of his own interpretation that he found it "strange that the proslavery construction of the Constitution, so utterly indefensible, upon history or by reason, should be so tamely acquiesced in by the courts."[12] Its force and elegance inspired Whigs like William H. Seward, who noted that it opened "a broad field of inquiry." Seward, like many others, had thought the Constitution to be proslavery and inflexible. When compared to the constitution of New York, which was revised every twenty-five years, and to those of states that incorporated organic law, the U.S. Constitution appeared frozen in time. Chase's interpretation imagined a wholly different original intent, one that had compromised with slavery gracefully in order to see it die gracefully. For Seward, this suggested that the Constitution's proslavery construction could be defeated without the formal and difficult process of amendment. When the "public conscience" was "restored to healthful action . . . there [would] soon be found a way for its manifestations."[13] For Seward and Chase, it was up to the people to promulgate this view of the Constitution, to express their sovereign will by electing officers who would restore the antislavery Constitution. They also saw the courts as another venue for constitutional expression, although the federal courts had clearly demonstrated their hostility. If, wrote Chase, the proslavery construction of the Constitution "finds sanctuary in Courts of Justice it must be dragged out, and denounced before the people." The result, Chase continued, was that it must fall. "If courts will not overthrow it, the people will, even if it be necessary to overthrow the courts also."[14]

Before overthrowing the courts, one might appeal to them, as Chase had done and continued to do. He argued his position forcefully in *Jones v. Van Zandt* in 1847, a case that became standard reading among antislavery lawyers. Paine cited it and noted the contribution of Robert Rantoul, who had argued *Sims's Case* in 1851.[15] Much of Paine's argument can be traced to these two cases, but he also departed from them in several important ways. He emphasized the nature of constitutional arrangements between states and the national government and how they impinged on citizens and their liberty. He stressed the connection between states and their citizens, particularly with regard to the broadly defined police power. Paine also took on the argument—often made by reluctant antislavery judges—that they had no choice but to enforce the Fugitive Slave Act.

Paine argued that the Fugitive Slave Act of 1850 was unconstitutional on three grounds. First, he asserted that Congress had no power to legislate on the subject. Second, the statute subverted due process by denying alleged fugitives the right to a trial by jury. Third, court commissioners were themselves unconstitutional officers. Although Paine listed his grounds in this order, he structured his oral argument differently, beginning with the legitimacy of commissioners, moving to the question of congressional authority, and ending with the violations that the law occasioned on a citizen's right to due process. This allowed him to begin with the most formal—and formally credible—argument and to end with a rhetorical plea for liberty that resonated both within the courtroom and beyond its walls.

He grounded all three points in the doctrine of state sovereignty. The national government, a limited creation of the states, could not usurp powers not specifically given it by the Constitution. This, opined Paine, was a doctrine "not denied in theory by any one" and in need of no proof. Rather, he said, "the great point of the controversy upon this subject is whether the Federal Government is the exclusive judge of the extent of its own powers, or whether the States have not also the right to judge upon that matter."[16]

This was the crux. Paine drew heavily from the Virginia and Kentucky Resolutions as well as from Madison's "Report of 1800" to demonstrate that the state had a concurrent right to decide when the federal government had encroached on its sovereign authority.[17] Beginning with the problem of court commissioners, Paine argued that they could not be considered officers of the courts because they did not have a judge's constitutionally required tenure or fixed salary. Justice Smith interrupted Paine at this point and asked whether Article II, Section 2, Clause 2, which provides that "Congress may, by law, vest the appointment of such inferior officers as they may think proper, in the President alone, in the courts of law, or in the heads of departments" had any bearing on his argument. Paine answered no. The critical point was the nature of the functions the officers performed. If the functions were judicial, then the office would have to conform to Article III of the Constitution. Because the commissioners ruled on the status of the state's residents, they were properly judicial officers.

Paine moved on to congressional power to legislate on the subject. He interpreted the fugitive slave clause of the Constitution as imposing directly on the states the duty of "delivering up" a fugitive from labor. There was no enabling clause attached to the fugitive slave provision, nor was the power enumerated in Article I. Paine argued further that it could not be considered an implied congressional power, for it created a criminal jurisdiction that the federal government had not previously possessed. Smith interrupted Paine to ask him if he believed Congress had any power to legislate *at all* on the subject. Paine emphatically answered no.

Paine then spoke at length about the right to trial by jury and recourse to the writ of habeas corpus. Even "admitting that congress has the power to legislate, and that a fugitive case is one to which the judicial power extends, still the law is unconstitutional, because it provides that any person claimed, may be reduced to a state of slavery without a trial by jury."[18] Trial by jury in criminal cases was guaranteed by the Sixth Amendment. Paine acknowledged that a status determination before a commissioner was not a criminal trial, but pointed out that the Seventh Amendment guaranteed a jury trial in civil cases in which the amount in controversy exceeded twenty dollars. The Fugitive Slave Act of 1850 also violated the civil protections of citizens contained within the Fourth and Fifth Amendments. Clearly, said Paine, the federal government had exceeded its constitutionally prescribed authority and, in doing so, had usurped the sovereign powers of the states. Then, dovetailing this point nicely with his opening remarks, Paine argued that the federal government could not be the sole judge of its own power, inviting the interposition of Justice Smith and the Wisconsin Supreme Court on constitutional grounds.

This case marked the emergence of Byron Paine as the leading lawyer in Wisconsin's antislavery cause, and it was chiefly through this argument—circulated among abolitionists in the North—that he gained national prominence. Charles Sumner wrote the young lawyer to commend him on his performance and to request copies of his argument in the case.[19] On June 7, after pondering the oral arguments for a week, Justice Smith granted Booth his writ of habeas corpus and declared the Fugitive Slave Act of 1850 unconstitutional. Despite the shocking presumption—that a state judge sitting in vacation could oppose the entire U.S. Congress—most understood that Smith's ruling applied only to the commissioner's court. William Cramer of the *Daily Wisconsin* complained that "we can see no particular object of these proceedings, unless it be to get up an excitement and to manufacture public sentiment or sympathy. If Mr. B. should be discharged from custody, it would not effect or control the Grand Jury in finding a bill against him. Consequently it can have no earthly effect except to add notoriety to the case—and counsel."[20] The general feeling in Madison was that the full bench would quietly overrule the decision.[21]

It was something of a shock, then, when the Wisconsin Supreme Court upheld Smith's decision in a 2-to-1 ruling. Chief Justice Edward Whiton's majority opinion accepted as its foundation the doctrine of state sovereignty: "It will not be denied that the citizens of the state naturally and properly look to their own state tribunals for relief from all kinds of illegal restraint and imprisonment. These courts are clothed with power sufficient for their protection."[22] Whiton did not feel the need to provide lengthy citations for this point, indicative of the common understanding of habeas corpus as primarily a state power. Several years later, Rollin Hurd published a treatise on this subject that gathered the sources for this view. The states had a right and duty to test by habeas corpus all forms of imprisonment, even if under color of federal law.[23] Whiton's one citation was to a fugitive slave case. Chief Justice Lemuel Shaw, of Massachusetts, had decided in *Sims's Case* that any person was entitled to petition for a writ of habeas corpus, even if held under color of process by a U.S. court. Whiton, however, rejected the further conclusion that Shaw drew: if it appeared from the face of the petition that the prisoner would not be entitled to a discharge, then the petition should not be granted.[24] This, felt Shaw, was the fatal defect in Sims's petition: once it became clear that the petitioner was held by virtue of U.S. civil process, the state court had to relent. Shaw conceded that a state could interpose between its citizens and the national government, but only in a "clear case."

For Whiton, Booth's was the clear case to which Shaw alluded. A state's citizen complained of illegal imprisonment by the federal government. The federal government held the citizen by virtue of a warrant from a federal commissioner under the authority of a law that had extended the criminal jurisdiction of the United States under the implied powers doctrine. By this reasoning, Whiton rejected Sharpstein's argument that the writ of habeas corpus could not be issued when it appeared that the prisoner was held by a U.S. court in a matter over which it had exclusive jurisdiction.[25] The state courts had leave to determine whether the imprisonment was legal and to inquire as to whether they held jurisdiction in the matter. Justice Samuel Crawford, the lone dissenter on the Wisconsin Supreme Court, agreed with Sharpstein and with the decision of Chief Justice Shaw in *Sims*: if the imprisonment was illegal, the proper recourse was to the courts of the United States. This rankled Smith, who countered that "the respective states were regarded as the essential, if not the sole guardians of the personal rights and liberties of the individual citizen."[26] The state had no choice but to intervene in the matter because the citizen's allegiance to the state translated into a corresponding duty to protect the citizen.

Paine defended his argument for interposition by invoking the people's right to protest unconstitutional enactments. He cited the Virginia and

Kentucky Resolutions denouncing the Alien and Sedition Acts, passed by Congress in 1798.[27] The Sedition Act had prohibited publication or utterance of any false, seditious, or malicious statements about the government, either house of Congress, or the president. Jefferson and Madison, alarmed by the Federalists' attempt to use congressional legislation to protect their power, protested the law by resorting to the legislatures of the sovereign states. The Virginia Resolution, passed on December 24, 1798, called them "palpable and alarming infractions on the Constitution." The Kentucky Resolution, passed on December 3, 1799, used much the same language. It also specified that although Kentucky would usually bow to the laws passed by Congress, "in momentous regulations like the present, which so vitally wound the best rights of the citizen, it would consider a silent acquiescence as highly criminal." The Kentucky legislature declared that it would not cease to "oppose in a constitutional manner" such unconstitutional laws. These resolutions drew alarmed responses from other states not willing to go so far; Madison's "Report of 1800" attempted to demonstrate before the country that the resolutions were not as extreme as some believed them.[28] They had been advanced with the utmost care to oppose "*deliberate, palpable* and *dangerous*" breaches of the Constitution by Congress.[29] They had followed numerous petitions from citizens across the republic asking for immediate repeal of laws they believed unconstitutional. In short, the resolutions were the voice of the people, standing up to enforce the Constitution as its last defenders.[30]

For both Paine and the Wisconsin justices who declared the Fugitive Slave Act unconstitutional, the Virginia and Kentucky Resolutions' qualifications were as important as the theoretical right to revolution. Paine warned that questions of constitutional construction, when involving "a conflict between the powers of the whole and of each sovereign part," must "be approached with solemnity and anxious care, with moderation and forbearance."[31] Justice Smith, in his June 7 opinion granting Booth's writ of habeas corpus, included a strongly worded admonition. Citizens calling on state courts to interpose themselves had to do so in good faith. They did not have a right to invent fictitious imprisonment for the purpose of testing a law. Nor did they have the right to test *any* law they disliked. Interposition could occur only when the state's sovereign right of self-defense had been violated. It gave the people a means by which to protest unconstitutional enactments that, reasoned Paine, would prevent the citizen from the necessity of resorting to revolution. In other words, state interposition sought to preserve rather than rend the peace.

To most antebellum Americans who believed in the necessity of Union, such a claim was ludicrous. To raise the banner of states' rights evoked memories of the nullification crisis of 1832–33. South Carolina's stand against the tariff of 1828, led by the irascible John Calhoun, had threatened to bring the state to blows with Andrew Jackson and the federal government. Some opponents of the Fugitive Slave Act cited Calhoun openly, and others later admitted his influence on their thinking. It has led scholars to pair Wisconsin's resistance with South Carolina's.[32] Still, there were palpable differences between both the justification for and operation of both theories.[33] Calhoun's protest was not over a matter of fundamental liberty but over a customs tax, a power explicitly granted to Congress by the Constitution. His solution created an extraconstitutional method for resisting federal law by state convention. It proposed that in almost any case of doubtful constitutional construction, the state could assert its own interpretation and be overruled only by other states. This method created a new kind of states' rights, one that existed in tension with other understandings of states' rights.[34] Moreover, its espousal of a new kind of federalist machinery implicitly abandoned the Madisonian synthesis evident in the "Report of 1800."[35]

In contrast, Paine's argument for interposition remained theoretically rooted in Jeffersonian and Madisonian protests, both by conscious citation and by implicit logic. Paine argued that the right of self-defense sanctioned an ultimate right to revolution. This was to be avoided, however, by separating powers and providing a number of constitutional checks on the exercise of power. At any stage, the people could interpose themselves in a constitutional manner: legislatures could pass resolutions denouncing certain federal laws, juries could refuse en masse to convict people of certain crimes, judges might refuse to sanction certain laws. But in one noticeable way, Paine departed from this Jeffersonian and Madisonian understanding of protest. He noted that "whatever objections might be urged against the actual exercise of the right of resistance by the legislative or executive departments of the State, cannot be urged with equal force against the action of its Judiciary."[36] Paine accorded special status to the courts as protectors of rights and interpreters of the Constitution. It was a subtle distinction, but one that implied an expanded role for the judiciary, if not judicial supremacy in matters of constitutional interpretation.[37]

Whiton and Smith approached the issue more cautiously than Paine, admitting to the citizen's right to habeas corpus without elaborating on the state's right to interpose. In Smith's first opinion, sitting in vacation, he made little mention of the rights of states vis-à-vis the national government. He did declare that "every jot and tittle of power delegated to the Federal Government will be acquiesced in, but every jot and tittle of power reserved to the States will be rigidly asserted and as rigidly sustained."[38] He also expressed his belief that the U.S. courts and the state courts came into collision on certain matters, something Smith considered natural in a dual-sovereignty system. He recognized the Constitution of the United States as the fundamental law of the land but also recognized that the citizen had the right to "try every enactment of the legislature, every decree or judgment of a court, and every proceeding of the executive or ministerial department, by the written fundamental law of the land."[39] The citizen had to follow the law and correct procedure, and Smith noted the dangers of such a doctrine. The citizen disobeyed a directive of the legislature at his peril and bore the consequences of his action if "his judgment should prove to be erroneous."[40] Both Smith and Whiton agreed on the peculiar nature of the double allegiance within the federal structure. A citizen of Wisconsin was duty-bound to recognize the U.S. Constitution and the Congress as the national legislature, but had the right to avail himself of his state courts to resist encroachments.

Whiton's opinion borrowed much from Paine's argument and hence drew the bulk of its sources from legal arguments that antislavery activists had circulated for some time. He found that the court commissioner was a novel office purporting to exercise a criminal jurisdiction. Paine, Whiton, and Smith all advanced a strict interpretation of the Constitution to demonstrate that these commissioners held a pretended power. Under Article III, Section 1, Congress was prohibited from investing judicial power in any department except the judiciary. Here, Paine's argument and Justice Whiton's ruling followed the familiar argument of the antislavery lawyer Robert Rantoul. Commissioners, despite being appointed by U.S. district courts, did not have the same tenure as judges. They sat at the pleasure of the courts. As Justice Smith put it, they were "irresponsible and unimpeachable." For some reason, neither Paine nor Whiton nor Smith chose to stress that the Fugitive Slave Act of 1850 specified that the commissioner was to receive a smaller fee for releasing an alleged fugitive than for returning the alleged fugitive to the claimant. This, argued Rantoul in *Sims,* made the commissioner a party interested in the outcome.[41] But whatever force this argument carried, it did not touch the issue that concerned the Wisconsin bench the most: the power of any U.S. court or officer to determine the status of a state resident without the aid of a jury.

The jury trial was the most important piece of the puzzle for Whiton.[42] He began his decision by speaking broadly about the protections a sovereign state could afford its citizens, and he ended with the trial by jury as a crucial component of due process. In his argument before Justice Smith, Paine had cited a long list of authorities securing due process and, in particular, the right of trial by jury. In his ruling, Whiton made it clear that he did not wish to discuss whether slaves were persons in the legal sense of the word or how the act impinged on fugitives' rights. Rather, he stated, "we propose to examine the operation of the act upon a free citizen of a free state, and to show that by it such a person may be deprived of his liberty without 'due process of law.'"[43] Under the 1850 act, this was the case. The proof of escape provided to a federal judge or a commissioner and a short description of the fugitive could result in the seizing of a freeman. The claimant could then take the alleged fugitive before a commissioner, whose summary determination either freed the alleged fugitive or sent him to slavery. For Whiton and for Smith, this violated due process. The freeman's membership in the state polity authorized recourse to the state for redress. As Paine and Smith put it, the judicial department had the autonomy and hence the added responsibility of being the last barrier between national police power and the citizen's liberty.

The stickier question was whether Congress had a right to legislate at all upon the subject. Paine and Smith took the hard states' rights line—the fugitive slave clause directed that free states could not free fugitive slaves by virtue of their laws but should deliver them up, and Congress had no constitutional warrant to legislate on the matter. This argument, of course, ran into an immediate and almost insurmountable difficulty in that Congress in 1793 had passed a Fugitive Slave Act, which subsequently had been upheld in the U.S. Supreme Court. Paine had no qualms about asserting that Congress had exercised a pretended power, and Smith agreed with him. Whiton left the subject of congressional power alone because he did not need to broach it to prove that the Fugitive Slave Act of 1850 violated the due process of citizens of Wisconsin. The notion of accepting as constitutional the "settled way" of governance was on its way out.

Justice Crawford gave more weight to authority than did his colleagues and dissented from the court's ruling. He did not find the reasoning of his brethren sufficient to overcome the long line of authorities upholding the Fugitive Slave Act. He did "confess" that the 1850 amendments to the Fugitive Slave Act "raised doubts" in his mind, but "failed to produce that conviction which should justify a court, or judge, to pronounce a legal enactment void."[44] There were precedents, said Crawford, for Congress establishing judicial officers, such as the appointment of justices to territorial courts and the granting of jurisdiction to state magistrates under the Fugitive Slave Act of 1793. Regarding the question of trial by jury, Crawford analogized this to the same process that took fugitives from justice across state lines. Fugitives from labor and justice were deprived of their "personal liberty without the intervention of a jury, but it is considered essential to the complete enforcement and fulfillment of the constitutional compact."[45]

Crawford had made explicit what supporters of the Fugitive Slave Act generally refused to admit: that the law subjugated legal protections of liberty in order to enforce constitutional compromises. His analogical reasoning was, at least in practical terms, an absurdity. A free black transported to a slave state was presumed a slave and at the mercy of his master. Crawford even acknowledged that "a case might arise" in which a freeman was "snatched from his liberty and reduced to the condition of slavery."[46] Crawford did not find these suitable grounds to declare the law void: "the duty of a judicial officer is to expound the law, not to make it."[47] Here was classic judicial conservatism born of legal formalism, a common trait in antebellum judges. It was reflected in the courts' unwillingness to consider constitutional challenges to the Fugitive Slave Act throughout the antebellum era and, more generally, in judicial reluctance to meddle in legislative matters.[48] Crawford essentially surrendered the right to test federal statutes against the Constitution.

Paine had already made clear he considered this position a failure of nerve. In a conversational tone, he noted that he had read Chief Justice Shaw's decision in the *Sims* case with great interest, since the syllabus announced that the opinion resolved the question of trial by jury. It did no such thing. Shaw, claimed Paine, merely rested on Story's pronouncement in *Prigg* that the process at some point would provide for trial by jury. Story's decision, of course, had neglected the issue of trial by jury altogether.[49]

Paine registered his disgust: "Here we have this great right disposed of in a paragraph. The massive bulwarks of the constitution, are overthrown by a single exhaltation [*sic*] of judicial breath!"[50]

Paine did more than just argue that Shaw had been wrong. He suggested that the U.S. courts had no business ruling on matters that belonged properly to the police powers of the states. Boldly, he established his states' rights position in the teeth of Chief Justice John Marshall's most strident nationalist decisions. He cited *McCulloch v. Maryland, Dartmouth College,* and *Gibbons v. Ogden:* three cases in which Marshall had broadly construed the powers of the United States. What Paine cited was Marshall's admission in each of these cases that his opinion should in no way be construed to limit the unsurrendered police power of the state. Although Marshall did not articulate what these police powers entailed, he gave them a broad reading in *Barron v. Baltimore,* an 1833 decision in which he declared that anything not expressly prohibited to the states was necessarily reserved to them.[51] *Barron v. Baltimore* rejected the claim that Fifth Amendment protections applied to the states as well as to the United States. Of particular interest was Marshall's understanding of how liberties were protected. It was the duty of state governments, rather than the federal government, to protect the citizens. Had the people "required additional safeguards to liberty from the apprehended encroachments of their particular governments: the remedy was in their own hands."[52] They would have called a convention and overhauled their own constitution. It was ludicrous, Marshall wrote, to assume that they would have to depend on the federal government, with its cumbersome amendment process, to provide protections. This implicit assumption was itself a first principle—the very nature of constitutional government allowed for the airing of grievances through a variety of procedures.

The Taney Court had elaborated the police power further. In *New York v. Miln,* the Court considered the constitutionality of a New York statute requiring masters of passenger vessels to provide a list of passenger names, occupations, and last place of legal residence when arriving in port. Miln's attorneys claimed that such a requirement impinged on interstate and international commerce, a domain in which the sovereignty of the states had been surrendered to the national government. The Supreme Court disagreed. Writing for the Court, Justice Philip Barbour found no collision between New York's law and that passed by Congress.[53] But this was not the Court's reasoning: "We choose rather to plant ourselves on what we consider impregnable positions. They are these: That a state has the same undeniable and unlimited jurisdiction over all persons and things, within its territorial limits, as any foreign nation; where that jurisdiction is not surrendered or restrained by the constitution of the United States." Barbour went further. It was "not only the right, but the bounden and solemn duty of a state, to advance the safety, happiness and prosperity of its people, and to provide for its general welfare. . . . All those powers which relate to merely municipal legislation, or what may, perhaps, more properly be called *internal police,* are not thus surrendered or restrained; and that, consequently, in relation to these, the authority of a state is complete, unqualified, and exclusive."[54]

Here was a slightly more substantive understanding of the "unsurrendered police power of the state" to which Marshall had alluded. It alarmed Justice Story enough to write a dissent defending his, and his mentor's, understanding of the expansive definition of the commerce clause.[55] But even Story admitted that states had the right to inquire into and determine the status of those entering the state. He admitted further that states had the right to legislate against the introduction of paupers, criminals, or other dangerous classes of people. Even when the Supreme Court struck down state legislation taxing immigrants to defray the expenses of quarantine in the *Passenger Cases* of 1849, it adamantly reasserted the right of states to pass quarantine laws.[56] True, the states had surrendered the right to regulate interstate commerce; but as Justice John McLean, writing for the Court, made clear, "it does not follow, as is often said, with little accuracy, that, when a state law shall conflict with an act of Congress, the former must yield."[57] Giving up the right to regulate commerce, continued McLean, did not mean parting with the power of self-preservation. States "may guard against the introduction of any thing which may corrupt the morals, or endanger the health or lives of their citizens."[58]

Put another way, federal courts had to presume state legislation regarding the police power to be valid, unless parties could show that it violated a power delegated in the Constitution to the national government. This principle suggested more than just a method of judicial interpretation. It understood states to be the fountain of sovereignty, the primary legislators and interpreters of their own rights. Counsel for Massachusetts in the *Passenger Cases* made this clear when he argued that the national government had no business interfering with states' internal police regulations. He reminded the Court that Congress had attempted to stretch its power unconstitutionally before—namely, in passing the Alien and Sedition Acts. These statutes were unconstitutional, he reasoned, because it had been left to the states to determine whether to admit aliens and how to regulate their conduct.[59] Chief Justice Roger Taney granted this argument some favor. His dissent complained that a tax to defray the expenses of quarantine did not impinge on the commerce clause. Trenchantly, he declared that the police power was plenary and beyond congressional control. "Any treaty or law of Congress invading this right," said Taney, "and authorizing the introduction of any person or description of persons against the consent of the State would be an usurpation of power which this court could neither recognize nor enforce."[60]

This was a powerful threat. Not all the Supreme Court's decisions affirming the police power carried such warnings to Congress, even when the majority opinion upheld states' rights. In the 1841 case of *Groves v. Slaughter,* the Court refused to use the commerce clause to invalidate a provision in Mississippi's constitution preventing the importation of slaves before a certain date. As a matter of their police powers, the Court declared, the states had a right to decide what kinds of people it would allow within its territorial limits, even if the exercise of this right impinged on the interstate slave trade.[61] In 1845, the Supreme Court declined to take jurisdiction in a religious liberty case originating in New Orleans. Justice John Catron, in a short opinion, declared that the Bill of Rights did not apply to municipal laws and that the states bore responsibility for defining and protecting civil liberties.[62] On these points, the Supreme Court was perfectly clear, direct, and uniform in its decisions, with one exception: the Fugitive Slave Act. There, Taney's threat to strike down any congressional legislation impinging on the states' police power rang hollow. More important for Taney was the necessity of securing slaveholders' constitutional right to their fugitive property.

Others were not so sure. Antikidnapping legislation from its inception had rested upon the states' "complete, unqualified, and exclusive" right to protect their citizens. As McLean made clear in his dissent in *Prigg,* the matter was "a most important police regulation. And if the master violate it, is he not amenable? The offence consists in the abduction of a person of colour."[63] McLean's frustrated dissent exposed the breakdown in comity that had put the two powers in conflict. Nor was McLean the first to raise this question. The entire history of the Fugitive Slave Act in the courts, at least until *Prigg,* had indicated that free blacks claimed under the law had remedies available to them in their home states.[64] McLean's dissent clung to the conceptual separation of fugitive slave rendition from the protection of free blacks embodied in antikidnapping legislation.

The Wisconsin Supreme Court had taken a bold step on an old constitutional plank. They did not venture out too far, however. When Booth pressed the issue by applying for a second writ of habeas corpus to release him from the custody of the U.S. district court, the Wisconsin court refused to intervene. Both Whiton and Smith made it clear in their opinions that restraint by a U.S. commissioner was one thing, but restraint by grand jury indictment was another.[65] It appeared from the warrant issued by Judge Miller that the district court had properly obtained jurisdiction. The state court declined to interfere with that jurisdiction. It did so over counsel's objections that no jurisdiction existed because the Fugitive Slave Act of 1850 had been rendered void by the court's own decision. Smith analogized this objection to a fictitious case before his own court. If a case was pending there, would "any one pretend that the parties in such case may go to another tribunal and have that question determined for us?"[66] No. Once jurisdiction had attached, proceedings could not be disturbed.

Smith did note in his opinion that the Wisconsin court had found the Fugitive Slave Act unconstitutional, but that the decision was not binding "upon the courts of another sovereignty over which we have no control." The ruling of the Wisconsin Supreme Court was law in Wisconsin, continued Smith, and "it would be illegal and unwise to entertain a suspicion that other courts independent of this would be less mindful of the great constitutional guaranties of personal liberty, than we ourselves have been."[67] In reality, the federal courts had not, in any instance, been mindful of these constitutional issues. There was, however, a practical element in the court's refusal to intervene: in July 1854 the federal government still needed to convince a jury of Sherman Booth's guilt. Noting that discharge by habeas corpus "was by no means an acquittal," Smith and Whiton declined to interfere with a trial by jury. Verdicts in favor of the defendants would keep the two courts from coming into direct collision.

In November 1854 and January 1855, however, juries found both Ryecraft and Booth guilty. Once again, Booth asked the Wisconsin Supreme

Court to intervene. This time the justices granted the petition, fully aware that the collision avoided in the July previous was now upon them. On January 27, the U.S. marshal complied with the court's writ "without acknowledging the jurisdiction of the honorable court in the premises."[68] On February 3, 1855, the Wisconsin Supreme Court unanimously released Ryecraft and Booth from imprisonment. Each justice wrote his own opinion, placing weight on different legal factors in the decision to grant the petition. All three, however, agreed that the conviction rested upon defective indictments. Neither of the two counts on which Ryecraft and Booth were convicted specified that Glover was a fugitive slave. "Who is this Glover thus aided?" asked Justice Crawford rhetorically.[69] More important, why was the federal government indicting Wisconsin citizens without proper statutory authority? Crawford entertained no doubts that the writ of habeas corpus allowed the state court to examine the legitimacy of the procedure.

There was still the question why the court felt it could intervene in January 1855, but not in July 1854. Smith made clear in his concurrence that the question of jurisdiction distinguished this decision to discharge from the court's earlier refusal to do so. In that decision, the court did not have the indictment before it and therefore had made no ruling on it. Crawford made no mention of this point, but focused instead on the federal government's inability to gain a conviction on the first count of the indictment. That count specified a crime under the seventh section of the Fugitive Slave Act of 1850, whereas the other two (for which the prosecution won jury convictions) did not. The defective indictment meant that the federal process was illegitimate—in essence, a nullity. Hence, the prisoners were owed a discharge. The decision invited a collision that might be unpleasant, but Crawford fully expected such things in America's constitutional system. In a final accounting, he laid out the possibility of appeal to the U.S. Supreme Court, "whose decision," he trusted, "should and would be acquiesced in by all parties."[70]

Whiton concurred with the portion of Crawford's decision that outlined the defects of the indictment. The federal courts did not have the power to enlarge their own jurisdiction. He also took note of the argument that state courts could never interrupt the process of a federal court, even "in a case where not even the forms of law were observed." Whiton responded with a touch of anger: "in my opinion, the state governments and state courts are not reduced to this humiliating condition."[71] Whiton then made the reasoning for his opinion clear in an appended note. He declared that the doctrine of federal supremacy of laws could not force a state to relinquish its right to self-protection. Such a rule would "present the spectacle of a state claiming the allegiance of its citizens, without the power to protect them in the enjoyment of their personal liberty upon its own soil."[72] Smith wrote an even more forceful concurrence that put Whiton's point explicitly in terms of the constitutional arrangements between the people, the states, and the United States. The duty of every government to protect liberty was essential, and it belonged not to the federal government "but has always been conceded to the states, without which they could not exist, because it is obvious that they could claim no allegiance or support from their citizens whom they had not the power to protect."[73]

The Wisconsin court's 1855 decision was not about the constitutionality of the Fugitive Slave Act but about the constitutionality of state courts interposing themselves when federal courts illegally detained that state's citizens. On this point, the court was unanimous.[74] Smith's opinion laid bare its theoretical underpinnings. He called attention to the place of habeas corpus in the state's fundamental law, noting that the court's power to issue the writ emanated from the Wisconsin constitution rather than from the revised statutes. It was beyond the legislature's power to revoke or substantively limit its operation. Addressing the question of the power of the court, he began with what he considered elementary and impregnable positions: (1) it was the government's duty to protect its citizens in their personal liberty; (2) this duty required the ability and the power to provide such protections; (3) the means for such protection was distributed in the American federal system, but this distribution did not abrogate essential duties; (4) whatever powers not delegated to a limited sovereignty remained with the original sovereignty, and in the case of the American system, that meant the states; (5) the states had never relinquished the inherent sovereign power to protect the liberty of their citizens; (6) if the state had the sovereign duty to protect its citizens, then it had the power to protect them as well.[75]

There were revolutionary kernels within this decision. Whiton and Smith both referenced Thomas Jefferson and James Madison, not only for their expositions of the separation of powers but also for their notions of interposition. Smith freely quoted the Virginia and Kentucky Resolutions and argued that collision in the federal system was natural. As for those who fretted about dissolution of the Union, "the real danger to the union consists, not so much in resistance to laws constitutionally enacted, as in acquiescence in measures which violate the constitution." Resistance, "when it can be done by constitutional means," would work to avert recourse to the right of revolution.[76] Here were all the elements of popular constitutional resistance: the recourse to fundamental principles; the affirmation of liberty as a fundamental right; the right of resistance by constitutional means; the necessary interposition of state institutions.

Antislavery activists celebrated the Wisconsin court's decision, but they could not be too sanguine. District Attorney Sharpstein prepared an appeal, and abolitionists dug in for the anticipated legal battle. On February 9, 1855, a public meeting was called in Milwaukee to discuss what their next steps should be. After passing resolutions saluting the Wisconsin Supreme Court for its bold stand and pledging pecuniary support to those "singled out" by the federal government for punishment, the crowd discussed what would happen next. Byron Paine discussed several strategies. Someone at the meeting asked what was to be done if federal officers refused to recognize the state court's discharge. He replied that the state court's decree was valid and binding until it "had been reviewed by the Supreme Court at Washington." Most expected the Supreme Court to overturn the court's decision, and some threatened violence against federal officers. Paine counseled against it and instead suggested that they "immediately apply to the Supreme Court at Madison for another writ of *Habeas Corpus.*" Continue to resist constitutionally, Paine was saying. If federal marshals refused to obey the writ of habeas corpus, "then obtain a writ of attachment, and let the sheriff call upon the power of his County, if needed, and if such call was made there would be strong arms enough found to serve and sustain the Sheriff."[77]

Paine's constitutionalism admitted the U.S. Supreme Court's appellate authority, but it refused to acknowledge its finality. If the Supreme Court struck down Booth's release on a writ of habeas corpus, he said, then simply get another. If the U.S. marshal refused to honor it, then the county sheriff—assisted by able citizens—could compel him to do so. Abolitionists used similar legal tactics across the North to aid fugitives in their flight.[78] They did so believing that they had gained at least the color of legal authority, but few were naïve enough to believe that they were not using legal technicalities to forestall or subvert a statute that mandated the return of fugitives to slavery.[79] Much the same was true of people in Wisconsin. Still, it would be anachronistic to think of Byron Paine, Sherman Booth, and all those who participated in Glover's rescue and Booth's trials as believing that they were acting against the law. Instead, they based their actions on a particular understanding of the Constitution and resistance. Paine believed that the U.S. Supreme Court could not close down avenues of resistance when questions of fundamental liberty were at stake. If the national government usurped authority, it was up to the states rather than the Supreme Court to enforce the proper understanding of the Constitution. State officers, reasoned Paine, would be bound to protect the fundamental liberty that was the province of state authority.[80]

Among the citations in Abram Smith's 1855 opinion were numerous references to Jefferson. Anticipating an objection, he wrote that some might say "that Mr. Jefferson is not judicial but rather political authority." Smith answered that "Mr. Jefferson was a lawyer by profession. All his writings show him to be deeply versed in the fundamental principles of law, and the rules of administrative justice. More especially was he eminently distinguished for his accurate conception of the principles upon which our government is founded."[81] This was a revealing defense. When Jefferson and his contemporaries expounded the Constitution, they had not thought in terms exclusively legal. Constitutional exposition had been the province of all three branches and a necessary part of determining the limits of governance. When government overstepped constitutional limits, it was the duty of the people to resist first through constitutionally prescribed means and then, if necessary, through more radical measures. From 1854 to 1855, resistance to the Fugitive Slave Act in Wisconsin had hewed to this tradition. Smith justified his participation in this resistance by resorting to fundamental principles, and to Jefferson.

Smith was claiming a great power for his court—the ability to declare a federal law unconstitutional—but he was not excluding other avenues of constitutional interpretation. He wrote that the legislative and executive branches "as coordinate departments with the judicial" had every right to interpret the Constitution. To argue that the judiciary's interpretation trumped that of the other two branches, said Smith, would substitute "judicial dicta for the mandates of the constitution and the sovereignty of the people constitutionally exercised."[82] Still, it did reveal just how much authority the courts had gained. It was Paine, after all, who had suggested to Smith that the courts should serve as the first line of defense for fundamental rights. That the court took this issue seriously there can be no doubt. In the span of a year, the court had augmented its own power tremendously. It claimed the power to review congressional law and to invalidate federal court proceedings. It had declared an act of Congress unconstitutional.

Still, it was only a court decision. Whiton and Smith had argued around Story's doctrine of preemption and rested on the police power of the states. It was this plenary power, they reasoned, that gave states the right to protect their citizens in the enjoyment of their liberty. It was the U.S. Constitution that reserved these powers to the states, and no subsequent Congress or Supreme Court could take it away, whatever laws they passed or decisions they handed down. At the core of these decisions lay technical arguments of complicated law. Although the decisions were printed by abolitionists and distributed throughout the state and throughout the North, many readers were perplexed by their complexities. Rufus King admitted in a private letter that he was not "lawyer enough to decide whether it be technically right."[83] Doubtless many others felt the same. But whether people opposed or lauded the decision, they were well aware that it was not the final statement on the constitutionality of the Fugitive Slave Act.

The Constitution before the People

> The election of a Supreme Court Judge is more important to the protection of life, liberty and property, than any other election by the people. We can live under the administration of a despotic President, protected by a firm, independent, liberty loving Supreme Court. But when this last defence of the people's liberties, and the rights of a sovereign State are surrendered to the Slave Power, the sun of Freedom has set, and the darkness of Despotism overshadows the last bulwark of Liberty.
>
> —Rufus King, Sherman Booth, and Horace Rublee, *Milwaukee Sentinel*, March 9, 1859

ON FEBRUARY 5, 1855, U.S. district court judge Andrew Miller found his courtroom crowded for the first time since he had sentenced Sherman Booth to one month in prison and a $1,000 fine several weeks earlier. Members of the press and public had come to hear his reaction to the Wisconsin Supreme Court's release of Booth on a writ of habeas corpus. He obliged them with a prepared statement. While he conceded that "the sovereignty and rights of the several states are the life of the Republic, and the people have in their state constitutions and laws provided checks against incroachments [*sic*] on the part of the general government," he vigorously denied the right of a state court to overturn federal court proceedings. He quoted Wisconsin's habeas corpus statute, which specified that if a state court found that a petitioner was held by federal process, then it was that court's duty to remand him. He also stated the doctrine of comity of courts: when jurisdiction was concurrent, the court to which jurisdiction first attached retained it. Although the harassment of U.S. officers continued, Miller blamed the "local excitement" on extremists and "magistrates and officers of very limited practical knowledge of the peculiar jurisdiction of the Federal Courts." Fortunately, he added, "such difficulties have generally been settled through the virtue, patriotism and intelligence of the people."[1]

Miller both staked out the independence of the federal judiciary and acknowledged that its authority depended upon the people's goodwill and support. This meant victories at the polls against abolitionists who had encouraged resistance. The precarious position that Democrats occupied in Wisconsin made such victories unlikely. Political realignment had begun before the Glover rescue, but the attempted enforcement of the Fugitive Slave Act quickened its pace. Antislavery meetings held across the state, such as the April 13 Anti-Slave-Catchers' Mass Convention in Milwaukee, led to a statewide convention in Madison during July 1854, in time to form a party and nominate candidates for the November elections. The Madison conference drew together the remnants of Wisconsin's Free Soil and Whig parties, and some Democrats crossed lines to join the new party. The conference announced the mission of the new party, resolving to accept the issue of freedom or slavery "forced upon us by the slave power" and pledging cooperation and association under the new name of "Republicans." The platform adopted by the assembly was of Free Soil and Liberty Party parentage, demanding that slavery be confined to its present borders, that it be excluded from the territories, and that no future slave states be admitted to the Union. It also called for the "repeal and entire abrogation of the Fugitive Slave Law." This was Salmon P. Chase's constitutionalism on a political platform, a desire to return the government to those first principles of liberty that the Kansas-Nebraska Act and the Fugitive Slave Act had abrogated.[2]

It worked. The Republicans flexed their muscle in the November elections, winning two of three congressional races and breaking the Democratic majority in the Wisconsin legislature. There was no question that the electorate had realigned. The only Democrat to win a congressional seat—Daniel Wells of the southeastern district—was an anti-Nebraska man himself.[3] These victories gave the Republicans a secure footing right before the 1855 election of a U.S. senator by the Wisconsin legislature. Despite difficulties in holding together an alliance of Whigs, Free Soilers, and disaffected Democrats, the Republicans decided on Charles Durkee, an abolitionist Free Soiler, as their man.[4] It was a strong start for the Republicans, who had openly declared their opposition to the proslavery construction of the Constitution embodied in the Kansas-Nebraska Act and the Fugitive Slave Act.

Such was the state of Wisconsin politics when Judge Miller convened his court on February 5, 1855. His insistence that the "virtue, patriotism, and intelligence of the people" would prevail most likely looked forward to the judicial elections to be held that April: the seat held by Samuel

Crawford, the one dissenter in the Wisconsin Supreme Court's holding that the Fugitive Slave Act of 1850 was unconstitutional, was open. Despite the gains by Republicans in the previous elections, many Democrats believed that the people would stop short of supporting judicial officers who flouted federal authority. Edward G. Ryan wrote privately to Attorney General Caleb Cushing that the guilty verdicts against Ryecraft and Booth had done much to "subdue the spirit of resistance to the Fugitive Slave Law in the region and to restore a healthy tone to our political opinions." He urged Cushing to use his influence to obtain a speedy ruling from the U.S. Supreme Court in the case of *Ableman v. Booth* affirming the constitutionality of the Fugitive Slave Act, if at all possible "before the political election in April, when Judge Crawford's successor is to be elected." It would be "a simple act of justice to that Judge to sustain him in his firm and lone dissent from the decision of our Supreme Court."[5]

The battle over a fugitive slave and an abolitionist printer was not over. The resistance that had begun on the courthouse steps on March 11, 1854, and ended in the Wisconsin Supreme Court would be put to the people. It would not be the last time. Throughout the 1850s, the issue of constitutional resistance was raised in the legislature and during elections. No one imagined that the Wisconsin Supreme Court's pronouncement on the constitutionality of the Fugitive Slave Act was final. There was the U.S. Supreme Court, which had appellate jurisdiction and had demanded the record for review. The Wisconsin legislature might denounce the opinion and revise the statute of habeas corpus to disallow such intervention in the future. It might pass a law making the rescue of a fugitive slave from federal custody a state crime. State officers might charge Booth and Ryecraft with riot. Finally, and most importantly, the Wisconsin Supreme Court justices faced elections, the first of which came scarcely two months after their decision in Booth and Ryecraft's habeas corpus hearing. And the final arbiter of the constitutional position taken by the court was, of course, the people themselves.

⸺

The Republicans were aware that the April election would be a referendum on the fugitive slave issue. They nominated Orsamus Cole, a popular antislavery Whig who had voted against the Fugitive Slave Act in Congress and supported the Republican position on state sovereignty. Booth, according to his own account of the Republican caucus meetings, led the states' rights faction of the party that had demanded Cole's selection in closed-door meetings.[6] The Republicans won a close election that split right down party lines—80 percent of Democrats voted for Crawford and 90 percent of Republicans voted for Cole, giving him a narrow victory.[7] The first political test of the supreme court's decision returned a victory for Republican constitutionalism.

The Wisconsin Supreme Court, meanwhile, was pushing its constitutional resistance to a new level. John Sharpstein had already appealed the decisions of the Wisconsin Supreme Court, and the U.S. Supreme Court had agreed to hear both *Ableman v. Booth* and *U.S. v. Booth*. Sharpstein was still worried. He wrote a letter to the solicitor of the Treasury, informing him of the "high handed" decision to release Booth on a writ of habeas corpus, which he called "practical nullification." He asked for instructions on "what measures shall be employed to quell this insurrection."[8] The official response was to continue quietly, according to procedure. But clearly the federal officers expected trouble, as Sharpstein had been instructed, back on September 20, 1854, to obtain a transcript of the record of *Booth v. Ableman*.[9] He had sent the official copy off to Washington on November 8.[10]

On March 5, 1855, the solicitor of the Treasury sent detailed instructions regarding the Wisconsin Supreme Court's release of Booth and Ryecraft from federal custody a month earlier. He noted the possibility "that when the writ of Error is served, the Supreme Court of your State may refuse to recognize it and direct the clerk not to send up the Record." He advised Sharpstein to obtain "a transcript of the record, and every paper connected with [*U.S. v. Booth*]," but cautioned him to keep such affairs quiet, as "this is a precautionary measure and you will make the application as on your own account and without reference to instructions from this office."[11] Very early on, federal officers in Washington had anticipated resistance from state officers. They had good reason. There was a rich history of state resistance to perceived constitutional encroachments on its authority, beginning with Georgia's refusal to accept the Supreme Court's ruling in *Chisholm v. Georgia* in 1794 and the resistance of Virginia and Kentucky to the Alien and Sedition Acts in 1798 and 1799. States had engaged in resistance to unfavorable Supreme Court decisions in every decade of the antebellum era.[12] It took no great stretch of the imagination for federal officers to anticipate concerted resistance from the Wisconsin Supreme Court.

Legal options were beginning to run out for federal officers. In March 1855, trials on charges of riot brought against the principals in the Glover rescue had ended in jury acquittals.[13] For what it was worth, juries had now refused to convict rescuers under state law; and, although they found that Booth and Ryecraft had unlawfully removed a fugitive from the federal marshal's custody, two different juries had refused to produce a guilty verdict on the one count of the indictment that specified a crime under the Fugitive Slave Act. Was this tantamount to jury nullification? The guilty verdicts on the remaining two counts qualify such a conclusion, but acquittal on the first count had provided a jurisdictional hook for the Wisconsin courts to intervene.[14]

On June 1, 1855, Sharpstein received a letter from the clerk of the Wisconsin Supreme Court. The clerk told him that he had received the writ of error and that the court had instructed him to make no return until they met again on the nineteenth.[15] When they did meet, they refused to enter the writ on the record. On July 25, Sharpstein wrote Streeter to notify him of the court's brash action. He expressed confidence that this attempt "to determine the appellate jurisdiction of the Supreme Court of the United States awakens a feeling in the minds of all sane men which it will be difficult for the Justices of that court to withstand in coming elections." Politics rather than law was the reason for the supreme court's stand, claimed Sharpstein, who noted that they relied "upon the people of this state to sustain them." The upcoming political elections would be a "desperate contest" in which the state's Democratic Party faced "the combined forces of abolitionists, whigs, know nothings, and disciples of free love." Sharpstein, if nothing else, was consistent in zealous hyperbole. He also identified the importance of the judicial doctrine of state interposition. One of the rallying cries for the alliance, claimed Sharpstein, was "support your Supreme Court."[16] Nevertheless, he recognized the difficulty of sustaining such a position and predicted that the Democrats would prevail.[17]

Sharpstein was right about the impending success of the Democrats, albeit for the wrong reasons. When antislavery Republicans raised their second-favorite reform issue—temperance—they were very nearly hoisted by their own petard.[18] Temperance advocates pushed adoption of a prohibition statute modeled after Maine's 1851 Act for the Suppression of Drinking Houses and Tippling Shops. Called simply the Maine Law, this statute extended police regulations to prohibit the manufacture and sale of any alcoholic beverages except those especially licensed for medical use.[19] Republicans passed the bill on March 3. Governor William A. Barstow, a Democrat, vetoed it. When the legislature returned an amended bill on March 27, he again vetoed it and wrote a strong message condemning the law as unconstitutional.[20]

Temperance was the passion of a generation of reformers who embraced a host of issues. However sincere their intentions, however, Republicans had put themselves in the unenviable spot of supporting sweeping legislation that targeted the habits and customs of Wisconsin's sizable German population. That population, along with other enemies of temperance, freely celebrated the veto, cheering in saloons and lighting bonfires in the streets of Madison, Milwaukee, and other cities. A torchlight parade in Madison visited the assembly and the governor, and Barstow briefly addressed the crowd. The revelers then gathered around a bonfire outside a German saloon, resisted attempts by the city marshal to break up the ceremony, and listened to speeches from Democratic senators and the mayor of Milwaukee. The *Madison Journal* sardonically noted that it foreshadowed the November electoral contest, in which Democrats would "hope to ignore all other issues and to be 'borne on to fortune' upon a tide of rum." The Republicans, he assured his readers, would not be goaded. "Their principles are too broad and important to be laid aside," and the prohibition issue "will not be made a test of political orthodoxy."[21]

But the Republicans made it a party issue and stirred the embers of opposition in the German community, most of whom interpreted it as outright nativism.[22] In the 1850s, nativism had crystallized into its own third party: the Know Nothings. Cloaked in secrecy, they pledged to purify America and save its republican institutions from the corrupting influence of foreigners. These goals would be achieved not only through stricter immigration laws but also through a longer period of naturalization that would prevent the foreign born from collecting political rights too early. Their secrecy earned them the derisive nickname "Know Nothings," for their claim to know nothing about their organization when asked.[23] Know Nothings were not a formidable presence in Wisconsin politics, but their existence and purpose were enough to inspire dread among Wisconsin's foreign born.[24] This fear explained in part the reaction to the murder of a German family by the supposed Know Nothing, George DeBar. His lynching in

August of 1855 by a mob of Germans, despite the presence of two militia companies (both of German guards) called up by the judge overseeing the case, exacerbated an already tense situation right before the Republican state convention.[25] Democrats decried the lynching and blamed the violence on the example provided by abolitionists during the Glover rescue, and the Republicans had to contend with charges of association with the Know Nothing Party.

Republican leaders had already evinced concern about the influence of Know Nothings. Sherman Booth warned of "dark lantern boys" packing local party meetings and electing fellow Know Nothings as delegates. To counter this threat, Booth asked for a mass meeting in place of a convention. Party leaders defeated this idea, but there is some evidence that Booth's fears were justified. Know Nothing leader John Lockwood distributed a secret directive for lodge members to turn out and take control of Republican caucuses. Several Know Nothings were elected as delegates. Elisha Keyes, a delegate and secretly a Know Nothing, later claimed that his organization controlled the convention.[26] However preposterous, the underhanded tactics and avowed secrecy of the party frightened Booth enough to announce in the summer of 1855 that he would seek the Republican nomination for governor.

Booth had a number of other reasons for seeking the nomination, not least of which was his prodigious ego. It was odd timing, however. Although Booth had been released on a writ of habeas corpus, the federal marshal had never formally acknowledged the authority of the writ and might, of his own authority, rearrest him at any time. Booth also faced a civil action that brought him back before the U.S. district court in April 1855. Benammi Garland asked for $4,000: the sum of his fees and expenses, Joshua Glover's alleged price on the auction block, and the $1,000 civil penalty authorized by the Fugitive Slave Act of 1850. The lawyers presented their case in four days, but the jurors would not return a verdict. On April 23, Judge Miller dismissed the jury and ordered a new trial. On July 5, he empaneled a new jury, which heard arguments over the next two days. Miller gave the jury a strong charge, the import of which was that they must find for the plaintiff. This time, the jury returned a verdict against Booth. Booth's attorneys complained of Miller's instructions and asked for another trial, but Miller declined. On August 6, 1855, judgment was formally rendered against him for $1,000, plus costs, which amounted to $247.50.[27] Achieving the office of governor would afford Booth a potent means of resisting the execution of this judgment, which the Wisconsin Supreme Court had no jurisdiction to review. This raised troubling conflict-of-interest issues that Booth never addressed publicly.

Legal troubles aside, Booth was far too controversial a figure to head the Republican cause in 1855. He had made many enemies and made party leaders nervous. Rufus King refused to back him, and the nomination went to the popular Coles Bashford. Throughout the Republican convention, however, Booth wielded his influence to demand of party leaders that they publicly repudiate the Know Nothings. Booth and his faction stood united on this front, and few seemed willing to oppose them. If Elisha Keyes and his organization really did control the convention, then they did not risk their position by openly objecting to Byron Paine's resolution, unanimously adopted, that declared the Republican Party for equal rights and opposed "to all secret political organizations which favor such proscription or adopt secret measures."[28]

Paine's resolution was only a part of the Republican Party's very public repudiation of nativism. On the whole, though, the issue detracted from the party's platform, which vowed to "accept this issue [of freedom] forced upon us by the slave power." To combat the Fugitive Slave Act and the extension of slavery into the territories, the party resolved to "use such constitutional and lawful means as shall seem best adapted to their accomplishment." The last resolution invited "all persons, whether of native or foreign birth," into the party.[29] But nativism would not go away. The Republicans received an unwanted endorsement from the Know Nothings shortly before the election and had to deal with charges that Coles Bashford, their gubernatorial candidate, was secretly a Know Nothing. The Republican press published testimonials about the nominee's tolerant character, and on November 5, Bashford himself circulated a letter stating firmly that he was not and had never been a Know Nothing.[30]

The damage was already done. The Republicans lost their majority in the assembly, retained only a slim majority of one in the senate, and carried none of their candidates for state offices, save the governorship. In that close race, the Know Nothing endorsement may have helped the Republicans: the biggest jump in votes for Bashford came from those counties that had Know Nothing lodges.[31] But few could miss the writing on the wall. The Maine Law and the association with Know Nothings had turned out German voters en masse. Turnout for Democrats surged 32 percent, shaking the hold that Republicans had gained on the state only months before. The Republican *Milwaukee Sentinel* published an "Ode to Lager Beer" that sardonically noted the malted beverage's transformative power. Under its spell, "each tipsy cobbler is a Roger Sherman" and "weazen-faced schneiders emulate a Clay." It had transformed the election as well, bringing the Democrats back into power. "The very devil plays with politics," the writer lamented, noting that in Milwaukee "we preserve our liberties with LAGER BEER."[32] Whatever the poem's aesthetic merits, it was prescient, perhaps more so than the author intended. The Republicans had staked a claim to being the defenders of the American constitutional order, which they predicated on rights, inclusion, and liberty. Temperance cut to the heart of the issue by intruding on nearly all these principles. Barstow's vetoes and the 1855 repudiation at the ballot box sent a sobering message to Wisconsin's abolitionists. If they were to assert their constitutionalism in the name of the people, then they would have to include them all.

Despite their losses in the November election, Republicans managed a narrow victory in the gubernatorial race—at least until supplemental returns arrived late and gave the governorship to William Barstow. Coles Bashford charged the canvassers with fraud. The Wisconsin Supreme Court considered the case and, after a concerted political and legal battle, came to the determination that Bashford had been elected governor. A constitutional crisis was averted only when Barstow resigned his office and the lieutenant governor, who assumed the governorship after Barstow's resignation, stepped down when Bashford arrived. Republicans now controlled the executive and judicial branches, as well as one house of the legislature. But victory had come at great cost. Temperance and nativism had brought Germans to the polls in large numbers in the election of 1855, curbing the party's momentum. It was highly questionable whether Republican stock was rising or falling in the spring of 1856, a presidential election year, when turnout typically was higher and voters often reverted to traditional party loyalties. In 1856, many wondered whether the Republican Party was destined to eclipse the Whig Party or follow its predecessors to the third-party graveyard.[33]

It was the first fruits of the Kansas-Nebraska Act that kept the Republican Party strong in Wisconsin and throughout the North. Douglas's popular sovereignty had brought not an amicable solution, but confusion, conflict, and bloodshed to the territories. A disputed election in the fall of 1855 led to creation of two territorial legislatures in Kansas, each of which charged the other's supporters with treason. The murder of a free soil settler by a proslavery man in November 1855 touched off a series of confrontations that nearly led to outright warfare in the winter. News of these events spurred immediate action in Wisconsin. Milwaukeeans devoted to the cause of free soil established an emigrant aid society. People from all over the state pledged money, weapons, and clothes, and funded several trips.[34] In May 1856, more blood stained Kansas and even the national Capitol. On the Senate floor on May 19 and 20, 1856, Charles Sumner, of Massachusetts, decried "the crime against Kansas" in audacious language. Speaking with the passion of a revivalist, Sumner assaulted the "armed hordes from Missouri," who had arrived at the polls with "cannons, arms, flags, numbers, and all this violence."[35] All the props in the abolitionist tragedy of slavery versus freedom were evident: liquor, guns, corruption, and the inevitable savaging of liberty. Many recoiled at his personal denunciation of the aged and well-liked senator from South Carolina, Andrew Butler. It inspired the infamous thrashing Sumner received from Preston Brooks, of Georgia, several days later, staining the Senate in blood and shocking the conscience of the country. Southerners, incensed at Sumner's harsh rhetoric, applauded Brooks for his actions. Northerners were just as revolted by Brooks's resort to violence. The chasm between the cultures of North and South never seemed wider or deeper in the popular imagination. News arrived fast after Sumner's beating that proslavery forces had sacked Lawrence, the free soil stronghold in Kansas.[36]

Wisconsin's Republican Party leaders began 1856 by attempting to clarify their mission. At a legislative caucus in January 1856, they sought to purge Know Nothings from their ranks. Whatever battles went on behind closed doors, it was the public issue of temperance that mattered most. With reluctance, some of the more zealous temperance advocates placed the evil of drinking beneath that of slavery and concentrated on securing the Republican coalition. The popular signal came on Tuesday, February 24, 1857, during Milwaukee's first carnival celebration. It was a two-day fete, which began with the "Prince Carnival" holding court at the theater in Market Hall on Monday night and then on Tuesday reviewing his "'Invalid Guard,' grotesquely dressed." Holding a second levee that morning, the entire troop marched in procession at two o'clock from Market Square around the city, in no particular direction, until sundown. Thousands gathered and followed the parade. Among the participants were Bacchus and King Gambrinus, the mythical inventor of lager beer. They flanked two satirical apostles of temperance, "one of whom," the *Milwaukee Sentinel* glibly observed, "getting too much excited with his subject, fell out of his wagon on Wisconsin Street."[37] Replete with ridicule, the carnival gave temperance its proper funeral.[38]

Turnout for the November 1856 elections was extraordinarily high, and the Republicans made a strong showing. They did not win by converting many Democrats—foreign born or native—to their cause, and there is ample evidence that even those Democrats who had flirted with the Republicans in 1854 came back to their party for the presidential election. The surge for Republicans came mainly in increased participation and in the solid alignment of Whigs and Free Soilers in the Republican ranks.[39] The Republicans won the state's five electoral votes for president, returned large majorities for both the assembly and the senate, and sent three congressmen to Washington. Firmly in control of the legislature when it met in January of 1857, the Republicans could nominate another U.S. senator.

The nomination tested the party's ideological commitment to the principle of popular constitutional resistance to the Fugitive Slave Act. It was apparent from the first caucus meetings of Republicans, in which nine prospective candidates received votes. Booth led the radicals in supporting the abolitionist Edward D. Holton.[40] Many were concerned that the Republican coalition might fall apart if abolitionists dominated the party leadership. Holton himself shared those concerns and cheerfully announced that he would throw his support behind the most popular candidate. There was enthusiasm, albeit limited, for James R. Doolittle, who had been judge of the first judicial circuit the previous year and was a recent convert to the Republican Party. The party favorite appeared to be Judge Timothy Howe. The powerful Rufus King supported him and suggested that Doolittle should stay out of the election, because the state constitution did not allow sitting judges to seek other offices.[41] Howe emerged as the frontrunner in the first caucus vote on Thursday, January 15. He gained ground in the vote on January 17. At this point, however, Howe made it clear that he would not support the position that state writs of habeas corpus could interfere with federal court proceedings. Booth was outraged. At his instigation, the

Republican caucus put two resolutions to the candidates. The first endorsed Jeffersonian constitutionalism as expressed in the Virginia and Kentucky Resolutions and pledged the Republican Party to the restoration of "the purity of principles" of the republican predecessors. The second resolve held that Republicans considered it "an imperative duty" to stand by the supreme court of the state "to pronounce final judgment" in all matters regarding reserved powers of the state and to shield state residents from unconstitutional enactments of the national government.[42] The party test was not to be abolitionist, but constitutional.

Judge Howe heartily endorsed both resolutions. The Virginia and Kentucky Resolutions, said Howe, had been a popular enforcement of constitutional limits and arrested "a flagrant usurpation by the General Government of the rights reserved to the States." Howe also pointed out that this theory had been abused by nullifiers—an overt reference to South Carolina and the tariff crisis—but that "recent aggressions" required a "reassertion on our part of every right and power" reserved to the states "for the protection of its citizens and the preservation of liberty." He went on to endorse explicitly the stand of the state supreme court on the Fugitive Slave Act "and all other unconstitutional laws." Then, he equivocated. "Whether all decisions are irreviewable by a federal tribunal," wrote Howe, "is a decision upon which I must be excused from passing an opinion." It was a strange caveat, politically speaking. The resolution had not suggested that *all* decisions of the Wisconsin Supreme Court were final and not subject to appellate review. Howe's equivocation may have been unnecessary and certainly raised eyebrows among the Republican Party faithful.

Howe represented the conservative and unionist Republicans. He believed in the importance of the people and the state employing all constitutional means of resistance against the Fugitive Slave Act. But Howe felt that the Wisconsin Supreme Court had broken the rules. He took time to explain this. Because the state's habeas corpus statute mandated that petitioners held under federal process immediately be remanded, he did not believe that the Wisconsin Supreme Court had the jurisdiction to release Booth and Ryecraft. Lacking proper authority, the court had brought the two systems into needless conflict. Howe's opinion on the matter still gave the ultimate authority over the Constitution to the people and celebrated resistance against flagrant violations of constitutional rights by the people but drew the line at nullification. It was one of the best reasoned and most salient criticisms of the court's assumption of power on principle rather than by positive enactment.

Doolittle refused to answer until the caucus ruled on his eligibility. The question had been broached in the press, because article VII, section 10, of the Wisconsin constitution declared in no uncertain terms that judges "shall hold no office of public trust except a judicial office, during the term for which they are respectively elected." It further specified that any votes for such officers "given by the legislature or the people, shall be void." Opinions varied among Republicans as to whether this prohibition applied to federal offices, but they seemed united on one point—the joint convention of the legislature was the only body eligible to interpret this constitutional provision. Even the justices of the supreme court, who had intruded on the gubernatorial election a year earlier, acknowledged that this was not a case that would come before them, and so they freely gave their opinions—unanimously in favor of Doolittle's eligibility—to the press. The Republican caucus concurred and voted him eligible on January 19.

Doolittle immediately sent a short message heartily endorsing both resolutions. His stock rose in the next balloting. The next day, he sent a full reply to the caucus. "In the Old World it has been regarded that man was made for government," he began, "here that government was made for men." As such, equality of rights was the republican foundation for government, rather than the distribution of rights at the caprice of the sovereign. He endorsed the position of the court declaring the Fugitive Slave Act unconstitutional. He then noted that "the courts are constituted to declare the law and not to make it" and that the decision of one supreme court could not be absolutely binding upon another, nor even upon future courts. Otherwise, there would be no way to correct errors. "But what tribunal shall judge of the powers granted and the rights reserved?" he asked. Each government would have to judge for itself, and, if a state supreme court disagreed with the U.S. Supreme Court, "the only appeal is to the Bar of Public Opinion." He then explicitly disavowed any connection with South Carolina's nullification and threat of secession during the tariff crisis. "We stand upon our rights as a sovereign state in the union," said Doolittle, "and do not seek our redress by going out of the union."[43]

Like Howe, Doolittle believed in limits. He went further, though, in suggesting that the two supreme courts were coequal. Howe believed that the U.S. Supreme Court held the highest appellate authority and blanched at the idea that the two courts might continually overrule one another. Doolittle's extended endorsement of the resolutions won him a bare majority in the caucus vote, and Howe was defeated. On January 26, a joint meeting of the legislature elected Doolittle to the U.S. Senate. Once again, the Republicans had pushed forward the idea of popular constitutional resistance. The only hiccup occurred when the attorney general returned an opinion that Doolittle was ineligible for the office because of his current judgeship. Republicans attempted to keep the opinion out of the lieutenant governor's hands, first by vote and then by force.[44] It did not matter. The Democratic lieutenant governor declared the votes void and refused to certify the election. To give Doolittle his seat, Republicans passed a statute on February 12 authorizing the governor to sign the certificate of election for a U.S. senator. The day after the governor signed this act into law, his private secretary signed the certificate elevating Doolittle to the U.S. Senate.[45]

Thus began 1857, as the Republicans forcefully announced their espousal of states' rights and popular constitutional resistance in party caucus. The press paired it with the upcoming spring election for chief justice of the supreme court. Edward Whiton's reelection, the press surmised, would demonstrate the people's support for the constitutional stand taken by the supreme court.[46] The Wisconsin legislature took its own constitutional stand when it considered enacting a personal liberty law. The Republican majority in the Senate easily defeated Democratic amendments intended to declaw the bill. It passed by a 2-to-1 margin.[47] The bill went to the House, where Democrats attempted to amend it to read that the Fugitive Slave Act was constitutional and that the "judgment of the Supreme Court of this State upon the said Fugitive Slave Law is hereby repealed."[48] This proposal was soundly crushed, but it was an intriguing moment. The very suggestion that a judicial pronouncement could be repealed by the legislature demonstrated the fragility of the court's stand. If the intervening elections had yielded even slight Democratic majorities, the two branches might well have been arrayed against each other. However much power the court possessed, it was not in a position to defy both Congress and the Wisconsin legislature.

Instead, Wisconsin enacted a personal liberty law that granted even county courts the right to issue writs of habeas corpus to fugitives, made it the duty of district attorneys to seek their discharge, and established fines of $1,000 for the kidnapping of free blacks. The law mainly mirrored

Massachusetts's personal liberty law, but the last section was peculiar to Wisconsin. It provided that "no judgment recovered against any person or persons for any neglect or refusal to obey, or any violations of the act of Congress, commonly termed the Fugitive Slave Act [of 1850] . . . shall be a lien on any real estate within this State, nor shall any such judgment be enforceable by sale or execution of any real estate or personal property within the State."[49]

This last section, if not intended to aid Booth, was immediately helpful to him.[50] On February 2, 1857, Marshal Ableman had enforced the judgment of the U.S. district court in *Garland v. Booth* by seizing a printing press and portable steam engine from Booth and selling them at public auction. The only bidder was Benammi S. Garland, most likely represented by counsel, who bought the lot for $150. Booth still owed slightly more than $1,000 on the judgment, so Ableman attempted a second levy on April 4 by seizing Booth's steam press, fonts, paper, and all his printer's material. On April 7, he noted in his return on the writ in a forced, angular hand that "the forgoing property so levied upon was forceably [*sic*] taken from me by Herman L. Page, Sheriff of Milwaukee County."[51] Under the auspices of Wisconsin's personal liberty law, Booth had secured a writ of replevin from the Circuit Court of Milwaukee County and had arrayed the state's officers against the U.S. marshal. Wisconsin's stance against the Fugitive Slave Act had completely abrogated the law there. The fugitive was long gone, Booth and Ryecraft were at liberty, and not even the civil judgment in favor of Garland could be enforced.

Wisconsin's defiance came at just the moment when other northern states appeared to be wavering in their resolve against the Fugitive Slave Act.[52] Interest had not flagged, however, on the question of slavery in the territories. President Pierce had made it a cornerstone of his annual address to Congress in December of 1856. In his view, the 1856 election had been a referendum on constitutional issues. The people's sovereign voice had "asserted the constitutional equality" of states and citizens, whether free or slaveholders, from the North or South.[53] The Democrats' victory, he reasoned, necessarily signaled popular approval of Douglas's "popular sovereignty" principles that had opened up federal territory to slave settlement. "In the progress of constitutional inquiry and reflection," he asserted confidently, "it had now at length come to be seen clearly that Congress does not possess constitutional power to impose restrictions" on the right of citizens to take their slave property into the territories.[54] The Missouri Compromise, Pierce said, might have been a statute constitutionally passed by Congress, but it was a nullity in the way that any unconstitutional law was—it granted no right and took none away. It might have commanded the respect of citizens while it was on the books, but, after passage of the Kansas-Nebraska Act and the results of the 1856 election, its unconstitutionality was beyond doubt. Although on his way out of the presidential office, Pierce was effectively providing the executive's interpretation of the constitutional limits on congressional powers.[55] This provoked angry replies from Republicans who sharply disputed Pierce's interpretation of both congressional power and the meaning of the election.

Congress was bitterly divided over the territorial question, and the incoming President James Buchanan espoused Pierce's position. All eyes turned to the impending decision of the Supreme Court in the case of *Dred Scott v. Sandford.* Arguments had commenced in the December term, and it was clear that this case concerned more than the status of a single slave. Scott had predicated his suit for freedom on the fact that his owner willingly took him into federal territory that Congress had designated as free. There were myriad ways in which the Court might treat this issue, and some hoped that it would provide a definitive answer to the controversy that raged over Douglas's popular sovereignty principle. The decision came down on March 6. It took Taney two hours to read the opinion of the Court, and he did not release it immediately to the press for publication. Few, however, could miss the enormous import of his conclusions. Taney declared that African Americans were not citizens of the United States and, as such, had no standing to sue in U.S. courts. He also declared that the Missouri Compromise was unconstitutional because it took property from slaveholders who traveled into that territory without due process of law.

At long last, Taney had made good on his threat to strike down any act of Congress that impeded on constitutionally guaranteed rights of U.S. citizens or the reserved rights of states. Southerners celebrated the decision as a vindication of their rights. Northerners reacted angrily, sponsoring legislative resolutions and popular petitions that decried the decision's frightening ramification—that slavery was a national institution protected by the Fifth Amendment to the U.S. Constitution. The Democratic press both North and South urged respect for the judicial branch, and some asserted the right of the Supreme Court to decide constitutional questions. Republicans angrily denounced that view.[56]

People in Wisconsin protested the decision shortly after its full text was made available by publication of *Howard's Reports.* On June 17 in Milwaukee, a mass convention was held and resolutions offered up that condemned *Dred Scott* because it declared slavery a "National institution" worthy of federal protection in the territories while "free colored citizens are denied the rights of citizenship and protection by the Federal Government." It also connected *Dred Scott* with the Fugitive Slave Act of 1850, its enforcement by zealous federal officers, and the Kansas-Nebraska Act, evidence enough of the Slave Power's domination of all three departments of the federal government. The convention pledged to uphold the "true" Constitution, which meant that civil liberties found their last protection in the states and that the U.S. Constitution did not countenance slavery. The focus on rights and their protection occupied a good portion of the resolutions. It was "the duty of all Republican Governments to protect the Liberties of all the people from whom they require allegiance." It was the duty of Congress to prohibit slavery in the territories and "to protect with equal care the rights of all persons abiding therein, without regard to Birth, Creed, or Color." As for the Fugitive Slave Act, the Wisconsin Supreme Court had declared it unconstitutional: "there is, therefore, no law for the reclamation of Fugitive Slaves in Wisconsin, and whoever undertakes to return a fugitive to slavery is a kidnapper."[57]

Dred Scott galvanized the radical wing of Wisconsin's Republican Party, but it offended moderate antislavery sensibilities, as well. In its September convention, the Republican Party adopted the resolutions of the June 17 meeting and pledged itself to a militant constitutional resistance. But turnout in the November elections was anything but militant, as more voters stayed home than ventured to the polls. After the presidential election the year before, such a letdown was normal, but it did not help the Republican cause. Republican Alexander Randall won the gubernatorial election by fewer than a hundred votes, and the Democrats made some tangible gains after their ringing defeat in 1856. It was, nevertheless, a Republican victory. All three branches of the state government were solidly Republican, and the party had stood on its constitutional platform.

One issue, however, went down in defeat yet again: black suffrage. In addition to the personal liberty law, the Wisconsin legislature had passed a bill providing for a popular referendum on the question of black suffrage.[58] For abolitionists, this was the last, unimplemented portion of their constitutionalism. "The Republicanism of Wisconsin," editorialized Booth, "which has stood up so manfully for the support of our Supreme Court against the inhumanity and usurpation of the Fugitive Slave Act," should also "uphold the rights of the colored citizens of this state."[59] Sadly for Booth, the Republican Party did not endorse the suffrage question at the state convention, although delegates retained the plank eschewing proscription on the basis of race, ethnicity, or color. The Democratic press denounced the Republicans for their hypocrisy. "All real Republicans who believe in the equality of the African and the white or Caucasian races," editorialized one paper, "must toe the mark, and go the whole figure. No grimaces—no wretchings—no distortion; but go the whole figure, and swallow the whole nigger!"[60]

Republicans kept black suffrage at arm's length, partly because of the political queasiness the subject evoked. Not much had changed since the rescue of Joshua Glover. The minstrels still made their rounds, and racial attitudes remained deeply rooted in popular culture. But there were differences. Republicans like Sherman Booth and Rufus King had published articles, lectures, and arguments about the effects of slavery on the black race, suggesting that the defect was not racially, but culturally determined.[61] Wisconsin's blacks also began speaking up. The able and eloquent Byrd Parker, a black preacher from Oshkosh, spoke around the state in support of the referendum.[62] The "Bird of African plumage" irritated the Democratic press, perhaps because his abilities implied a mental equivalency with whites that one Republican editor made explicit: "those who heard him, and whose reason is not perverted by political prejudices, will admit that if Mr. Parker was put on a level with *some* white men he would be by no means *elevated*."[63] Many Democrats were horrified to find that William Noland—the very same barber who had refused service to one of the men who had arrested Joshua Glover—had been holding office for some time and competently enough to escape detection.[64]

Political agency was a positive step, but it still clung to context. One of Parker Byrd's arguments for the granting of suffrage was that it would not increase the chances of intermarriage and amalgamation.[65] On the eve of the election, the *Argus and Democrat* asked any who supported the extension of suffrage to consider a recently circulated story about a black man

in Racine who had attempted to rape a German-born girl in the city before a white man frightened him off. The girl did not show up before a
magistrate to report the crime, stated the *Argus,* "and there are suspicions
of foul play."[66] Insinuating murder may have been absurd, but the paper
was only preaching to the converted. The voters of Wisconsin resoundingly
rejected the extension of suffrage in 1857 by a vote of 45,157 to 31,964. Yet
there were encouraging signs. Michael J. McManus's sophisticated analysis of the breakdown of the vote showed that Republicans accounted for
95 percent of the prosuffrage tally and that fully 30 percent of the antisuf-
frage Republican vote was concentrated in a few western counties, where
hostility to blacks had existed since their first settlement there. McManus
also found that nearly 20 percent of each party who had voted in the gubernatorial race sat out the suffrage vote, while 8 percent of the antisuf-
frage tally came from men who abstained from the gubernatorial election.
Racial attitudes had called out people with strong feelings and revealed
deeply held ambivalences on both sides of the issue. But Republicans, it
appeared, were firmly committed.[67]

For the next year and a half, other matters occupied Wisconsin politics.
The panic of 1857 had clouded the election and very likely kept many voters away from the polls. Even worse was the political scandal over the La
Crosse & Milwaukee Railroad's outright purchase of the Wisconsin legislature and governor back in 1856. The Wisconsin legislature investigated
in 1858 and discovered that the railroad company had paid out more than
$800,000 in bonds and cash to the assemblymen and senators who had
voted to extend the company a land grant. Coles Bashford had received
$50,000—apparently for his signature on the grant—and not one assem-
blyman or senator who opposed the measure received any bonds.[68] The
embarrassing scandal garnered national attention and might have sunk
the Republicans, had not it implicated Democrats as well. Its great effect
was to cool the constitutional issues that dominated 1857.

These issues exploded again in January 1859, when Abram Smith's seat
on the supreme court was up for election. The Republican caucus met on
Friday afternoon, March 4, and nominated Byron Paine as their candidate. Paine's orations against the Fugitive Slave Act both in and out of
court in 1854 and 1855 had earned him celebrity status in Wisconsin, but
he had also quietly built his credentials since those dramatic years. In 1856,
he ran for the office of clerk of the state of Wisconsin and won. Later that

year, Governor Bashford appointed him county judge of Milwaukee to fill a vacancy. The next year, he stood for the judgeship and—in that heavily Democratic county—won. The Democrats nominated William Pitt Lynde, another Milwaukee lawyer who had built a flourishing private practice and had aspirations for public office. After serving as attorney general for the Wisconsin Territory, President James Polk had appointed Lynde U.S. attorney in 1845. He lobbied for adoption of the state constitution in 1848 and was elected to Congress after Wisconsin became a state. His busy law practice and the failing health of his father kept him out of the public spotlight for most of the 1850s, but, by 1859, he was ready to return to public affairs.[69]

There could be no clearer choice between two candidates. Lynde was a Democrat through and through and had vocally repudiated abolitionism as early as 1846.[70] Paine's positions were well known. From the start, both Democrats and Republicans sought to make the election a referendum on constitutional issues. The Republicans appointed a committee of three, including Rufus King and Sherman Booth, to prepare a public statement. The committee denounced mere partisanship in endorsing a candidate for judicial office. The issues in this case were too momentous, said the committee: "[I]t is not merely a political, but a legal and constitutional question, affirmed over and over again on the side of liberty and right, by the people of this State."[71]

The election became even more important when word arrived that Chief Justice Taney had reversed the Wisconsin Supreme Court's decisions in *U.S. v. Booth* and *Ableman v. Booth* on March 7, 1859. He did so without a formal record of *U.S. v. Booth* and no acknowledgment that the Wisconsin Supreme Court would accept his decision. He chastised the court for extending its own jurisdiction, noting that if state courts could claim this power against the United States, then "their supervising and controlling power would embrace the whole criminal code of the United States." He rejected the foundation of fundamental law cited by the Wisconsin court, writing that "there can be no such thing as judicial authority, unless it is conferred by a Government or sovereignty." The state, said Taney, lacked the power to confer such authority.[72] He then explained how the Constitution had established a hierarchical system of courts, culminating in the Supreme Court, to ensure uniformity of constitutional law across the states. Although the framers had granted this tremendous power to the federal government rather than to the state governments, in Taney's estimation the Supreme Court was also the last protector of states' rights. For, "by the very terms of the grant" of judicial power, "the Constitution is under their view when any act of Congress is brought before them, and it is their duty to declare the law void, and refuse to execute it, if it is not pursuant to the legislative powers conferred upon Congress."[73]

Taney had exercised this mighty power when he declared the Missouri Compromise unconstitutional in *Dred Scott*. If the Court might declare that Congress could not ban slavery in the territories because it violated property rights, then perhaps it might declare that the Fugitive Slave Act's suspension of habeas corpus and trial by jury similarly impinged on the liberties of freemen. Taney did not even consider the possibility: "it is proper to say that, in the judgment of this court, the act of Congress commonly called the fugitive slave law is, in all of its provisions, fully authorized by the Constitution of the United States."[74] After devoting thirteen pages of the decision to proving the supremacy of federal laws and institutions and claiming the full power of judicial review of congressional statutes, Taney dismissed the Wisconsin court's decision in one sentence. He insisted that national supremacy on this subject did nothing "to awaken the jealousy or offend the natural and just pride of State sovereignty." As for the vigilance of citizens in asserting their constitutional rights, Taney came close to scolding Wisconsinites: "now, it certainly can be no humiliation to the citizen of a republic to yield a ready obedience to the laws as administered by the constituted authorities."[75] Nowhere did he consider the implications of the law's effect on the state's police power or its traditional position in deciding matters of status and membership of its residents.[76]

News of Taney's decision arrived on March 11 and immediately escalated the stakes in the upcoming election. On Saturday, March 12, Newton S. Murphy, a young assemblyman from Walsworth County, introduced a joint resolution decrying the U.S. Supreme Court's decision as "an arbitrary exercise of power, unwarranted by the constitution even by implication." The Wisconsin Supreme Court had exercised the only sound opinion on the matter, he stated, and the "State of Wisconsin will never submit to such usurpations of the Supreme Court of the United States, without an appeal to the people."[77] The assembly opted for different language, and on March 19 it issued a joint resolution taking notice of the Supreme Court ruling and roundly rejecting it. "Such assumption of power and authority by the supreme court of the United States," read the resolution, "to become the final arbiter of the liberty of the citizen . . . is in direct conflict with that provision of the constitution of the United States which secures to the people the benefits of the writ of habeas corpus." They asserted the compact theory of the 1798 Kentucky Resolution and promised "positive defiance" of all unconstitutional enactments by the federal government.[78] The Wisconsin legislature was now aligned with the state's supreme court against the Fugitive Slave Act. But in the upcoming judicial election, such resistance would be placed squarely before the voters again. "To this decree, as to the DRED SCOTT decision, the People of Wisconsin are expected to yield a prompt and unhesitating obedience," wrote Rufus King, "and the approaching election for Supreme Court Judge will afford them a convenient opportunity for giving in their adhesion."[79] In short, the ballot box in the April election would be the last opportunity for the people at large to take a constitutional stand on the Fugitive Slave Act.

Abram Smith, the judge whose seat was up for election, announced shortly after news of Taney's opinion arrived that he would not submit his name as a candidate. In an address to the public, he recounted his six years of service, thanked the people for their trust, and declined to seek office again. He bemoaned that political parties were now running judges on their tickets and swore "that in *no event would I take a party nomination.*" The nomination of judges to gain political advantage threatened the independence and integrity of the bench. He acknowledged that, during his tenure, the court had taken on questions of the most delicate and novel nature and that he had ruled according to the "great conservative principles of popular liberty and State Sovereignty." That he had made enemies, he was sure, but if any judge had not, "it would have afforded the strongest possible evidence that he had failed to perform his full duty." Those same issues, said Smith, were at stake in the coming election. He ended by expressing the hope that his supporters would not allow their personal feelings to deter them from "giving a cordial and energetic support to the principles which they cherish and desire to see triumphant."[80] This was as obvious an indirect endorsement of Byron Paine as it was a necessary political move to ensure that the Republican vote was not split. The focus on constitutional issues in the judicial election of 1859 had made it political, and for the moment at least the two were joined at the hip.

This was the Republican message. The Democratic press, perhaps not wanting to come down on the side of *Dred Scott* and the Kansas-Nebraska Act, stressed the qualifications of the candidates. Lynde was a seasoned lawyer and public servant, whereas Byron Paine was a young man, prone to amusements and of a mind more literary than lawyerly.[81] Lynde had made a fortune on his investments and law practice, affording him independence from moneyed interests.[82] Republicans countered each of these charges, but they maintained that "every citizen should remember that in governments like ours, principles, and not men or money, are at stake."[83] And the principles were clear. Democrats feared that voting for Paine was voting to repudiate the Constitution by refusing the U.S. Supreme Court's authority and nullifying the Fugitive Slave Act of 1850. Republicans feared that voting for Lynde was voting to repudiate the state's stand on its reserved rights, particularly its protection of citizens' liberties. Although the issues often were oversimplified in the newspaper columns, many papers reprinted at length Paine's arguments before the Wisconsin Supreme Court in the Booth case, the statutes in question, and relevant portions of the Supreme Court decisions that supported their cases. The usual pettiness of partisanship aside, it was an election about ideas.

Both Paine and Lynde had, in the old-fashioned republican tradition, declined to campaign for the office. Carl Schurz, the German-born reformer active in the Revolution of 1848 and now settled in Milwaukee, went on the stump and, behind the slogan of "State Rights and Byron Paine," campaigned tirelessly for his candidate.[84] His speeches turned on notions of the popular origins of constitutionalism. "The protection of the natural rights of man is the principal aim and end of all political organizations," said Schurz, adding that this fundamental principle "comprehends the duties of man no less than his rights." It was the responsibility of every individual member of society to defend his rights, said Schurz, and it was this principle that underlay America's constitutionalism. He began by explaining the compact theory now so familiar to the states' rights cause but mediated it through a history of self-government in North America that, aided by legal tradition and geographical circumstances, had established the practical means to secure liberty: the Constitution. It was not the proper place of the Supreme Court or the Congress or the president, Schurz made clear, to claim the Constitution solely for themselves, particularly in matters pertaining to fundamental liberty.

Citing again the Virginia and Kentucky Resolutions, Schurz argued that when liberty was at stake, it was up to the states to decide whether their citizens' rights had been violated.

This was familiar territory. But important to Schurz's argument was his direct appeal to the people's role in defending their constitutional liberties. "I hope the people have not lost all the wisdom of vigilance," he implored the crowd. It was up to them to sustain the battle. The Slave Power was a formidable opponent, and it had dominated all the branches of the federal government in its quest for power. None was more dangerous than the Supreme Court, that "anomaly in our Constitutional system." Free from election and with a life tenure, a federal judge stood "above public opinion, above the will of the people, above laws and constitution." This was not a body to be trusted with fundamental law, particularly on the subject of personal liberty. As Schurz reminded the crowd, the Court had lent silent sanction to the Alien and Sedition Acts and to the Bank of the United States. The trouble was not that the federal judiciary was enlarging its own power, but that it had always construed the Constitution to enlarge the powers of the federal government. Now, the Supreme Court had made "a rapid stride onward" in augmenting its own power by declaring the Missouri Compromise illegal. Was this the body to trust with the protection of civil liberties? No. It was "the irresponsible authority," said Schurz, alluding to the Court's insulation from the ballot: "we must give it its pound of flesh, *but it shall have not a drop of christian blood.*"

Schurz's allusion drew applause, and it was the keystone to the arch. Constitutional interpretation in Schurz's conception was never far from the people. Against the notion of judicial supremacy he cited Madison's "Report of 1800" to argue that each branch had a coordinate right to interpret the Constitution. And on all matters in which fundamental law, reserved rights, and the liberty of the people were at stake, the states held the right to review for themselves whether the Constitution had been violated. The Court's claim to jurisdiction over the state supreme courts came, said Schurz, not from Article III of the Constitution, but from the Judiciary Act of 1789. This law, framed by those who feared that the states would overpower the fledgling national government, had not been intended to divest the states of their rights or to invest the Supreme Court with powers not granted to it under the Constitution. The stand taken by Virginia and Kentucky during the crisis brought on by the Alien and Sedition Acts demonstrated that the true danger had not been centrifugal, but centripetal.

Now, in 1859, the same logic could be applied to the stand taken by the state of Wisconsin—by its legislative, executive, and judicial branches—against the unwarranted and unconstitutional intrusion of the federal government on the civil liberties of its citizens. The people had a simple choice. On one side stood William Pitt Lynde, a man, Schurz admitted, of great learning, unimpeachable honesty, and a personal character above reproach. "But at the same time he is just the man to carry out the objects for which he was nominated," warned Schurz. "His disposition is of the yielding kind, his mind dependent on authority, and not infrequently following the lead of power." On the other side stood Byron Paine, the people's candidate who would hold firmly to constitutional principle and not relent to the irresponsible Supreme Court.[85]

It was an impressive speech, and Schurz remembered it as the best received of any he ever gave.[86] His arguments against judicial supremacy, although drawing liberally from Madison and Jefferson, exposed how much more power the Supreme Court had garnered by the 1850s. Madison had disposed of the argument that the Court was the highest interpreter of the Constitution in a few sentences. Schurz spent a quarter of his speech detailing instances of resistance to the Supreme Court by the states. Schurz also made the telling admission that, even if the Supreme Court was the final interpreter of the Constitution for the federal government, it could not be for the original parties to the federal compact, the states. Democratic opponents were not nearly as nimble. They were reduced to quibbling, incorrectly as most everyone knew, that Jefferson did not author the Kentucky Resolution. Because few were willing to attack Byron Paine directly, it was an election that would turn almost solely on the issue of Wisconsin's resistance of the Fugitive Slave Act.

Paine won decisively. In the largest turnout for an election for state office, he won 54 percent of the popular vote.[87] Without doubt, Paine's antislavery constitutionalism had the backing of Wisconsin's voters. It had been nearly five years since he had stood before the bench and argued the unconstitutionality of the Fugitive Slave Act. In 1859, his arguments won him a seat on Wisconsin's highest court.

—

Paine's victory at the polls was attributable, at least in part, to the people of Wisconsin rejecting Taney's decision in *Ableman v. Booth*. The express declarations of both parties on the legitimacy of resistance and their choice of candidates made it difficult to see the election in any other light. But the election was itself an indication of the fragility of the Wisconsin Supreme Court's stand on the matter. Had the people of Wisconsin strongly opposed the court's decision, then Crawford would have retained his seat, Whiton would have lost his, and Paine never would have been elected. The court's decision did not result in mass action or concerted protest— certainly not on the scale engendered by Joshua Glover's arrest and incarceration. Even if public distaste was mild, Democrats still had legislative means to oppose the court. Several had been introduced as resolutions before the legislature, although none succeeded.

Paine's election in 1859 was the culmination of popular constitutional resistance to the Fugitive Slave Act. The Wisconsin Supreme Court's decision had been only one piece of the resistance that had begun with the mass meeting shortly after Glover's arrest and that had gripped Wisconsin politics ever since. It was not the only political issue before Wisconsin voters—no one would pretend that—but it featured prominently in the Republican Party platform and was tested on numerous occasions. When abolitionists shed their devotion to temperance to focus on constitutional resistance to the extension of slavery into the territories and the enforcement of the Fugitive Slave Act, they settled firmly on this issue.

It was through these processes that resistance to Taney's decisions in *Dred Scott* and *Ableman v. Booth* took place. Over and over again, Republicans refused to accept Taney's pronouncements on the place of slavery in the Constitution. At issue was not just the meaning of the Constitution but the issue of who was its final interpreter. This was a typical reaction in the North, where Republicans were horrified that the U.S. Supreme Court had suggested that Congress had no power to keep slaves out of the territories. Wisconsin had taken this resistance further by refusing to allow the Supreme Court to review its rulings, which, it declared, rested on the unsurrendered powers reserved to the states by the Tenth Amendment. On the matter of fundamental liberty, it admitted no power of appeal to the U.S. Supreme Court.

This resistance went too far for conservative Republicans. Timothy Howe was their primary spokesman, and he was made to pay for his conservative views during the 1857 campaign for the U.S. Senate. State resistance to federal jurisdiction was not unprecedented—Wisconsin was not the first court to refuse to enter a writ of error on its record—but the move was extraordinary. It is telling that federal officers anticipated resistance, whereas Byron Paine initially admitted the U.S. Supreme Court's appellate authority (but also denied its finality). For conservatives, the stakes were considerable in the 1850s. Howe believed that the state could continue to resist constitutionally without resorting to nullification.

This ideological stance led Howe to refuse—silently—to endorse Paine during the judicial election of 1859. Sherman Booth made this public when he ripped Howe in print for his silence. Howe responded, but he had truly reached the nadir of his standing with the Wisconsin Republican Party. Yet it was not the end of the story. The means of resistance and the claims of Wisconsin's states' rights stand changed again with the coming of the Civil War.

SEVEN

Denouement

I am aware that the idea of state rights is at present exceedingly odious and unpopular. It is branded as a legal and political heresy, and held directly responsible for the attempt at secession with all its disastrous consequences. But the two claims are entirely distinct and dissimilar. Secession is revolutionary; state rights not. Secession seeks to withdraw and overthrow the powers admitted to have been delegated to the federal government. State rights makes no such effort. Secession throws off entirely all obligation under the constitution of the United States. State rights throws off none of that obligation, but concedes that that constitution and laws made in pursuance of it are the supreme law of the state, and that it is the sworn duty of its tribunals to regard and enforce them as such.

—Byron Paine, dissenting opinion in
Knorr v. Home Insurance Company of New York, 1869

THE RESCUE OF Joshua Glover had, by 1860, become a national event. Wisconsin's steadfast resistance had morphed from a fugitive slave rescue to the interposition of the state with such intensity that all federal officers—from a deputy marshal to the chief justice of the U.S. Supreme Court—had been stung by the defiance. Most off-putting to them was its success. Despite immense pressure, the stand against the Fugitive Slave Act survived again and again at the polls. The people of Wisconsin rejected the proslavery construction of the Constitution that had dominated the federal government throughout the antebellum era. The position was radical in its rejection of the Supreme Court's appellate authority but conservative in its assertion of the reserved right of the states to protect their citizens. Fugitives, this position acknowledged, had to be returned to slavery, but not by an army of federal officers encroaching on the reserved right of the states to protect their residents.

Most slaveholders saw such resistance not as a conservative stand against aggregating national power but as a direct attack on their peculiar institution. In February 1860, with the presidential election looming, Robert Toombs addressed the implications of the rescue of Joshua Glover on the Senate floor. The bellicose Georgian senator assailed all northern states for thwarting execution of the Fugitive Slave Act, but he singled out Wisconsin for particular opprobrium. John P. Hale, senator from New Hampshire, argued bitterly with Toombs. He said he did not object to carrying out the conditions of the fugitive slave clause, so long as it was done in "a fair and constitutional manner." Toombs pounced. What, he asked, was a fair and constitutional manner? Toombs then answered his own question: "I know it is one of those equivocations which is practiced here. When you come to the point, *he will talk to you about trial by jury;* he will talk about some plan that will defeat it; but as to carrying out that provision of the Constitution in its honest integrity, so as to deliver the fugitive, I do not believe that he is for it, or that his constituents are for it."[1] Toombs's displeasure was with those abolitionists who had marshaled every possible legal resource to defeat execution of the law. Those who sought to defeat the law often did so through courts, legislatures, and state officers. But in his exasperation, he had turned trial by jury into an equivocation, an inconsequential legal minutia instead of one of the fundamental building blocks of the American constitutional order. Wisconsin had made a powerful assertion to the contrary. Invoking the right of popular constitutional resistance, every branch of the state government had registered its disagreement, supported at the polls by a population that refused to waver.

It was this resistance by state officers that so irritated Toombs. When he complained that the Wisconsin Supreme Court's actions were "without precedent," he did not mean that their refusal to heed the U.S. Supreme Court's order was without precedent.[2] Toombs himself stated that he had never in his life considered "the Supreme Court of the United States as the ultimate arbiter of my rights, or even a safe depository of political power."[3] The unconstitutionality of Wisconsin's resistance was in its repudiation of the fugitive slave clause in the U.S. Constitution. For this, said Toombs, there was no precedent. He demanded an explanation or, better yet, an apology. James Doolittle spoke up for his state. He asked Toombs if he predicated his argument on the assumption that the Fugitive Slave Act of 1850 was constitutional. Toombs said yes. And if it were unconstitutional, continued Doolittle, then the entire proceeding in the district court was a nullity. Toombs may have sensed the trap, but he answered in the affirmative. "And Wisconsin is right," said Doolittle. "If your law is constitutional, then the proceeding of the Wisconsin court is wrong." Toombs declared he had nothing to say about that subject at that time. Doolittle also said he would reserve for another time the debate about the Fugitive Slave Act's constitutionality. "But the tone and manner of the honorable Senator," warned Doolittle, speaking to Toombs, "in speaking of the State of Wisconsin, had better change."[4]

Amid this heated exchange was a fundamental problem—no one could agree on an arbiter for the dispute. Each advanced a states' rights argument to bolster his case, but each rested it upon a markedly different foundation. For Wisconsin, the struggle began and ended with the same principle—in matters of grave constitutional importance, the people themselves had to decide the meaning of rights, liberties, and constituted relationships between dual sovereignties. They had assembled popularly to protest the Fugitive Slave Act at the time of Glover's arrest and declared that it violated rights sacredly guaranteed to the people of Wisconsin by the state constitution and by the U.S. Constitution. Popular action gave way to popular organization and, ultimately, to victory at the polls.

One cannot separate these fundamental principles of popular constitutional resistance from their substance—from their reasons for existence. The right to resist laws constitutionally enacted by Congress could not be reduced to empty appeals to states' rights. To do so risked dissolving the distinction between matters of personal interest and issues of fundamental liberty. Wisconsin's abolitionists understood this. The public discourse over states' rights—whether raised during the trials of Booth or the electoral contest between Paine and Lynde—forced its participants to articulate definitions of citizenship and of rights and to give constitutional resistance some kind of substance. At its heart, this was not a theoretical discussion about how the American dual sovereignty system might operate in the abstract. It was instead a gritty debate about the operation of everyday laws. It meant differentiating the rights of fugitive slaves from the rights of whites and free blacks. It meant articulating how the citizen must balance the duty to obey the laws with the duty to resist unconstitutional encroachments on his liberty. It meant defining democracy and the rule of law as an open and public process, transparent and subject to popular scrutiny at all times.

This had not always been pleasant. Abolitionists faced a populace likely to think of blacks as inferior humans, as objects of ridicule and scorn rather than the subjects of a serious constitutional debate. To some extent, abolitionists used this perception to their advantage. Focusing on Glover's body and the violence that had left it bloodied and exposed in the county jail, they played on their audience's sympathy. They could not expect to overcome the deeply ingrained racism of some northerners, but they made the constitutional rights of blacks an issue worth fighting for.

The appeal to sympathy lent moral credence to abolitionists' arguments, but Wisconsin's resistance to the Fugitive Slave Act was fundamentally constitutional. It involved popular action legitimated by parliamentary procedure, the act of petitioning, recourse to the courts, judicial review of a congressional statute, judicial scrutiny of federal legal process, and legislative resolution and statutory enactment. Wisconsin stood firmly on the notion that the responsibility for the protection of citizens' liberties lay with the state and that this protection was among the state's fundamental and reserved powers. Although it worked through the branches of government established by the Constitution, it relied on an understanding of vigilant citizenship that made it the duty of every citizen to protect his own rights. The active citizen, state sovereignty, the police power, fundamental law, states' rights—all these issues swirled together in and out of court, producing powerful notions of resistance that Wisconsin Republicans used, ultimately, to defend the rights of Wisconsin's black residents.

It was not to last. The collision inaugurated by the Fugitive Slave Act's operation brought Wisconsin and the United States into irreconcilable conflict just as the nation approached the fateful election of 1860. The success of the Republicans on the national stage occasioned a substantial retreat from popular constitutional resistance in Wisconsin. Although the retreat was varied and slow, there was simply no way to maintain a hold on constitutional resistance in the face of the crisis of the 1860s. Secession tainted the states' rights doctrine, and the Civil War stained it in blood. The real question became what principles—what portion of the substance of popular constitutional resistance—would be surrendered with states' rights.

Federal officers had been waiting in the wings to rearrest Booth since his release from custody in January of 1855. In March 1859, the U.S. Supreme Court's opinion—even if unacknowledged by the Wisconsin court and repudiated by the Wisconsin legislature—gave Marshal Ableman a legal arrest warrant. But it was another event in March 1859 that made Booth vulnerable. He seduced his neighbor's fourteen-year-old daughter. Her irate father pressed criminal charges. Edward G. Ryan, delighted with the opportunity to prove Booth a sanctimonious fraud, volunteered to aid the prosecutor in the criminal case. In July, the lurid affair came to trial amid great public excitement. Booth's defense attorney mounted an attack on the girl's chastity, a shameless blame-the-victim strategy that probably saved his client—the jury deadlocked at 7 to 5 for conviction—and ran the young girl out of town. Ryan may not have won his case, but his eight-hour oration shredded Booth's credibility.[5] Whatever celebrity his role in resisting the Fugitive Slave Act had brought him was now eclipsed by a sexual encounter that cast a pall over his self-righteous moralizing, judgmental politics, and the power he held within the Republican Party. He was more vulnerable than ever.

On September 22, the new U.S. district attorney in Wisconsin presented two motions to the Wisconsin Supreme Court, requesting that it take judicial notice of the U.S. Supreme Court's decisions in *Ableman v. Booth* and *U.S. v. Booth*. The new chief justice, Luther Dixon, voted in favor of the motions. He was opposed by Orsamus Cole and clearly would have been opposed by Byron Paine, but Paine recused himself because he had been counsel in the case back in 1854 and 1855. The motions failed on the 1-to-1 split, but Dixon wrote a long opinion explaining his position. He reduced the entire question to one of appellate jurisdiction. "The only question," wrote Dixon, was whether the U.S. Constitution conferred "on congress the power to provide by law for an appeal from the courts of the several states to the supreme court of the United States." Noting that the proper solution "was never perhaps since the commencement of our national career more vitally [important] than at the present time," Dixon held in the affirmative.[6] He also appealed to the public for moderation. Consciously echoing Whiton, he promised to remember that a frequent recurrence to fundamental principles was necessary to sustain government. But he denied that this case raised those principles: "I have not placed on one side of me the horrors of 'consolidation' and 'despotism,' and on the other those of 'dissolution' and 'anarchy,' and endeavored to make choice between them."[7] These considerations, he said, were best left to the other branches of government. The rest of his opinion applied a very standard reading of statutory and constitutional law that affirmed the appellate power of the U.S. Supreme Court.

Dixon had very little to say about breaches in fundamental law, but he appended to his decision a pamphlet published by an anonymous member of the Milwaukee bar who did. The argument was intended to demonstrate both the constitutionality of the Fugitive Slave Act and legitimacy of the Supreme Court's appellate jurisdiction. The writer admitted that he had grave doubts as to the constitutionality of some sections of the Fugitive Slave Act of 1850 but was bound to respect the fact that Congress had held authority over the subject since 1793 and that it had been upheld by the Supreme Court. But, lest anyone should accuse him of believing that the Supreme Court was infallible, he made his position clear. If Congress attempted to legislate on a subject beyond the purview of the powers granted it by the Constitution, "then I hold that neither the states, their officers, nor the people are bound by such action on the part of congress even though the supreme court should decide it constitutional. In such case resistance would be a proper and natural right."[8]

Belief in popular action as the best safeguard for constitutional rights remained a cornerstone of antebellum constitutional theory, and on this subject the moderate Timothy Howe—whose conclusions were close to those of Chief Justice Dixon—was in agreement with Byron Paine. The Supreme Court might be the court of last resort on all questions called before it, but its authority to interpret the Constitution did not necessarily trump that of other branches. Democrats pushed the Wisconsin legislature to repudiate the state supreme court's stand in the Booth cases. On January 14, 1860, a Democrat introduced a resolution in the Wisconsin legislature celebrating Dixon's opinion and assaulting the "ultra abolitionists" who wanted "to decide this and similar cases according to their political platform or the so called 'higher law.'"[9] The assembly referred the resolution to the Judiciary Committee, which rather unceremoniously tossed it back with a recommendation that it be tabled. "Your committee have not discussed the abstract merits of the said resolution," read the report, "being of the opinion that the same do not present a proper subject for legislative action or review."[10] This was certainly a more tepid reply than the spirited resolves of a year earlier, when the Wisconsin legislature had denounced the U.S. Supreme Court decision in the Booth cases.

For Booth, the long struggle was nearing a close. Federal marshals arrested him on March 1, 1860, and confined him in a federal building in Milwaukee. Booth's application for a writ of habeas corpus from the Wisconsin Supreme Court met the same fate as the district attorney's motions to enter the U.S. Supreme Court decision on the record—a bench split 1 to 1, with Paine recusing himself. Booth's friends forwent the legal niceties of removal and rescued him by force on August 1. All the careful distinctions Booth once had drawn between violence and order melted away as one of his rescuers referred to his gun as the writ of habeas corpus and his armed guard threatened to shoot down any federal officer attempting to take him.[11] Booth remained at large for more than two months, until he was arrested again while giving a speech at Berlin, Wisconsin, on October 8. The U.S. district court ordered him imprisoned until he paid the fine that he had owed since 1855, plus interest and fees. Only an eleventh-hour pardon by President Buchanan on March 11, 1861—when the country had far greater things to worry about than one abolitionist's fate—freed Booth from jail.[12]

Booth fared worse in civil court. The execution of the order in *Garland v. Booth* had been stopped by Booth's writ of replevin against Jonathan Arnold, filed in the circuit court. Both parties waived a jury, and the judge decided in favor of Booth. Arnold appealed the decision to the Wisconsin Supreme Court, which heard it in 1861. The court entertained many arguments from counsel that dealt directly with the problems between two statutes passed by the conflicting sovereignties. James Paine, still defending his old ally Booth, argued that the unconstitutionality of the Fugitive Slave Act of 1850 rendered the civil judgment in *Garland v. Booth* a nullity. Arnold argued that Wisconsin's personal liberty law went against both the U.S. and the Wisconsin constitutions and was thus void. Byron Paine again recused himself from ruling on a case involving his former client, and it appeared that the court would again divide 1 to 1.

This time, however, Cole voted with Dixon to reverse the judgment of the circuit court and order a new trial. He also wrote the opinion of the court, which tiptoed around the explosive issues of sovereignty and liberty and focused instead on one argument of counsel. Arnold argued that even if the Fugitive Slave Act was unconstitutional, the Constitution still granted the federal courts jurisdiction in suits between citizens of different states. Therefore, the Milwaukee circuit court had erred in interfering, regardless of any Wisconsin statute. Cole reported that this argument "struck me with much force."[13] Article III, Section 2, clearly gave the federal courts jurisdiction in cases involving citizens of different states. Because the current case fell under that description, there was no reason for the Wisconsin courts to interfere.

Was this an abandonment of the Wisconsin court's claim to be the last court of appeal on matters of reserved rights? After all, the issues of jurisdiction and comity of courts had been broached in 1854 and 1855, when the Wisconsin Supreme Court decided that the writ of habeas corpus could supersede federal court proceedings. Cole had been elected on the basis of his support for that position. In 1859, he still had been unwilling to admit the appellate power of the Supreme Court in the matter of *Ableman v. Booth* and *U.S. v. Booth,* but now he indicated in *Booth v. Arnold* that the only court competent to review the case was the Supreme Court. Cole did not even address the personal liberty law, which the Wisconsin legislature had most likely intended to frustrate civil claims. Section 11 of the act stated "nor shall *any* judgment [under the Fugitive Slave Act] be enforceable by sale or execution of any real estate, or personal property within this State."[14] The state had rested on its power to interpose itself in any case. Without expressly nullifying this law, Cole had found a way to conscientiously ignore it.[15] "So while holding that the fugitive slave law is an unconstitutional enactment," wrote Cole, "I am still constrained to decide that the district court had jurisdiction."[16] It was valid and binding jurisdiction, at least until a proper appellate court corrected the error.

This was a significant retreat for a supreme court that had declared itself the court of last appeal on the issue of reserved rights. Cole gave no indication that his argument would have extended to an analogous jurisdictional question raised in a habeas corpus hearing. The court did not have to disturb its precedent proclaiming the Fugitive Slave Act unconstitutional. Cole had already voted in 1859 to refuse to admit the U.S. Supreme Court's appellate authority and in 1860 he voted to grant Booth a writ of habeas corpus, both times reaffirming his readiness to protect the liberty of Wisconsin citizens, if not their moveable goods. It was that principle which divided the civil from the criminal case. No one associated replevin with fundamental law as they did habeas corpus. Most of this is inference, because Cole did not leave behind notes, letters, or other evidence clarifying his views. But nothing in his opinion was inconsistent with the constitutional resistance to the Fugitive Slave Act that the court had invoked in 1854 and that had reached its apogee in 1857. And there were other pressures bearing on the court in 1861 that discouraged it from taking a hard turn down the avenue of judicial resistance. The Gulf states had seceded from the Union on the premise of states' rights, and a northern court opinion rife with references to the same principles and the same thinkers would have fast become an embarrassment. Reversing the circuit court on a technical point of jurisdiction let the issue go quietly.

Wisconsin's governor also retreated from the hard-line position he had occupied not a year before, when he had suggested that he might call upon the Wisconsin militia if U.S. marshals refused to obey state laws. His address to the Wisconsin legislature in January 1861 decried secession and advanced the essentials of the theory of perpetual union.[17] But it was still a federal union, and the national government was a limited one. "The reserved rights of the States are not to be imposed upon or impaired by usurpations of the National Government," said Randall. The complicated dual allegiance of their federal system necessitated certain collisions and conflicts, but it also created a system of law and politics meant to absorb it. It was, after all, "the people" who "make and unmake constitutions and laws, by processes known only to the Constitutions of the several States or the United States."[18] Lately, the conflicts had become bloody. Citizens merely expressing their opinion were being "mobbed and hung upon the next tree." This was a far cry from the purpose for which Jefferson and the founders had nurtured the Constitution, "the purpose of protecting and not for the purpose of taking away inalienable rights, for the purpose of protecting and preserving civil and religious liberty, and not for the purpose of extending human slavery."[19] Amid this great clamor, the people had addressed this question in 1860. "As is the legal habit once in four years," said Randall, "the people, in the usual constitutional way, without force or violence; with no armed bands; with no hostile or wicked intent; with no serried ranks or glittering bayonets, elected a President." He was a "peaceable, quiet citizen, undeniably eligible to the office." He had promised not to use the national government to disturb slavery where it existed but believed that Congress possessed the authority to prohibit its extension into the territories. The people had agreed with him, and had elected him. "There is nothing unconstitutional in entertaining such views, or in expressing or avowing such opinions."[20]

Randall interpreted the 1860 election as a referendum on the constitutional issue of congressional power to prevent the extension of slavery into the territories. His election was the final arbiter of the question, not Chief Justice Taney's ruling in *Dred Scott* or any one state's opinion on the matter. This was the constitutional victory for which Wisconsinites had long struggled. Randall deployed the rhetoric of democratic voice versus anarchic violence earlier used to defend Glover's rescue. In the face of the election of Lincoln—a "peaceable, quiet citizen"—southerners invoked violence, "and armed men, making actual war upon the nation, threaten a dissolution of this Union, and the destruction of this government." Randall was differentiating southern states' rights from Wisconsin's in terms that rhetorically matched the abolitionists' arguments against the Fugitive Slave Act.

Randall was not content to fall back on platitudes and stock images. He noted the southern demand that the personal liberty laws of the North be repealed immediately and unconditionally. He responded forcefully. "Personal liberty laws are found, or should be found, upon the statutes of every State," said Randall, adding, for good measure, "[T]hey ought to be there." It was the highest duty of state legislatures "to provide by every constitutional means for the protection of the rights of person of the citizens." Randall admitted that if the legislature was "satisfied that any of the provisions of our personal liberty laws are in conflict with the Constitution," then it was their duty to change the law. Still, that duty was not a repudiation of the constitutional duty to protect the residents of Wisconsin. "We will make sacrifices of feeling to appease and conciliate our brethren, but *we will make no more sacrifices of principle.*"[21]

There was no question that the Republican Party had to rethink its stance regarding judicial and legislative nullification of the Fugitive Slave Act in the face of South Carolina's secession. The most telling sign was the senatorial election in 1861. Timothy Howe, the man who had lost in 1857 because of his refusal to espouse states' rights, received the nomination in 1861 for his unionist stance. It was his moment of triumph, especially because he had been on the outs with the party since his failed senatorial bid.[22] He had sulked in private life, and his last public statement had been a series of exasperated letters published in 1859, following a typically vicious attack upon him by Sherman Booth's *Free Democrat*.[23] Booth was furious that Howe had withheld his support from Byron Paine in the state supreme court election and accused him of repudiating the principles of republicanism. Howe published his responses in the *Oshkosh Democrat*, and Republican sheets across the state reprinted them. Howe's letters forcefully declared his attachment to the party. "With every fibre in me quivering with hatred of slavery," wrote Howe, "I would pursue [my opposition to slavery] to the very threshold of the Constitution, but I will not cross that threshold." The threshold was nullification, "the great and fundamental political heresy" that would disgrace the party and involve the state in a crime.[24]

Howe was not arguing that the U.S. Supreme Court could settle the territorial question or even the Fugitive Slave Act. He wanted "to reverse the decision of the Supreme Court of the United States in the case of *Dred Scott*, by the legitimate use of the ballot box."[25] He wanted Wisconsin's congressmen and senators to seek repeal of the Fugitive Slave Act. He admitted in a later letter that he did not initially object to extreme measures of resistance because he "felt that statute to be so disgraceful to the National character that if one would attack it, I cared little what weapons he employed."[26] Howe had changed his mind when state officers began resisting. His arguments sometimes lacked gravity—at one point he pleaded the statute of limitations on the idea of states' rights—but they did expose nullification's dangers. Lawmaking authority had not been vested in state officers bound to interpret the U.S. Constitution and enforce the laws made under its aegis. Still, Howe believed deeply in resistance and felt passionately that the ultimate arbiter of the Constitution would be the people acting in their sovereign capacity. He placed the limits of this resistance, however, at the arraying of state institutions against federal ones.[27]

Howe's views were decidedly more attractive in 1861 than they had been in 1857, and most voters in the state acquiesced to the choice of a unionist Republican as a U.S. senator. In this way, the Wisconsin legislature retreated from its 1859 position, quietly abandoning the mantle of states' rights for that of perpetual union. It also repealed the personal liberty law.[28] In its report suggesting repeal, the Judiciary Committee made clear that such a retreat was more of an advance to the rear. After all, repealing the law did not restrict the access of any person in the state to habeas corpus. What was more, the election of 1860 had reaffirmed the country's dedication to the very principles embodied in Wisconsin's personal liberty law. "Public opinion," proclaimed the judiciary committee, had worked "revolutions more wonderful than the sword has ever known."[29] By 1861, Wisconsin Republicans could congratulate themselves on the successful elevation of their principles by the final arbiter of the ballot box. *Dred Scott* and Douglas's popular sovereignty for the territories had been defeated, and slavery would expand no further.

The South, however, refused to defer to the ballot box. Southerners put the same construction on the election of 1860 that Governor Randall had. It was the election of a party opposed to slavery and meant that the Constitution would now be given an antislavery construction by the legislative and executive branches, regardless of any promises made by Lincoln to the contrary. The final substantive victory for those who had resisted the federal government in Wisconsin came on June 25, 1864, with repeal of the Fugitive Slave Act.[30] Even if the means effecting constitutional resistance had to be abandoned, the substance of its claims were realized.

There were those who held on to the means of resistance—the trenchant assertion of states' rights—until the bitter end. Byron Paine was chief among them. In an 1861 civil suit over an injury sustained during a railroad accident, Paine held with Cole—over the dissent of Chief Justice Dixon—that the federal courts could not remove issues from state courts.[31] Paine remained on the court for another three years, resigning in 1864 to take a commission as lieutenant colonel of the Forty-third Wisconsin Regiment and to fight in the last stages of the Civil War. In 1865, he returned to the supreme court as a lawyer for Ezekiel Gillespie, a leading figure in Milwaukee's black community. Gillespie had moved from Indiana to Wisconsin after passage of the new Fugitive Slave Act in 1850 and had opened a family grocery in downtown Milwaukee. He did not keep the business past the panic of 1857, but began working for Alexander Mitchell—one of Milwaukee's richest citizens—shortly before the Civil War.[32]

At Sherman Booth's instigation (or so Booth claimed), Gillespie attempted to vote in the 1865 election and was turned away at the polls. He filed suit, and Paine argued on his behalf that the 1849 referendum had granted blacks the suffrage and that the board of canvassers had no right to quash the election on grounds that fewer people voted on the suffrage issue than in the gubernatorial election. The court agreed. Peacefully, and quietly, Paine continued to go to the courts to claim civil rights.[33] History records more about Paine's achievements in court than about Gillespie's brave act of going to the polls. Gillespie did not speak much about his role, and no one paid attention to him. His obituaries did not mention it and focused instead on his service to Alexander Mitchell and the Chicago, Milwaukee & St. Paul Railroad.[34] Such was the mixed legacy of the war for the Constitution. Rights might be asserted and victories won, but blacks still lived in the shadows, only minor players in their own drama.

Paine returned to the bench in 1867 by appointment, and, in 1868, was reelected to the office of supreme court justice. There he held on to his states' rights theory until the end. In an 1869 civil suit of markedly little political import, Paine dissented from the majority, holding that federal courts had jurisdiction under a congressional statute—despite the fact that the parties were residents of different states. Taking full account of the Civil War and the unpopularity of the doctrine of states' rights, he laid out the interpretive framework of a dual sovereignty system and rejected the notion that, on the question of the states reserved rights, the U.S. Supreme Court might be the final arbiter. He acknowledged that there were doubts about whether the states might be the last court of appeal regarding their reserved rights. "I think the whole matter should be made the subject of a constitutional amendment," wrote Paine.[35]

Missing from his opinion, however, was any explanation of why a civil lawsuit between two parties from different states intruded on the reserved powers of the state. Paine's refusal to let go of the implications of popular constitutional resistance demonstrated why it was a bad doctrine for the court. Logic required its application in one case as well as another, ultimately drawing no distinction between a case that might reduce a person to perpetual bondage and a case involving an insurance claim. Lost was the notion, so carefully expressed by Madison and Jefferson, that state claims to resist unconstitutional enactments could be put forward only in clear cases of usurpation. Constitutional resistance was never comfortable in the rigid straitjacket imposed by lawyers. It worked well enough as a line of last defense for fundamental liberty, but it was not a legal doctrine particularly suited for tort law.

Ever the good judicial soldier, Paine continued to assert the reserved power of the states in the more tendentious cases of *Whiton v. Chicago & Northwestern Railroad Co.* and *In re Tarble* in 1870, the former concerning a congressional statute that removed civil cases to federal courts and the latter involving a habeas corpus writ issued by a state commissioner at the behest of a man whose underage son had joined the military.[36] In both cases, Cole and Paine held that state jurisdiction, while not paramount, was coequal with that of the U.S. Supreme Court on the matter of reserved rights. Once again, the U.S. Supreme Court disagreed. In 1872, Justice Stephen Field wrote the landmark decision that overruled the Wisconsin Supreme Court's stand on habeas corpus.[37] Salmon P. Chase wrote the lone dissent, holding to the last that state courts still had the power to test any kind of imprisonment with the ancient writ of liberty.[38]

By then, Byron Paine was dead. The man who had argued fundamental law before the Wisconsin Supreme Court at the age of twenty-six, who had been elected to the bench before he turned thirty, died from a severe attack of erysipelas (a skin infection) at the age of forty-three. He was widely beloved in the state, and respected even by his enemies. In his memorial, Edward G. Ryan praised his integrity and force of character, remarking that "there was no possibility of confounding him with the crowd of respectable mediocrity."[39] Of course, members of the bench and bar always seemed far more generous to each other in death than in life. Even the old slave catcher Jonathan Arnold received a laudatory memorial when he died in 1869, although it did begin by acknowledging that "an analysis of his character would be difficult, because in it are many apparent contradictions."[40] Paine had distinguished himself, and even Ryan recognized this. As for his jurisprudence, "the printed brief which he submitted in this court in [Booth's habeas corpus case] was the ablest argument I ever met against the constitutionality of the fugitive slave act."[41] Paine may have even convinced Ryan, if only a little. Although Ryan openly admitted his proslavery leanings well after the Civil War, he did don the states' rights mantle in at least one case. In *State ex rel. Drake v. Doyle,* Ryan asserted the absolute right of the states in licensing corporations, despite having to circumvent a congressional statute in so arguing. The U.S. Supreme Court agreed, then reversed itself several decades later.[42] In this way, over the decades, the last vestiges of Paine's jurisprudence died.

———

The principles for which Paine and Wisconsin at large had fought, however, did not die. It took a war to defeat slavery, and it took even more to secure the fruits of victory. Republicans still had to come to grips with one of the fundamental problems exposed by the arrest and rescue of Joshua Glover. The competing claims of dual sovereignties over Glover's body had created a jurisdictional war. Solving it meant not merely abolishing slavery and repealing the Fugitive Slave Act but redefining the relationship of the federal and state governments to the people. In 1866, the Republican Congress did just that when it passed a civil rights bill that defined, for the first time, U.S. citizenship. All those born on American soil were U.S. citizens. In a fitting act of irony, Republicans justified giving Congress plenary power to enforce civil rights by invoking the example of the Fugitive Slave Act of 1850. Just as the *Daily Wisconsin* had predicted back in 1854, "the same power" once used to enlarge slavery was now being used "for the strengthening of Liberty."[43] Congress achieved this in spite of President Andrew Johnson, who complained in his veto message that the civil rights bill unconstitutionally usurped the police power reserved to the states. Congress overrode the veto, but Johnson's objections raised the possibility that this constitutional victory could be repealed at a later date. Republicans sought to secure their interpretation of citizenship by amending the Constitution; in 1868, they succeeded when the Fourteenth Amendment was ratified. Citizenship was extended to all born in the United States, and the old distinctions of status imposed by states were swept away.

Here was a proper vindication of the principles for which Wisconsin had rebelled. Constitutional resistance had not been invoked merely to exalt the rights of the states but to defend the constitutional guarantee of liberty for Wisconsin's citizens. Glover's arrest and rescue had cast a bright light on the difficulties inherent in a federal union in which divided allegiance left the privileges and immunities of citizenship with each individual state. Actively enforcing the rights of residents of one state over those of another—especially when it was the right to property in humans over their civil rights—had helped bring the nation to crisis. The Fourteenth Amendment solved this theoretical problem by making citizenship national and ungraded and by granting Congress plenary power to enforce rights. In this way, it was the final adoption of the Constitution for which Wisconsinites had struggled. In 1870, the Fifteenth Amendment extended suffrage to all adult males, regardless of "race, color, or previous condition of servitude." The Republicans made good on their promise of freedom for all, or at least for the newly freed slaves.

The passage of the Civil War amendments was not the end of the story. If the rescue of Joshua Glover teaches anything, it is that the assertion and winning of constitutional rights is never easy. Removing slavery from the

Constitution proved difficult enough, but making a reality of the promise of universal citizenship was another matter entirely. That was another struggle, one that took more than a century. Throughout, the lessons learned from the rescue of Joshua Glover—from all manner of constitutional resistance in antebellum America—played their part. Blacks espoused democratic citizenship and increasingly asked federal courts to enforce their civil rights. Even when the courts turned them away, they organized and resisted on their own. They stood up in the face of enormous odds and horrible violence. They toiled amid tremendous cultural and intellectual prejudices largely inherited from the American experience with slavery. Still, in the name of liberty and with a firm belief that their own actions could change the constitutional order, they struggled on. We live with the triumphs and the tragedies of this struggle still.

The Ends of History

I do not see in [the death of slavery], nor in the other events of the [Civil War], any evidence of a special interposition of Providence. But I do see evidence of that which seems to me a wiser and a higher plan. A plan which has made it the unalterable law of oppression and wrong, that they should tend to their own destruction. . . . A plan that has made it the unalterable law of justice and right to tend to their own perpetuation, by making the common interest and safety of mankind dependent upon them, and thus gathering all men slowly but surely to their defence.

—Byron Paine, "The Radical and the Conservative," 1869

IN 1959, jazzman Charles Mingus recorded "The Fables of Faubus" on his album *Mingus Ah Um*. He recorded it as an instrumental because Columbia Records deemed the lyrics, which lampooned Arkansas governor Orval Faubus, too controversial. Faubus had become famous for dispatching the Arkansas National Guard to keep nine black students from entering Little Rock's Central High School in 1957. Mingus meant to skewer him and in 1960 released "The Original Faubus Fables" on the Candid label with its lyrics intact. As with much of Mingus's best music, it was simultaneously serious and comic, bold and playful. The musicians bantered back and forth in a kind of burlesque dialogue, asking each other to name someone sick and ridiculous. "Governor Faubus!" a musician hollered back. The song's bold musical construction continued with seemingly random shouts, sometimes unintelligible but always accusatory, equating Jim Crow segregation with nazism and indicting Faubus as a racist fool. The characterization stuck. Faubus's marshaling of state power to resist desegregation in 1957 turned him into an enduring symbol of racism and injustice.

Also in 1957, historian Alfons Beitzinger published a meticulously researched article on the rescue of Joshua Glover and the federal government's inability to enforce the Fugitive Slave Act in Wisconsin. Although he restricted his study largely to the sources generated by court proceedings, legislative debates, and official correspondence, his account did not differ much from my own. His conclusions, however, did. He characterized the entire affair as a law enforcement problem. He concluded that the rescue and the forcible resistance against the Fugitive Slave Act "remain[ ] a woeful reminder that in the presence of state and popular hostility the firm and prompt deployment of overpowering force within the framework of adequate administrative machinery alone can insure the full execution of the law."[1]

Now, half a century later, I have concluded something quite different. While I have stopped short of concluding the opposite—that the Booth cases are a woeful reminder that only sustained popular and state resistance can successfully thwart attempts by the federal government to subvert civil liberties under color of law—I have at least drawn different political lessons. These are, namely, that sustained popular resistance was evidence that the law had failed to achieve even the minimal consensus that contemporaries understood was necessary to ensure the respect for rule of law; that the duty of defending constitutional liberties devolved in the last instance to the people; and that resistance by state officers—including the judiciary—stemmed from an understanding of state sovereignty and the duty of states to protect liberty.

Who is right?

I have a personal stake in suggesting that Beitzinger's conclusions were at best narrow and at worst reductive. But before we dismiss them, we might do well to consider why he chose to reduce an event as complex as Joshua Glover's rescue to a law enforcement problem. Charles Mingus's arresting song suggests the reason. Reaction to the Supreme Court's ruling in *Brown v. Board of Education* in 1954 had been extreme in the American South. In Mississippi, "Citizens' Councils" formed for the express purpose of opposing *Brown.* Following the Supreme Court's ruling in *Brown II* that desegregation must commence with "all deliberate speed," southern politicians called for popular resistance to desegregation. The legislatures of Alabama, Florida, Mississippi, and Georgia passed resolutions claiming to have the right of interposition and declaring the Supreme Court's decision "null and void." North Carolina, South Carolina, and Louisiana passed similar resolutions protesting the decision and complaining of illegal encroachments on powers reserved to the states. In the face of hard-line segregationist action, moderates—including governors Thomas Stanley, of Virginia, and Orval Faubus, of Arkansas—abandoned their positions and moved to the right.[2]

The protest came to a head when southern congressmen and senators signed the Southern Manifesto in 1956. Citing historical precedents for segregated schools at the time of the Fourteenth Amendment, the manifesto condemned the Supreme Court for exercising "naked judicial power" against the law of the land. It commended "those states which have declared the intention to resist forced integration by any lawful means."[3] And resist they did. Itinerant segregationist speakers whipped the populace into a frenzy. Many demanded state interposition. Some state legislatures made compliance with desegregation orders illegal. The KKK was resurgent.

With this context in mind, Beitzinger's article takes on a different sheen. By divorcing morality from law and submerging the question of the Fugitive Slave Act's constitutionality, Beitzinger was able to present Glover's rescue solely as a law enforcement problem. By tracing the federal government's institutional responses to the Wisconsin case, Beitzinger was able to conclude that the government's inflexibly legalistic response had incapacitated it. In the face of "state and popular resistance" to federal law, only overpowering force could ensure the execution of the law. Given the "state and popular resistance" to desegregation after *Brown,* Beitzinger's article provided historical evidence for those who urged President Dwight D. Eisenhower to support the Supreme Court and use federal power to enforce desegregation. Civil rights enforcement was a role the executive had not yet assumed, and there were no signs it would do so in 1957. But without it, the success of desegregation was anything but secure.

The case that became etched in Americans' memory occurred in Little Rock, Arkansas, and inspired Mingus's *Original Faubus Fables.* The case does not begin with resistance, however. Little Rock's school board had begun complying with *Brown* the day after the decision was handed down and adopted a gradual desegregation plan in May 1955. It was then that segregationists sprung into action. Citizens' councils formed. Speakers from Georgia and Texas urged resistance. Lawsuits were filed in both state and federal court. Governor Faubus, a moderate on race issues, found himself with a potentially explosive situation on his hands when the NAACP filed a lawsuit, *Aaron v. Cooper*, on behalf of black students who were not admitted to Little Rock's Central High School.[4] Simultaneously, he faced a challenge in the gubernatorial race from archsegregationist James Johnson. Nevertheless, Faubus maintained a moderate position on race: although he denied that *Brown II* compelled the state to act, he supported desegregation if it was the result of local choice. Faubus trounced his opponent at the polls, but several popular initiatives passed on the ballot, including a constitutional amendment introduced by Johnson that essentially overruled *Brown II* and directed the state legislature to draft laws opposing desegregation.[5]

In April 1957, the U.S. Court of Appeals for the Eighth Circuit upheld the district court judge's ruling in *Aaron v. Cooper* that approved the school board's plan for desegregation and gave the district court supervisory authority.[6] On September 3, 1957, the school board's request for a delay in implementing the integration plan was rejected by the district court. The court instead ordered integration forthwith. Arkansas and the federal government were now headed for unavoidable collision.

What followed was one of the most memorable events in the desegregation struggle. Governor Faubus earned Mingus's "sick and ridiculous" tags for dispatching the Arkansas National Guard to keep nine black students from entering Central High School. From that point on, he was in direct defiance of a federal court order. To defend his actions, Faubus invoked the police powers doctrine. Because the state had the sovereign right to regulate the health, welfare, and morals of the people within its jurisdiction, Faubus had the power to act in the face of impending disorder, even if it meant ignoring a federal court order. Private negotiations led to the withdrawal of the Arkansas National Guard, and ultimately Eisenhower was forced to deploy the 101st Airborne to ensure the safety of the "Little Rock Nine." A new round of litigation started, including the return of *Aaron v. Cooper* to the courts.

The 1958 Arkansas gubernatorial contest turned on the issues of desegregation and states' rights. Faubus dropped any pretense of moderation and condemned the Supreme Court. He argued that only Congress or "the people" could force desegregation and denied that *Brown* bound him, as Arkansas's governor, to act. On June 21, Judge Harry J. Lemley granted the school board's petition for a postponement of desegregation in *Aaron v.*

Cooper.[7] On August 18, the court of appeals overturned Lemley's decision by a vote of 6 to 1.[8] The court blocked implementation, however, until the Supreme Court could hear an appeal. The Supreme Court agreed to hear the case and expedited its hearing. The bench called a special term and ordered a September 7 deadline for the filing of briefs. The bench heard oral arguments on September 11. After just a thirty-minute conference, the Court upheld the circuit court's decision. The following day, the Court ordered the school board to implement the desegregation plan. Faubus responded by signing legislation giving him authority to circumvent the order. Ultimately, Little Rock's citizens voted to close the schools.

On September 29, 1958, the Supreme Court convened and delivered its written decision in *Cooper v. Aaron,* drafted by Justice William J. Brennan and signed by every member of the court. The opinion directly answered Faubus's claim that he was not bound by *Brown.* Article VI, stated the Court, made the Constitution the supreme law of the land. *Marbury v. Madison* had established the principle that "it is emphatically the province and duty of the judicial department to say what the law is." The Supreme Court interpreted this as meaning that it was the final expositor of the Constitution, and "that principle has ever since been respected by this Court and the Country as a permanent and indispensable feature of our constitutional system." The Supreme Court's interpretation of the 14th Amendment in *Brown,* therefore, was the supreme law of the land. To support its contention that the states could not advance an alternate interpretation or resist the order, the Court cited *Ableman v. Booth.*[9]

Beitzinger's argument and *Cooper v. Aaron* appear to converge. In *Cooper,* the Court drew a line of authority extending from *Marbury* in 1803 through 1958 to demonstrate that its authority was paramount. Ironically, the Court could cite Taney's proslavery *Ableman v. Booth* to defend its order to desegregate. A year earlier, Beitzinger had published a historical account in which he characterized Wisconsin's resistance to the Fugitive Slave Act as extralegal and reckless and he vindicated *Ableman* as the last word on the constitutionality of the Fugitive Slave Act. *Ableman* and *Cooper,* their holdings and their histories, seem perfectly analogous. To condemn *Ableman* would be to condemn federal judicial supremacy and, hence, to condemn *Brown* and *Cooper.* Implicitly, praising resistance to the Fugitive Slave Act in all its forms—active resistance by a vigilant citizenry, state interposition, consistent popular attempts to overrule the Supreme Court at the ballot box—might lead one to admire the resistance of southerners to *Brown* and to federal orders to desegregate.[10]

So much for the moral neutrality of history. But before we resign ourselves to condemning Wisconsin's resistance in the 1850s as unconstitutional in order to vindicate the use of federal power to enforce racial justice in the 1950s, it is necessary to list some palpable differences between the two cases and to suggest some means of reconciling them.

The Supreme Court cited *Ableman* to prove that the its own interpretation of the Fourteenth Amendment as prohibiting segregation in public schools was the "supreme law of the land."[11] The case was certainly on point. But Taney's argument, when scrutinized, rests on a slightly different foundation than Brennan's. Taney began by noting that the separation between federal and state jurisdiction was as clear "as if the line of division was traced by landmarks and monuments visible to the eye."[12] Hence, state courts had no business interfering with federal courts as a matter of jurisdictional comity. In *Ableman,* the jurisdictional clash involved a dispute over the legitimate scope of congressional power versus state power. Taney claimed the right to arbitrate this dispute between two sovereignties. He assured his readers that his opinion should do nothing "to awaken the jealousy or offend the natural and just pride of State sovereignty."[13] He promised that he would just as readily strike down congressional attempts to infringe on the states' authority as he would (in the present case) correct states' invasion of congressional power.

Taney's articulation of judicial supremacy was powerful enough, but it did not rest on a muscular assertion of the right of courts to review the substance of federal (or, presumably, state) statutes.[14] This might explain why Taney did not cite *Marbury v. Madison* to demonstrate that the judiciary's interpretation of the Constitution was binding on the other branches of government. In fact, Taney cited no authorities whatsoever. He rested, instead, on the time-tested role of the court as regulator of federalism. The Court might delineate the powers held by each government, but it deferred to the legislature the right of determining how to (ab)use those powers.

This is the weakness behind Taney's boldness. One can almost see *Dred Scott* peeking from beneath the cloak of judicial supremacy. Taney's attempt to resolve the problem of slavery in the territories in *Dred Scott* divided the Court internally and left it embattled nationally. By 1859, many southerners supportive of the ruling were still claiming that the Supreme Court could not bind the states with its constitutional interpretations. The practice of coordinate construction among the branches meant that the slavery question could be settled only by an appeal to the people. This was certainly the way Democrats had interpreted the elections of 1852 and 1856. In 1859, the settlement of the slavery issue lay in the election of 1860 and ultimately in the Civil War, not in the pronouncement of the Supreme Court.

Putting aside for a moment the question of judicial supremacy, there was another issue hidden away in the details of *Ableman v. Booth.* The Fugitive Slave Act of 1850 had subverted the old constitutional settlement that had left the protection of certain classes of persons (namely, free blacks) to the states.[15] The states' police powers included the paramount right to protect citizens against foreign encroachments on their liberty. The protection of liberty was fundamental in the U.S. Constitution, and this power had not been surrendered to Congress. Taney brushed over this point, as if constitutional law was ordinary law, as if the protection of a citizens' liberty against the possibility of perpetual bondage could be analogized to a criminal prosecution for stealing the mail. However sound the logic of Taney's opinion in *Ableman v. Booth,* it suggested that personal liberty—one of the primary reasons for constitutional government in the first place—was a matter of secondary importance left in the hands of a sovereign that claimed no right nor duty to defend it. This was untenable to many in 1859. It should still be so today.

Things were different in 1958. Slavery no longer existed, and the Fourteenth Amendment had made citizenship a matter of federal law. With the nationalization of citizenship went the duty of protecting the rights of American citizens. However incomplete the legal revolution was in 1868, however long it took for Congress to act, the Fourteenth Amendment shifted the duty to protect the rights of citizens to the federal government. In 1954, *Brown v. Board of Education* had directly addressed this point. When citizens of the United States complained of the violation of their civil rights, the Court responded as the last protector of those rights—not just as the arbiter of jurisdictional disputes. Viewed from this angle, the Supreme Court's assertion of federal supremacy in *Cooper v. Aaron* and its claim to hold the exclusive right to judge the Constitution bears little resemblance to Taney's opinion in *Ableman v. Booth,* which was largely a technical argument about jurisdiction and was concerned more with the Judiciary Act of 1789 than the tacitly claimed right of judicial review.

But what of resistance? As Hendrik Hartog has pointed out, claiming rights most usually means claiming them against some other vested right.[16] The right of free blacks in the 1850s to the full protection of the state against kidnapping generally meant impeding or, at least, delaying fugitive slave rendition. Likewise, the claim of blacks in the 1950s to the right to an equal education meant upsetting local traditions that stretched back at least a half century. The merits of each argument aside, the forms of resistance matter. At least a partial analogy can be drawn between the 1850s and the 1950s. Resistance to the Fugitive Slave Act involved citizen action, voluntary association in the form of vigilance committees, itinerant abolitionist lecturers drumming up popular resentment, the filing of numerous court actions, and ultimately the interposition of the state legislatures by resolution and hostile statutes. Resistance to desegregation also began with a groundswell of radical opinion, the formation of "Citizens' Councils," itinerant segregationist lecturers drumming up popular resentment, the attempt to forestall it judicially, and ultimately the interposition of the state legislatures by resolution and hostile statutes. On first blush, it appears that justifying resistance in the first instance necessarily justifies it in the second.

Although there are many differences between the resistance effected by abolitionists and that of segregationists, two major points separate them. The first is the cultural bounding of resistance. Wisconsin's abolitionists justified their actions as being peaceful and transparent. They met in public, published their resolutions and arguments, and labored to keep resistance nonviolent. They castigated the federal government for carrying out arrests at night, attempting to hold secret trials, and violently enforcing the law. Segregationists made no such claims. If one takes the Little Rock episode as emblematic, desegregation was a very public affair, and local officers (members of the school board) implemented the plans. Although they were following a federal court order, they were not (as was the case with the Fugitive Slave Act of 1850) completely shut out of the process. Segregationists relied not only on public organization but on the night-riding KKK's acts of terrorism to cow the black population into submission. In the face of federal weakness, segregationists openly called for violence and intimidation.

Measuring violence—especially in its cultural context—is tricky. But the historical circumstances merit the attempt. Jim Crow segregation was a legal regime built for race control, and it encouraged violence because it depended on violence to enforce its arbitrary and capricious rules. Charles Mingus certainly understood this. Shrieking saxophones and ominous drum rolls permeate "The Original Faubus Fables," as the musicians plead for a halt to the stabbings and the shootings. Their pleas testified not just to intimidation faced by civil rights activists in the case of Little Rock desegregation but to nearly a century of gruesome lynchings in the American South meant to keep the black population in a state of terror. The spectacle of violence was horrific—the mutilation, the castration, the cutting off of fingers and ears as souvenirs, the burning alive of black men for crimes they may or may not have committed. This was the violence that Mingus feared and loathed. This was the violence that met civil rights activists in the South. To compare it with the breaking of a Milwaukee jail in 1854 that took no lives and resulted in no more damage than necessary to remove a fugitive slave from federal marshals is absurd.

Not all abolitionists eschewed violence. Some—like John Brown—advocated it on a chilling scale. Some abolitionists tore up the Constitution. Their frightening self-righteousness would demolish any obstacle in their fight against slavery. This was not the case in Wisconsin. Booth's radicalism was constrained by a constitutional party of lawyers who conceded certain rules. Until the Wisconsin Supreme Court took the bold step of refusing to recognize the writ of error from the U.S. Supreme Court, they had believed that they would have to pursue other means. But this leads us to a collateral criticism of Beitzinger's argument: there is little evidence that the "prompt deployment of overpowering force" would have achieved successful execution of the Fugitive Slave Act. This was, after all, what the federal government had attempted in Boston. Its direct end was a courthouse wrapped in chains, bloodshed during the botched rescue of Anthony Burns, and outrageous costs of enforcement. And still, no fugitive slave would be taken from Boston after Burns's rendition. Rescues persisted in other parts of the country as well, despite the show of force in Boston. Would the prompt deployment of overpowering force have convinced others to stop resisting? The evidence suggests that it is unlikely.

The second difference lies in the theoretical underpinnings of the states' rights theory. In the 1850s, the *imperium in imperio* encompassed a wider scope of police powers than it did in the 1950s. Regardless of theoretical claims to federal supremacy, the central government lacked the apparatus and authority to extend its power into vital areas of local governance before the Civil War. After passage of the Fourteenth Amendment, a half-century tradition of progressive government, the establishment of the Federal Bureau of Investigation and New Deal administrative agencies, federal supremacy had established deep roots in traditional police issues. Importantly—vitally—the states' rights claims reflected this change. In 1850s Wisconsin, the state rested itself on the right to protect citizens' liberty. In contrast, the Southern Manifesto could complain only that the Supreme Court was interfering with matters traditionally belonging to local governance.[17]

The undeniable similarity lies in the means of resistance. The notion that one might constitutionally resist an order of the Supreme Court clearly animated segregationists as it had abolitionists a century earlier. Faubus asserted (then and later) that he was bound by a mandate of the people. But one could argue that, within Little Rock, the community consensus had been for gradual desegregation and that Governor Faubus had subverted this consensus.[18] After galvanizing the community against a perceived outside threat, he briefly gained broad popular approval for his actions. This approval, however, disintegrated in 1959 in the face of the extreme tactics employed—mob rule, violence, and ultimately the closing of the schools. In Wisconsin, popular consensus against the Fugitive Slave Act did not dissipate with time. The only factor that consistently threatened the consensus was the Republicans' adoption of the temperance issue, which earned the enmity of the German population. Against the Fugitive Slave Act, popular resistance was sustained until after the start of the Civil War, when the constitutional issues that had animated the resistance were being settled with force and arms.

All this speaks to the complexity surrounding *Ableman v. Booth* and *Cooper v. Aaron*—a complexity that makes comparison difficult. We need not worry about reconciling them by drawing a straight line from one to the other. Only those concerned with buttressing the notion of judicial supremacy need do that. Rather, the palpable differences between the two cases indicate how, at each point in time, people in the United States made claims for rights. What the Court articulated in *Cooper v. Aaron* was not the timeless constitutional principle of judicial supremacy, but a muscular new role for the Court as the defender of civil rights. A century earlier, the Wisconsin Supreme Court had done something similar. In fact, the 1850s marked the first time that courts began striking down legislation because it violated civil liberties. It was a watershed for judicial review, and state courts—not the Supreme Court—led the way.

Above all else, any comparison of *Ableman v. Booth* and *Cooper v. Aaron* must look first and last not at the pronouncements of the courts, but at the constitutional assertions of the people. The civil rights struggle of the 1960s did not begin or end in the courts. It began and ended with the people who fought to gain their rights. So, too, with the struggle against the Fugitive Slave Act. Of course, the courts were important. They provided the vital setting for the American civil rights movement. But we must be careful not to confuse that setting with the substance of the struggle itself. The civil rights struggle hardly could have succeeded in America had it not been for its permeation of law, politics, and culture. This was Charles Mingus's battle—to communicate the soul of resistance against racism across space and time. He was joined by other artists in the 1960s in a cultural movement that resembled, however imperfectly, the sentimental turn in antislavery literature in the 1850s that warred against slavery. These considerations, I believe, separate Beitzinger's conclusions from my own. I have searched for the meaning of the rescue in a broader range of sources and in a different context. It is here that I found a dialogue between the people and the courts, between officers judicial, legislative, and executive, and between the federal government and the states. It is within this dialogue that constitutional processes have worked themselves out. It is here that we must look for the meaning of the Constitution. And hopefully, for meaning in our history.

NOTES

CHAPTER I

1. Arnold and Hamilton, one of Milwaukee's most prominent law firms, represented Garland and published a statement of facts in the Milwaukee papers after the rescue. See *Milwaukee Sentinel,* March 13, 1854. Judge Miller's arrest warrant for Glover repeated this same set of facts. See *In re Booth,* 3 Wis. 144, 149 [3 Wis. 157, 162] (1854). The case was decided during the January term of 1855, but a later editor included it in the 1854 volume of the *Wisconsin Reports* with the other Booth cases. The Lexis-Nexis citation for the Booth cases differs from the printed reports. Lexis-Nexis reports the page numbers from an earlier edition, which are preserved in brackets in the printed volumes of the *Wisconsin Reports.* I record both paginations in this book, beginning with the printed reports and followed by the Lexis-Nexis citation.

2. The ownership of the shanty is difficult to trace. At the public meeting in Racine, the authorities claimed it was owned by Duncan Sinclair. Milwaukee newspapers later claimed that Glover owned the shanty himself. I have found no other record of it.

3. The principal source for this narrative, which virtually every historian has used since the event itself, is the article "High Handed Outrage! Attempt to Kidnap a Citizen of Racine by Slave-Catchers," *Racine Advocate,* March 12, 1854. I take the description of citizens' activities in Racine at face value. For the narrative of the arrest or capture of Glover, I use only what information can be confirmed by other sources.

4. The city of Racine prosecuted an assault and battery case against Garland, and the facts as presented in "High Handed Outrage!" were supposedly put together by the city attorney, indicating that evidence of the arrest also came from William Alby. See John G. Gregory, *History of Milwaukee, Wisconsin* (Chicago: S. J. Clarke, 1931), 747.

Principal scholarly accounts of Glover's arrest have drawn rather uncritically from the article in the *Racine Advocate,* which claimed that there was no service of process on Glover and that Deputy Marshal Kearney immediately (and seemingly without provocation) struck Glover on the head. In subsequent testimony during the Ryecraft trial in November of that year and the Booth trial of January

1855, it became clear that Glover had indeed tried to grab the gun pressed to his head and that this had initiated the struggle.

5. Stanley W. Campbell, *The Slave Catchers: Enforcement of the Fugitive Slave Law, 1850–1860* (New York: W. W. Norton, 1970).

6. Robert R. Russel, "The Issues in the Congressional Struggle over the Kansas-Nebraska Bill, 1854," *Journal of Southern History* 29 (May 1963): 187–210.

7. William Cronon, *Nature's Metropolis: Chicago and the Great West* (New York: W. W. Norton, 1991), 68–70.

8. Frank H. Hodder, "The Railroad Background of the Kansas-Nebraska Act," *Mississippi Valley Historical Review* 12 (June 1925): 3–22.

9. One might well ask, then, how it passed. Douglas and the Democrats made it a test of party loyalty, although southern and northern Democrats voted for different reasons. See Roy F. Nichols, "The Kansas-Nebraska Act: A Century of Historiography," *Mississippi Valley Historical Review* 43 (June 1956): 204–12.

10. Eric Foner, *Free Soil, Free Labor, Free Men: The Ideology of the Republican Party before the Civil War* (1970; repr. with new introduction, New York: Oxford University Press, 1995), 154–60; William E. Gienapp, *The Origins of the Republican Party, 1852–1856* (New York: Oxford University Press, 1987), 75–79.

11. "Impressions of our State," *Daily Wisconsin,* June 7, 1854. The description was written by a correspondent of the *New York Evening Post* on the occasion of the opening of the Milwaukee & Mississippi Railroad from Milwaukee to Madison. The correspondent also complained that Milwaukee's beautiful brick was "miserably caricatured and scandalously libelled [*sic*] in the material of the Trinity building in New York."

12. Statistics taken from Milwaukee Chamber of Commerce, *An Exposition of the Business of Milwaukee* (Milwaukee: A. Baylies, 1863). Western settlement in the 1830s proceeded both in the quick construction of urban centers and in rural settlement. William Cronon described it as "reading Turner backwards," suggesting that rapid urban development spurred the commercial development of the rural frontier. See Cronon, *Nature's Metropolis,* 46–54.

13. "High-Handed Outrage!" *Racine Advocate,* March 12, 1854.

14. Diane S. Butler, "The Public Life and Private Affairs of Sherman M. Booth," *Wisconsin Magazine of History* 82 (Spring 1999): 168–72.

15. Testimony of Charles C. Cotton in *U.S. v. Booth,* as reported in the *Daily Wisconsin,* January 11, 1855.

16. Vernon L. Volpe, *Forlorn Hope of Freedom: The Liberty Party in the Old Northwest, 1838–1848* (Kent, Ohio: Kent State University Press, 1990), 47–57, 93–95.

17. The handbill was printed in both Sherman Booth's *Daily Free Democrat* and Rufus King's *Milwaukee Sentinel* on March 13, 1854. The handbills were also admitted into evidence in two different trials.

18. Liberty required constant vigilance, and history was often read this way—as a series of struggles against the dangerous consolidation of power. See Daniel John McInerney, *The Fortunate Heirs of Freedom: Abolition and Republican Thought* (Lincoln: University of Nebraska Press, 1994), 27–58; Dorothy Ross, "Historical

Consciousness in Nineteenth-Century America," *American Historical Review* 89 (October 1984): 916–18. Contrary to what McInerney and Ross have argued, this view did not preclude notions of progress and historical change. See Joyce Appleby's arguments in the introductory chapter to *Liberalism and Republicanism in the Historical Imagination* (Cambridge, Mass.: Harvard University Press, 1992), 1–33. See also the rhetorical analysis of abolitionism in Stephen John Hartnett, *Democratic Dissent and the Cultural Fictions of Antebellum America* (Urbana: University of Illinois Press, 2002), 33–39. In Wisconsin, the debate over the Fugitive Slave Act (and, among other issues, temperance) was influenced by liberal assumptions about the inevitability of progress. I explored this more fully in my dissertation. See Howard Robert Baker II, "The Rescue of Joshua Glover: Lawyers, Popular Constitutionalism, and the Fugitive Slave Law in Wisconsin" (Ph.D. diss., University of California, Los Angeles, 2004), 55–63.

19. Sherman Booth chronicled his efforts in his newspaper, the *Daily Free Democrat,* March 13, 1854.

20. Abolitionists frequently claimed that the meeting was several thousand strong, and various other independent sources confirm this. See *Daily Free Democrat,* March 13 and 22–24, 1854; "U.S. v. Sherman Booth," *Daily Wisconsin,* January 11, 1855; *Milwaukee Sentinel,* November 21, 1854. U.S. district attorney John Sharpstein, in a letter to Bill Streeter, solicitor of the Treasury also confirmed both the size of the meeting and the number of respectable citizens in the crowd and among the organizers. See J. R. Sharpstein to W. B. Streeter, March 20, 1854, Solicitor of the Treasury Manuscripts, Letters Received from U.S. District Attorneys, Marshals, Clerks of Court, 1853–1881, Wisconsin, RG 206, National Archives, College Park, Maryland (hereafter NA).

21. For contemporary descriptions of the courthouse square, see Milwaukee's *City Directory* 1847–48 (p. 58); 1848–49 (p. 11), Milwaukee County Historical Society, Milwaukee, Wisconsin (hereafter MCHS).

22. *Milwaukee Sentinel,* February 23, 1847.

23. "Affray," *Milwaukee Sentinel,* April 4, 1848.

24. Throughout this book, I use "native-born American" in the sense in which it was used in the 1850s—an English-speaking American citizen born in the United States.

25. "Letter of Charles A. Brandeker," *Milwaukee Sentinel,* March 7, 1850.

26. "Letter of A. T. Phillipe" and "Letter of A. Henry Bielfeld," *Milwaukee Sentinel,* March 11, 1850.

27. "Police Doings for 1851," *Milwaukee Sentinel,* January 8, 1852.

28. "Letter of Charles A. Brandeker."

29. "A Strike and a Riot," *Milwaukee Sentinel,* July 12, 1853.

30. Ibid.

31. David Grimsted, "Rioting in Its Jacksonian Setting," *American Historical Review* 77 (April 1972): 364. On the fear of escalating urban violence and the survival of democracy, see Paul A. Gilje, *The Road to Mobocracy: Popular Disorder in New York City, 1763–1834* (Chapel Hill: Published for the Institute of Early

American History and Culture by the University of North Carolina Press, 1987). For a general interpretation of these matters, see Paul A. Gilje, *Rioting in America* (Bloomington: Indiana University Press, 1996); David Grimsted, *American Mobbing, 1828–1861: Toward Civil War* (New York: Oxford University Press, 1998). For an alternative, but unconvincing, view, see Kimberly K. Smith, *The Dominion of Voice: Riot, Reason, and Romance in Antebellum Politics* (Lawrence: University Press of Kansas, 1999). Smith argued that antebellum mobs were an orderly method of political expression and that historians have overplayed their violence. She argued mainly from a rhetorical and theoretical stance and relied on a rather thin evidentiary base that did not sustain her conclusions.

32. The starting points for the study of crowds and the legitimating notions they held are George F. E. Rudé, *The Crowd in History: A Study of Popular Disturbances in France and England, 1730–1848* (New York: Wiley, 1964); Edward P. Thompson, "The Moral Economy of the English Crowd in the Eighteenth Century," in *Customs in Common* (New York: New Press, 1993), 185–258. Thompson's work on the "food riot" (originally published in *Past and Present* in 1971) demonstrated that crowds enforced discipline, preventing members from stealing and oftentimes simply forcing merchants to sell grain at the fair—rather than market—price. This kind of crowd action was not as common in America, but it did occur in Boston in 1710, 1713, and 1729. See Pauline Maier, "Popular Uprisings and Civil Authority in Eighteenth-Century America," *William and Mary Quarterly* 27 (January 1970): 5. For a recent critique of the Thompson/Rudé model, see Suzanne Desan, "Crowds, Community, and Ritual in the Work of E. P. Thompson and Natalie Davis," in *The New Cultural History*, ed. Lynn Hunt (Berkeley: University of California Press, 1989), 47–71.

33. Rioters usually claimed to be acting for the maintenance of public order rather than its disturbance, as in the Boston Bawdy House Riot of 1734 or the 1773 attack on a smallpox hospital built on Essex Island. See Maier, "Popular Uprisings," 5–7.

The social elite were notoriously ambivalent about such affairs. They often lent support to rioters when the cause seemed just. See Thompson, "Moral Economy," 238–41. Their ambivalence toward such crowds had deep cultural and psychological roots. Elites certainly feared the disorder and violence that mobs brought with them. But mobs often replicated the prevailing social order, even if inverting it for the duration of the event. In that sense, the mob's ability to make the underclass "kings for a day" ultimately lent authority to the prevailing hierarchy. See Gordon S. Wood, *The Radicalism of the American Revolution* (New York: Vintage Books, 1991), 89–91, 213–14.

34. Edward Countryman, *The American Revolution* (New York: Hill and Wang, 1984), 74–79; Maier, "Popular Uprisings," 14; John Phillip Reid, *In a Rebellious Spirit: The Argument of Facts, the Liberty Riot, and the Coming of the American Revolution* (University Park: Pennsylvania State University Press, 1979), 50–56, 90–99; Gordon S. Wood, *The Creation of the American Republic, 1776–1787*, 2d ed. (Chapel Hill: University of North Carolina Press, 1998), 319–28.

Crowd action was disciplined in extraordinary ways. For instance, a Boston mob released men they had "arrested" on suspicion of complicity with British tax collectors when the mob's leaders learned that the men were innocent. See Maier, "Popular Uprisings," 14. There may be no better example of this than the Boston Tea Party, in which only tea was thrown overboard and the other cargo remained untouched; one person found stuffing tea into his pockets was made to throw it overboard and was punished for his transgression. See John Phillip Reid, *The Constitutional History of the American Revolution*, vol. 3, *The Authority to Legislate* (Madison: University of Wisconsin Press, 1991), 296–97.

35. Joyce Appleby, *Inheriting the Revolution: The First Generation of Americans* (Cambridge, Mass.: Harvard University Press, Belknap Press, 2000), 26–31; David Waldstreicher, *In the Midst of Perpetual Fetes: The Making of American Nationalism, 1776–1820* (Chapel Hill: University of North Carolina Press, 1997), 177–207. On the rise of voluntary associations providing permanent charity see Lori D. Ginzberg, *Women and the Work of Benevolence: Morality, Politics, and Class in the Nineteenth-Century United States* (New Haven, Conn.: Yale University Press, 1990), 14–16; Conrad Edick Wright, *The Transformation of Charity in Postrevolutionary New England* (Boston: Northeastern University Press, 1992), 113–80.

36. Malcolm J. Rohrbough, *The Trans-Appalachian Frontier: People, Societies, and Institutions, 1775–1850* (New York: Oxford University Press, 1978), 114–28. See generally, Noble E. Cunningham, *The Process of Government under Jefferson* (Princeton, N.J.: Princeton University Press, 1978). For an example of recourse to popular assembly to secure squatters' property claims in Wisconsin, see James Willard Hurst, *Law and the Conditions of Freedom in the Nineteenth-Century United States* (Madison: University of Wisconsin Press, 1956), 1–7.

37. For a detailed exploration of the laws governing voluntary association, see Baker, "Rescue of Joshua Glover," 32–116.

38. The records of several voluntary associations can be found in the MCHS. One of Milwaukee's most famous was the Young Men's Association. See "Library Catalogue—Young Men's Association," MCHS. Praise for the Young Men's Association was ubiquitous. See "Young Men's Association," *Daily Wisconsin*, April 4, 1854.

39. King George III's refusal to hear petitions from the American colonies had become a prime constitutional issue in the 1770s. See John Phillip Reid, *Constitutional History of the American Revolution*, vol. 2, *The Authority of Rights* (Madison: University of Wisconsin Press, 1986), 22.

40. On the question of class conflict along cultural lines, see Michael Feldberg, *The Philadelphia Riots of 1844: A Study of Ethnic Conflict* (Westport, Conn.: Greenwood, 1975), 84–88.

41. Grimsted, "Rioting in its Jacksonian Setting," 365–66.

42. This was the operating assumption of the Federalists in the early republic. See Gilje, *Road to Mobocracy*, 100–12. This fear that democracy was too fragile to keep order was voiced less frequently but more vehemently by the time of the Civil War. See Grimsted, *American Mobbing*, 250–55.

43. Richard Maxwell Brown, *Strain of Violence: Historical Studies of American Violence and Vigilantism* (Oxford: Oxford University Press, 1977).

44. Businesses advertising in the city directories of the 1850s listed their addresses by building in this central market area rather than by street address. The 1850s city directories are available at the MCHS. See also Kathleen N. Conzen, *Immigrant Milwaukee, 1836–1870: Accommodation and Community in a Frontier City* (Cambridge, Mass.: Harvard University Press, 1976), 140.

45. The collective value of real estate, improvements, and personal property in the First Ward increased dramatically between 1853 and 1854, from $674,622 to $1,005,680. Milwaukee (Wis.) assessor, assessment rolls, 1852–1860, 1862, manuscript 720, MCHS.

46. There were also several consulates for the German states in Milwaukee. See John Warren Hunt, *Wisconsin Gazetteer* (Madison, Wis.: Beriah Brown, 1853), 149.

47. *Milwaukee Sentinel*, March 8, 1854.

48. Ibid.

49. Although missing tax rolls make it impossible to determine how much Bielfeld owned, the *Milwaukee Sentinel* of April 14, 1864, reported that one of Bielfeld's buildings burned down in a city fire.

50. *Milwaukee Sentinel*, February 1, November 29, 1847. Conzen, *Immigrant Milwaukee*, 196.

51. "Letter to the editor, A. Henry Bielfeld," *Milwaukee Sentinel*, February 27, 1846.

52. *Milwaukee Sentinel*, August 28, 1848. Bielfeld had also delivered 1848's Fourth of July oration in German. See *Milwaukee Sentinel*, July 6, 1848.

53. Byron Paine kept many of his speeches and arguments, which are collected in his personal papers. See Byron Paine, "Discussion of Fugitive Slave Law"; "Debate on the Question: Would the North be justifiable in dissolving the Union, in event of the annexation of Texas"; and "On Liberty and Slavery," in the folder Political Speeches and Arguments, Byron Paine Papers, 1845–1869 (hereafter Byron Paine Papers), Wisconsin State Historical Society Archives, Madison, Wisconsin (hereafter WSHSA). He supported adoption of the Maine Liquor Law in Wisconsin, as noted in "Temperance Meeting," *Milwaukee Sentinel*, October 8, 1853.

54. *Milwaukee Sentinel*, September 16, 1853. The paper reprinted a review by the *Racine Advocate* and then commented on it. Rufus King had complained in the *Milwaukee Sentinel* of May 31, 1853, that the *Daily Free Democrat* had been too strong in its praise of Byron Paine's abilities.

55. In an entirely separate matter, the *Daily Wisconsin*—a paper not friendly to abolitionists—remarked that Byron Paine was one of the most respected members of the community. See *Daily Wisconsin*, April 13, 1854. Upon learning that Byron Paine's name had been advanced for clerk of the assembly, the *Daily Wisconsin* noted that "[t]he Republicans could not find a man better qualified than Mr. Paine." *Daily Wisconsin* January 9, 1855.

56. *Madison Democrat*, quoted in the *Milwaukee Sentinel*, December 15, 1854. Evidence of this opinion abounds.

57. "Great Meeting in the Court-House Square!" *Daily Free Democrat,* March 13, 1854.

58. *Milwaukee Sentinel,* November 28, 1854. Byron Paine wrote this in a review of Judge Miller's opinion in the Ryecraft case, which cited one of Judge Nelson's opinions.

59. "Speeches of the Mass Convention of Freemen, in Young's Hall," *Daily Free Democrat,* April 15, 1854.

60. Byron Paine recalled this during Sherman Booth's first habeas corpus trial. See Byron Paine, *Argument of Byron Paine, Esq. and Opinion of Hon. A. D. Smith on the Unconstitutionality of the Fugitive Slave Act* (Milwaukee, Wis.: Sherman M. Booth, 1854), 19.

61. "Resolutions of the Great Meeting in the Courthouse Square," *Daily Free Democrat,* March 13, 1854.

62. Even if "not without a dissenting voice," none of the public reports or private accounts of the meeting which I have cited in this chapter disputed that the crowd adopted the resolutions.

63. Milwaukee assessment rolls, 1854, Milwaukee (Wis.) assessor, assessment rolls, 1852–1860, 1862, manuscript 720, MCHS. From 1852 to 1856, Herbert Reed reported 200, 300, or 400 dollars' worth of movable goods. He advertised in the Milwaukee city directories of the 1850s, as well (MCHS). He was related by marriage to Abram D. Smith, the judge who later ruled the Fugitive Slave Act of 1850 unconstitutional. I owe this information to conversations with Ruth Dunley.

64. "Resolutions of the Great Meeting."

65. Sharpstein to Streeter, March 20, 1854.

66. Reports in the *Milwaukee Sentinel* and *Daily Free Democrat* did not mention anything about the fluctuation in the assembly's numbers, but multiple witnesses in the Ryecraft trial remembered the crowd's depletion by four o'clock. See "U.S. v. John Ryecraft," *Milwaukee Sentinel,* November 19, 1854.

67. James Angove much later claimed credit for obtaining the loose piece of timber that broke down the jailhouse door. In testimony at later trials, Herbert Reed was fixed with the blame for operating the battering ram. Angove was never charged in the rescue. He did, however, work for John A. Messinger. For Angove's account, see "Helped Save Glover," *Milwaukee Sentinel,* June 10, 1900. Online facsimile available at Wisconsin History, Wisconsin Historical Society, http://www.wisconsinhistory.org/turningpoints/search.asp?id=1033.

68. "Report of the Ryecraft Trial," *Milwaukee Sentinel,* November 21, 1854. The testimony cited is from the first day of trial, November 17.

69. During the trial of Sherman Booth, Parsons and other witnesses testified to substantially the same set of facts. The *Daily Wisconsin* reported that Parsons testified that he "saw nothing indicating violence, nor heard threats made" in "U.S. v. Sherman Booth."

70. This smacks of some embellishment, but it is verified in three independent sources: *Daily Free Democrat,* March 13, 1854; *Daily Wisconsin,* March 14, 1854; and the testimony of George S. Mallory during the trial of John Ryecraft, as reported

in the *Milwaukee Sentinel*, November 18, 1854. It was also retold in Vroman Mason, "The Fugitive Slave Law in Wisconsin, with Reference to Nullification Sentiment," *Proceedings of the State Historical Society of Wisconsin* 43 (1895): 125. Mason reported having interviewed principals and witnesses as well as reviewing written sources in the preparation of his article.

71. Chauncey C. Olin, "A History of the Early Anti-slavery Excitement in the State of Wisconsin from 1842–1860," microfilm, reel 1 P82-5062, Wisconsin Historical Society Library.

72. "Der arme Negerslave befreit," *Der See-Bote*, March 15, 1854.

73. "The Rescue Case," *Daily Wisconsin*, March 13, 1854.

74. *Daily Free Democrat*, March 13, 1854.

CHAPTER 2

1. William Blackstone, *Commentaries on the Laws of England, in Four Books* (Oxford: Clarendon Press, 1768), 3:3.

2. Max Farrand, *The Records of the Federal Convention of 1787* (New Haven, Conn.: Yale University Press, 1911), 1:486.

3. Jack N. Rakove, *Original Meanings: Politics and Ideas in the Making of the Constitution* (New York: Vintage Books, 1997), 86–89.

4. David Brion Davis, *The Problem of Slavery in the Age of Revolution, 1770–1823* (Ithaca, N.Y.: Cornell University Press, 1975), 84–91, 122–26. The acquiescence of northern representatives in several matters regarding slavery has received harsh criticism from revisionist scholars. See Paul Finkelman, *Slavery and the Founders: Race and Liberty in the Age of Jefferson*, 2d ed. (Armonk, N.Y.: M. E. Sharpe, 2001), 81–83; Gary B. Nash, *Race and Revolution* (Madison, Wis.: Madison House, 1990), 42. Whether this made the Constitution a "proslavery" document remains a matter of argument. See Earl M. Maltz, "The Idea of the Proslavery Constitution," *Journal of the Early Republic* 17 (Spring 1997): 38–40.

5. Somerset v. Stewart, 98 Eng. Rep. 499 (K.B. 1772), reprinted in Melvin I. Urofsky and Paul Finkelman, *Documents of American Constitutional and Legal History* (New York: Oxford University Press, 2002), 1:44–45.

6. Davis, *Problem of Slavery*, 216–42; Paul Finkelman, *An Imperfect Union: Slavery, Federalism, and Comity* (Chapel Hill: University of North Carolina Press, 1981), 6–17.

7. Farrand, *Records of the Federal Convention of 1787*, 2:443.

8. Ibid., 2:446, 453–54; Paul Finkelman, "Slavery and the Constitutional Convention: Making a Covenant with Death," in *Beyond Confederation: Origins of the Constitution and American National Identity*, ed. Richard Beeman, Stephen Botein, and Edward C. Carter II (Chapel Hill: University of North Carolina Press, 1987), 221; William M. Wiecek, "The Witch at the Christening: Slavery and the Constitution's Origins," in *The Framing and Ratification of the Constitution*, ed. Leonard W. Levy and Dennis J. Mahoney (New York: Macmillan, 1987), 181–82.

There was one further modification to the fugitive slave clause. On September 15, the members changed the language from "No person legally held to service or labour in one state" to "No person held to service or labour in one state under the laws thereof." This was a small concession to those who did not want to suggest that slavery was "legal" in any kind of fundamental sense. See Rakove, *Original Meanings*, 91–93.

9. The most thorough account of the historical context and legislative history of the 1793 fugitive slave law is Paul Finkelman, "The Kidnapping of John Davis and the Adoption of the Fugitive Slave Law of 1793," *Journal of Southern History* 56 (August 1990).

10. State officers thought of the general government as a kind of federalist umpire. Although the dispute involved several court actions, no one thought to submit the matter to the courts for resolution. Nor did anyone think it strange that the federal government might, in matters involving relations between the states, advise state officers as to their duties.

11. An Act respecting fugitives from justice, and persons escaping from the service of their masters (Fugitive Slave Act), 1 Stat. 302 (1793).

12. Robert J. Kaczorowski, "The Inverted Constitution: Enforcing Constitutional Rights in the Nineteenth Century," in *Constitutionalism and American Culture: Writing the New Constitutional History*, ed. Sandra F. Van Burkleo, Kermit L. Hall, and Robert J. Kaczorowski (Lawrence: University Press of Kansas, 2002), 29–63. Kaczorowski argues that the Fugitive Slave Act was the only real enforcement of a constitutional right in the antebellum era. This argument reads a little too much into the 1793 statute. The federal government did not actively enforce this constitutional right of slaveholders, except in a few instances. For instance, the State Department put clauses in Indian treaties stipulating that fugitive slaves would be returned, and federal officers were primarily responsible for enforcing the fugitive slave law in Washington, D.C., and the territories. But it was state officers—who also took an oath to the U.S. Constitution—who primarily enforced these provisions in its first four decades of operation. See Don E. Fehrenbacher, *The Slaveholding Republic: An Account of the United States Government's Relations to Slavery* (New York: Oxford University Press, 2001), 214–16.

In another very important way, the Fugitive Slave Act was not only the enforcement of a private right. Its framers clearly thought in terms of directing state officers as to their duties to fulfill a constitutional compromise. Free states may not have been obligated to recognize slavery, but they were obligated to return fugitive slaves. While this *necessarily* involved a private right, it was not *primarily* thought of in that way.

13. This was universal by 1860, with the sole exception of Delaware. Courts affirmed that black skin or African features carried the presumption of slavery in North Carolina in 1802, in Virginia in 1806, and in Kentucky in 1835. Statutory definitions of mulattoes as quadroons (one-quarter blood African) often led to their enslavement (although sometimes for only a limited time) in southern states during the eighteenth century. See Thomas D. Morris, *Southern Slavery*

and the Law, 1619–1860 (Chapel Hill: University of North Carolina Press, 1996), 21–29.

14. Ira Berlin, *Generations of Captivity: A History of African-American Slaves* (Cambridge, Mass.: Harvard University Press, Belknap Press, 2003), 161–68; Steven Deyle, "The Ironies of Liberty: Origins of the Domestic Slave Trade," *Journal of the Early Republic* 12 (Spring 1992): 41–45.

15. Carol Wilson, *Freedom at Risk: The Kidnapping of Free Blacks in America, 1780–1865* (Lexington: University Press of Kentucky, 1994), 9–11.

16. *Annals of Congress*, 4th Cong., 1st sess., 1025 (April 18, 1796).

17. Ibid., 2d sess., 1732 (December 29, 1796).

18. Ibid., 1731 (December 29, 1796).

19. Ibid.

20. Ibid., 1895 (January 18, 1797).

21. Ibid., 2020 (January 30, 1797). Manumission presented its own set of legal challenges that emphasized the dual nature of slavery as a private property right and a matter of public policy. See Morris, *Southern Slavery and the Law*, 371–99.

22. Thomas D. Morris, *Free Men All: The Personal Liberty Laws of the North, 1780–1861* (Baltimore: Johns Hopkins University Press, 1974), 32. Morris located this report in the National Archives, College Park, Maryland. It does not appear in the *House Journal*, nor is there any indication why the report was never presented to Congress.

23. This point is made persuasively by Paul Finkelman in "Kidnapping of John Davis," 400.

24. *Annals of Congress*, 7th Cong., 1st sess., 423 (January 15, 1802).

25. Ibid., 15th Cong., 1st sess., 827–28 (January 28, 1818).

26. This was not always to be the case. Southerners worried about the consolidation of power in the national government precisely because it could be turned against slavery. It was upon this principle in the 1830s that Calhoun formulated his theories on state sovereignty and the limits of federal power to direct the states. See William M. Wiecek, "'Old Times There Are Not Forgotten': The Distinctiveness of the Southern Constitutional Experience," in *An Uncertain Tradition: Constitutionalism and the History of the South*, ed. Kermit L. Hall and James W. Ely (Athens: University of Georgia Press, 1989).

27. *Annals of Congress*, 15th Cong., 1st sess., 825 (January 28, 1818).

28. Ibid., 830 (January 29, 1818).

29. Ibid., 826 (January 28, 1818). Clagett's complaint was raised at a later time by James Burrill, of Rhode Island.

30. Ibid., 231–33 (March 6, 1818).

31. Fehrenbacher, *Slaveholding Republic*, 213–14, Morris, *Free Men All*, 35–41.

32. Judges did not feel trapped by prevailing positivist leanings to accept the fugitive slave law, as argued in Robert M. Cover, *Justice Accused: Antislavery and the Judicial Process* (New Haven, Conn.: Yale University Press, 1975). Rather, I argue that the constitutionality of the law was to be found in the compromises hammered out in Congress and in the state legislatures. A suggestive, but not

thoroughly researched, essay on this subject is Anthony J. Sebok, "Judging the Fugitive Slave Acts," *Yale Law Journal* 100 (April 1991): 1835–54. Sebok analogizes the "change" in the constitutionality of the fugitive slave law to changing societal conditions, which really serves as an argument for the constitutionality of both *Plessy v. Ferguson* and *Brown v. Board of Education*.

33. John Codman Hurd, *The Law of Freedom and Bondage* (1858; repr. Boston: Little, Brown, 1968), 2:5–6, 74–75. The Virginia statute was reaffirmed in the late 1790s along with a number of laws making antislavery agitation illegal as well. Delaware passed a more effectual antikidnapping statute and apparently worked to enforce it. A variety of cases brought on appeal during the nineteenth century indicated not only that kidnapping was a real problem but that some states vigorously enforced their laws. See, e.g., In re Jones, 2 Del. Cas. 622 (1821); State v. Clark, 1 Del. Cas. 549 (1818); State v. Griffin, 3 Del. 560 (1841); State v. Harten, 4 Del. 582 (1847); State v. Jeans, 4 Del. 570 (1847); State v. Jones, 1 Del Cas. 546 (1818); State v. Tindal, 2 Del. Cas. 169 (1802); State v. Updike, 4 Del. 581 (1847); State v. Whaley, 2 Del. 538 (1837); State v. Whitaker, 3 Del. 549 (1840).

34. Hurd, *Law of Freedom and Bondage,* 2:106–7. For Mississippi's law, see 2:146. Hurd's treatise says nothing of enforcement, nor does it appear from a cursory glance at the appellate court records that the law was much enforced.

35. Morris, *Free Men All,* 28–29.

36. An Act to Prevent Manstealing, § 3, Laws of Indiana, 1816. Reprinted in Stephen Middleton, *The Black Laws in the Old Northwest: A Documentary History* (Westport, Conn.: Greenwood, 1993), 228–29.

37. In re Susan, 23 F. Cas. 444 (C.C.D. Ind. 1818) (No. 16,632).

38. Glen v. Hodges, 9 Johns. 67 (N.Y. Sup. Ct. 1812).

39. In re Susan, 23 F. Cas. 444.

40. This fundamental point was not disputed in the early nineteenth century. See David P. Currie, *The Constitution in Congress: The Federalist Period, 1789–1801* (Chicago: University of Chicago Press, 1997); David P. Currie, *The Constitution in Congress: The Jeffersonians, 1801–1829* (Chicago: University of Chicago Press, 2001); Adam S. Grace, "From the Lighthouses: How the First Federal Internal Improvement Projects Created Precedent That Broadened the Commerce Clause, Shrunk the Takings Clause, and Affected Early Nineteenth Century Constitutional Debate," *Albany Law Review* 68, no. 1 (2004): 97–153.

41. Federalist jurist James Kent offered a full-blown theory of judicial review and judicial supremacy in "An Introductory Lecture to a Course of Law Lectures," reprinted in Charles S. Hyneman and Donald S. Lutz, *American Political Writing during the Founding Era, 1760–1805* (Indianapolis, Ind.: Liberty Press, 1983), 942. See also Maeva Marcus, "Judicial Review in the Early Republic," in *Launching the "Extended Republic": The Federalist Era,* ed. Ronald Hoffman and Peter J. Albert (Charlottesville: Published for the United States Capitol Historical Society by the University Press of Virginia, 1996), 25–32. Kent, of course, cannot be taken at his word. Although the *idea* of judicial review was well established by 1800, the *conditions* that would allow it to operate were not. See Gordon S. Wood,

"The Origins of Judicial Review Revisited, or How the Marshall Court Made More out of Less," *Washington and Lee Law Review* 56 (Summer 1999): 795–96.

On the rise of a Madisonian departmentalism that rejected judicial supremacy, see Larry D. Kramer, *The People Themselves: Popular Constitutionalism and Judicial Review* (New York: Oxford University Press, 2004), 105–14. The notion that judicial review was not fully established by 1800 has been one of the central arguments of many revisionists. See Jack N. Rakove, "The Origins of Judicial Review: A Plea for New Contexts," *Stanford Law Review* 49 (May 1997): 1031–64; Sylvia Snowiss, *Judicial Review and the Law of the Constitution* (New Haven, Conn.: Yale University Press, 1990); Jack M. Sosin, *The Aristocracy of the Long Robe: The Origins of Judicial Review in America* (New York: Greenwood, 1989); Christopher Wolfe, *The Rise of Modern Judicial Review: From Constitutional Interpretation to Judge-Made Law,* rev. ed. (Lanham, Md.: Rowman and Littlefield, 1994).

42. Theodore W. Ruger, "'A Question Which Convulses a Nation': The Early Republic's Greatest Debate about the Judicial Review Power," *Harvard Law Review* 117 (January 2004): 828–30. When the Ohio Supreme Court attempted to review state debt relief legislation, the justices came within an inch of impeachment. See Donald F. Melhorn, *"Lest We Be Marshall'd": Judicial Powers and Politics in Ohio, 1806–1812* (Akron, Ohio: University of Akron Press, 2003); William T. Utter, "Judicial Review in Early Ohio," *Mississippi Valley Historical Review* 14 (June 1927). A similar event occurred in Kentucky. See Arndt M. Stickles, *The Critical Court Struggle in Kentucky, 1819–1829* (Bloomington: Indiana University, 1929).

43. "Report of the Judiciary Committee of the House for the State of Indiana on the Governor of Indiana and the Acting Governor of Kentucky." Reprinted in Middleton, *Black Laws in the Old Northwest,* 237.

44. An act relative to fugitives from labor, Laws of Indiana 1824. Reprinted ibid., 242–43.

45. Blackstone, *Commentaries,* 3:129. For an excellent discussion of this writ, see Morris, *Free Men All,* 11–13.

46. Wright v. Deacon, 5 Serg. & Rawle 62, 63 (1819).

47. Ibid.

48. Commonwealth v. Griffith, 19 Mass. 11 (1823).

49. These legislative actions are thoroughly covered in Morris, *Free Men All,* 45, 52–56. In 1837, New Jersey supplemented its personal liberty law by requiring a trial by jury on the demand of either party. See Hurd, *Law of Freedom and Bondage,* 2:66–67.

50. Immediatism meant both abolition without delay and, for abolitionists, the rejection of intermediate agencies. In short, immediatism demanded direct action. See David Brion Davis, "The Emergence of Immediatism in British and American Antislavery Thought," *Mississippi Valley Historical Review* 49 (September 1962): 209–30.

51. Johnson v. Tompkins, 13 F. Cas. 840, 848 (E.D. Pa. 1833) (No. 7,416).

52. Cover, *Justice Accused,* 159–64.

53. *Report of the Case of Charles Brown, A Fugitive Slave, Owing Labour and Service to William C. Drury, of Washington County, Maryland* (Pittsburgh: Alexander Jaynes, 1835), reprinted in Paul Finkelman, ed., *Fugitive Slaves and American Courts: The Pamphlet Literature* (New York: Garland, 1988), 1:41–95.

54. Jack v. Martin, 12 Wend. 311, 321 (N.Y. Sup. Ct. 1834).

55. For instance, he cited *Livingston v. Van Ingen,* 9 Johns. 507, 507, 561, 566, 568, 575 (N.Y. 1811), without considering their qualifications or even their applicability to the case of fugitive slave rendition. His analogical argument assumed that the commerce and fugitive slave clauses of the Constitution conferred the same kind of authority on Congress.

56. Jack v. Martin, 12 Wend. at 321.

57. In re Martin, 16 F. Cas. 881, 884 (undated) (No. 9,154). Justice Thompson took notice that the case of *Jack v. Martin* had been decided by the New York Supreme Court but was still pending in the New York Court for the Correction of Errors. That would date it sometime between 1834 and 1835.

58. Bryan Camp, "Law and Politics and Judicial Reform in the 1846 New York Constitution Convention" (paper presented at the 25th Annual Conference on New York State History, Skidmore College, Saratoga Springs, N.Y., June 10–12, 2004).

59. Jack v. Martin, 14 Wend. 506, 538 (1835).

60. Ibid., 523.

61. Although unreported, the decision was circulated among abolitionists and reprinted as a pamphlet. It can be found in Finkelman, *Fugitive Slaves and American Courts* 1:97–103. On Hornblower's decision, see Paul Finkelman, "State Constitutional Protections of Liberty and the Antebellum New Jersey Supreme Court: Chief Justice Hornblower and the Fugitive Slave Law," *Rutgers Law Journal* 23 (Summer 1992).

62. Morris, *Free Men All,* 94–95.

63. Charles Francis Adams, ed., *Memoirs of John Quincy Adams* (Philadelphia: J. B. Lippincott, 1876), 11:336, cited in Paul Finkelman, "*Prigg v. Pennsylvania* and Northern State Courts: Anti-Slavery Use of a Pro-Slavery Decision," *Civil War History* 25 (March 1979): 5.

64. Joseph C. Burke, "What Did the Prigg Decision Really Decide?" *Pennsylvania Magazine of History and Biography* 93 (January 1969): 73–85. Historians still disagree as to exactly what *Prigg* did decide. Paul Finkelman notes that it "appears that Story did not have a solid majority behind him on every specific issue." See Finkelman, "*Prigg v. Pennsylvania* and Northern State Courts," 6. He explicates the matter more completely in Paul Finkelman, "Sorting out *Prigg v. Pennsylvania,*" *Rutgers Law Journal* 24 (Spring 1993): 605–65.

Cf. Don E. Fehrenbacher, *The Dred Scott Case: Its Significance in American Law and Politics* (New York: Oxford University Press, 1978), 43–47; Earl M. Maltz, "Slavery, Federalism, and the Structure of the Constitution," *American Journal of Legal History* 36 (October 1992): 474–76.

65. Prigg v. Pennsylvania, 41 U.S. (16 Pet.) 539, 621 (1842).

66. Joseph Story, *Commentaries on the Constitution of the United States; with a Preliminary Review of the Constitutional History of the Colonies and States, before the Adoption of the Constitution* (Boston: Hilliard, Gray, 1833). Story went to great lengths to popularize this view. It appeared almost word for word in his textbook for secondary education. See Joseph Story, *The Constitutional Class Book: Being a Brief Exposition of the Constitution of the United States, Designed for the Use of the Higher Classes in Common Schools* (Boston: Hilliard, Gray, 1834), 141.

67. I owe to Paul Finkelman the observation that Story subtly altered his historical analysis in *Prigg v. Pennsylvania,* making it into a sine qua non for the Constitution. See Paul Finkelman, "Story Telling on the Supreme Court: *Prigg v. Pennsylvania* and Justice Joseph Story's Judicial Nationalism," *Supreme Court Review* 1994: 256–59.

68. On Story's misinterpretation, see Wiecek, "Witch at the Christening," 182.

69. Prigg v. Pennsylvania, 41 U.S. (16 Pet.) 539 at 613. Story declared the clause to be self-executing and thus clothed the slaveholder with enough authority to arrest his fugitive anywhere in the federal union. But such a right was qualified by state laws insofar as it might impinge on the state's responsibility to keep the peace. The natural inference was that state legislation was required. Story positions the founders in such a way to show that it was their intent to pass such legislation. Ibid., 617.

70. Ibid., 623 (1842).

71. William M. Wiecek, "Slavery and Abolition before the United States Supreme Court, 1820–1860," *Journal of American History* 65 (June 1978): 42. Finkelman interprets Story's holding to mean that the states could not pass additional regulations but could aid in fugitive slave rendition. See Finkelman, "*Prigg v. Pennsylvania* and Northern State Courts," 10. I respectfully dissent. Story, I believe, was indicating that states could arrest or expel fugitives from their boundaries under police regulations independent of rendition. Even if it is implied that the two powers might work in concert (and Story thinks it is), it is conceptually separated by the headings of "fugitive slave rendition" on the one side and "police regulations to arrest fugitive slaves, paupers, etc." on the other.

72. Story's nationalism and judicial conservatism hardly need comment. On the subject, see R. Kent Newmyer, *Supreme Court Justice Joseph Story: Statesman of the Old Republic* (Chapel Hill: University of North Carolina Press, 1985), 371–76. On early instrumentalism, see Craig Evan Klafter, *Reason over Precedents: Origins of American Legal Thought* (Westport, Conn.: Greenwood, 1993).

73. Prigg v. Pennsylvania, 41 U.S. (16 Pet.) 539 at 621.

74. Finkelman, "Story Telling on the Supreme Court," 270–73.

75. Sturges v. Crowninshield, 17 U.S. (4 Wheat.) 122 (1819).

76. E.g., Cooley v. Bd. of Wardens, 53 U.S. (12 How.) 299 (1851); Gibbons v. Ogden, 22 U.S. (9 Wheat.) 1 (1824); Sinnot v. Davenport, 63 U.S. (22 How.) 227 (1859).

77. R. Kent Newmyer, *John Marshall and the Heroic Age of the Supreme Court* (Baton Rouge: Louisiana State University Press, 2001), 255.

78. Prigg v. Pennsylvania, 41 U.S. (16 Pet.) 539 at 622. See Karen Orren, "'A War between Officers': The Enforcement of Slavery in the Northern United States, and of the Republic for Which It Stands, before the Civil War," *Studies in American Political Development* 12 (1998): 358–59. Orren's conceptual framework makes officers' duties and rights central. I agree with Orren that antebellum Americans often thought in these terms, but that understanding does not explain adequately the use of constitutional means to oppose the fugitive slave law, especially in Wisconsin.

79. Prigg v. Pennsylvania, 41 U.S. (16 Pet.) 539 at 627.

80. Ibid., 629.

81. Moore v. Illinois, 55 U.S. (14 How.) 13 (1852).

82. Prigg v. Pennsylvania, 41 U.S. (16 Pet.) at 649.

83. Morris, *Free Men All,* 109–27.

84. Hurd, *Law of Freedom and Bondage,* 2:32, 2:50, 2:72–73.

85. Justice Woodbury made it seem as if the people of the states had surrendered the power of determining fugitive slave rendition to the federal government at the Constitutional Convention: "the federal power over [slavery] is limited and regulated by the people of the States in the constitution itself, as one of its sacred compromises, and which we possess no authority as a judicial body to modify or overrule." *Jones v. Van Zandt,* 46 U.S. (5 How.) 215, 231 (1847).

86. James Brewer Stewart, "From Moral Suasion to Political Confrontation: American Abolitionists and the Problem of Resistance, 1831–1861," in *Passages to Freedom: The Underground Railroad in History and Memory,* ed. David W. Blight (Washington, D.C.: Smithsonian Books, 2004), 81–86. The conversion of many to a more abolitionist stance was sometimes more subtle and personal than believing in a kind of grand conspiracy. It could come from personal experience. Take, for instance, the story of Rowland Gibson Hazard, a Rhode Island merchant who made frequent overland trips from Charleston to New Orleans to sell his cloth. In the 1840s, he was approached by a black sailor from Rhode Island who had been consigned to a chain gang in Charleston because he had no certificate of freedom. Hazard inquired into the matter and ultimately found twenty such men in Charleston, for whom he initiated, and won, a court action. See Myron O. Stachiw, "'For the Sake of Commerce': Slavery, Antislavery, and Northern Industry," in *The Meaning of Slavery in the North,* ed. David Roediger and Martin H. Blatt (New York: Garland, 1998), 40. For a theoretical model of how this became a historical trend, see Thomas L. Haskell, "Capitalism and the Origins of Humanitarian Sensibility, Part 2," *American Historical Review* 90 (June 1985): 547–66.

87. Although reliable numbers are impossible to come by, contemporaries and historians noted an increase in resistance by both blacks and whites. See Larry Gara, *The Liberty Line: The Legend of the Underground Railroad* (1961; repr. with new preface, Lexington: University of Kentucky Press, 1996), 152–55, Lois E. Horton, "Kidnapping and Resistance: Antislavery Direct Action in the 1850s," in *Passages to Freedom: The Underground Railroad in History and Memory,* ed. David W.

Blight (Washington, D.C.: Smithsonian Books, 2004), 154–64; Nikki M. Taylor, *Frontiers of Freedom: Cincinnati's Black Community, 1802–1868* (Athens: Ohio University Press, 2005), 138–54.

88. *History of Milwaukee, Wisconsin* (Chicago: Western Historical Company, 1881), 237, 240. Goodnow's account was reprinted in several of Wisconsin's county histories compiled in the 1880s. On this affair, see also Chauncey C. Olin, "A History of the Early Anti-Slavery Excitement in the State of Wisconsin from 1842 to 1860," microfilm, reel 1 P82-5062, Wisconsin Historical Society Library.

89. Paul Finkelman, "Fugitive Slaves, Midwestern Racial Tolerance, and the Value of 'Justice Delayed,'" *Iowa Law Review* 78 (October 1992): 89–141.

90. Fehrenbacher, *Slaveholding Republic*, 225; Paul Finkelman, *Slavery in the Courtroom: An Annotated Bibliography of American Cases* (Washington, D.C.: Library of Congress, 1985), 63–64, 69–69.

91. Leslie Friedman Goldstein, "State Resistance to Authority in Federal Unions: The Early United States (1790–1860) and the European Community (1958–94)," *Studies in American Political Development* 11 (Spring 1997): 149, 159–66; Dwight Wiley Jessup, *Reaction and Accommodation: The United States Supreme Court and Political Conflict, 1809–1835* (New York: Garland, 1987). See also Barry Friedman, "The History of the Countermajoritarian Difficulty, Part One: The Road to Judicial Supremacy," *New York University Law Review* 73 (May 1998): 356–405.

The issues that caused dissension among the states often were connected to issues far less tendentious, at least from the sectional standpoint, than fugitive slaves. For instance, the Ohio Supreme Court refused to enter the U.S. Supreme Court's judgment in the 1854 case of *Piqua Branch of the State Bank of Ohio v. Knoop* (57 U.S. [16 How.] 369 [1854]) for more than two years. *Piqua Branch* was a case about corporations and the right of states to regulate them, and it occasioned the stiffest resistance by state courts for several years. Similar struggles cropped up in the far West. The Supreme Court's distance from the western states meant that appeals were being taken far away from the hands of local authority. See Charles Warren, *The Supreme Court of the United States History*, rev. ed. (Boston: Little, Brown, 1937), 2:524–28.

92. Michael F. Holt, *The Political Crisis of the 1850s* (New York: W. W. Norton, 1978), 69–72, 82–87. For an account of the initial debate over the fugitive slave law and its subsequent retreat into obscurity in the Senate, see Fehrenbacher, *Slaveholding Republic*, 228. One scholar has claimed that the entire compromise—the fate of the Union, even—hinged on the adjustment of the Texas–New Mexico border. See Mark J. Stegmaier, *Texas, New Mexico, and the Compromise of 1850: Boundary Dispute and Sectional Crisis* (Kent, Ohio: Kent State University Press, 1996), 2.

93. *Congressional Globe*, 31st Cong., 1st sess., 481 (March 7, 1850).

94. Ibid., 2d sess., 1239 (August 21, 1850).

95. Ibid.

96. Ibid., 1st sess., 234 (January 28, 1850).

97. Fehrenbacher, *Slaveholding Republic*, 227.

98. An Act to amend, and supplementary to . . . the Act entitled "An Act respecting Fugitives from Justice, and Persons Escaping from the Service of their Masters," 9 Stat. 462 (1850) (hereafter Fugitive Slave Act of 1850). Section 7 spells out criminal penalties.

99. Ibid., section 5.

100. William M. Wiecek, *The Sources of Antislavery Constitutionalism in America, 1760–1848* (Ithaca, N.Y.: Cornell University Press, 1977), 258–66.

101. Joseph P. Thompson, *The Fugitive Slave Law: Tried by the Old and New Testaments* (New York: William Harned, 1850); J. G. Forman, *The Christian Martyrs; Or, the Conditions of Obedience to the Civil Government: A Discourse* (Boston: Wm. Crosby and H. P. Nichols, 1851); Charles P. Bush, *The Fugitive Slave Law: A Sermon, Preached in the Fourth Congregational Church, Norwich, Conn., June 25th, 1854* (Norwich: Woodworth and Perry, 1854). The constitutional issue was not unimportant—writers just spilled less ink on the subject. One very good exception was the American and Foreign Anti-Slavery Society's pamphlet, *The Fugitive Slave Bill: Its History and Unconstitutionality* (New York: William Harned, 1850).

102. Leonard Bacon, *The Higher Law: A Sermon Preached on Thanksgiving Day, November 27, 1851* (New Haven, Conn.: B. L. Hamlen, 1851), 8–9.

103. Robert H. Abzug, *Cosmos Crumbling: American Reform and the Religious Imagination* (New York: Oxford University Press, 1994), 150–62; Gary Collinson, "Anti-Slavery, Blacks, and the Boston Elite: Notes on the Reverend Charles Lowell and the West Church," *New England Quarterly* 61 (September 1988): 419–29; Chris Padgett, "Comeouterism and Antislavery Violence in Ohio's Western Reserve," in *Antislavery Violence: Sectional, Racial, and Cultural Conflict in Antebellum America*, ed. John R. McKivigan and Stanley Harrold (Knoxville: University of Tennessee Press, 1999), 206–7.

104. *Senate Journal*, 31st Cong., 2d sess., January 15 and 16, 1851, 85–88.

105. Gary Collinson, *Shadrach Minkins: From Fugitive Slave to Citizen* (Cambridge, Mass.: Harvard University Press, 1997), 11–126.

106. Gary Collinson, "'This Flagitious Offense': Daniel Webster and the Shadrach Rescue Cases, 1851–1852," *New England Quarterly* 68 (December 1995): 609–25. On Webster's equation of the rescue with treason, see Stuart Streichler, *Justice Curtis in the Civil War Era: At the Crossroads of American Constitutionalism* (Charlottesville: University of Virginia Press, 2005), 52–60.

107. Leonard W. Levy, "Sims' Case: The Fugitive Slave Law in Boston in 1851," *Journal of Negro History* 35 (January 1950): 72.

108. Finkelman, *Slavery in the Courtroom*, 103–7.

109. Campbell, *Slave Catchers*, 65–79, 111–47.

110. *Congressional Globe*, 32d Cong., 1st sess., appendix, 1103 (August 26, 1852).

111. Sumner asserted a rigid separation of powers to argue against the constitutionality of the fugitive slave law. His argument was that the present Congress was not constrained by the Supreme Court, by previous Congresses, or the country's long acquiescence to the law. It had the authority on its own to determine the law

unconstitutional. The idea that constitutional interpretation could be so fluid was just as terrifying to many as the idea that it could be fixed by one department.

112. *Congressional Globe,* 32d Cong., 1st sess., appendix, 1123 (August 26, 1852). The entire debate is found on pages 1102–25.

113. Inaugural Speech of Franklin Pierce, The Avalon Project, Yale Law School, http://www.yale.edu/lawweb/avalon/presiden/inaug/pierce.htm.

114. "Opinion on Extradition of Fugitives from Service," May 27, 1854, Caleb Cushing Papers, legal file, Attorney General's Office, box 235, May 1854, folder 2, Manuscripts Division, Library of Congress, Washington D.C. (hereafter LC).

115. "Opinion," June 3, 1854, Caleb Cushing Papers, legal file, Attorney General's Office, box 235, June 1854, folder 1, Manuscripts Division, LC. This was part of President Pierce and Attorney General Cushing's policy regarding the enforcement of the fugitive slave law. See Larry Gara, *The Presidency of Franklin Pierce* (Lawrence: University Press of Kansas, 1991), 106–11.

116. Fehrenbacher, *Slaveholding Republic,* 236.

117. See Campbell, *Slave Catchers.*

118. The most detailed—and interesting—account of the failed rescue of Anthony Burns is Albert J. Von Frank, *The Trials of Anthony Burns: Freedom and Slavery in Emerson's Boston* (Cambridge, Mass.: Harvard University Press, 1998).

119. "Opinion," June 3, 1854, Caleb Cushing Papers, legal file, Attorney General's Office, box 235, June 1854, folder 1, Manuscripts Division, LC.

CHAPTER 3

1. *Chapman's Chanticleer* (Indianapolis), February 9 and 19, 1854.

2. "Uncle Tom's Cabin," *Milwaukee Sentinel,* March 3, 13, 14, and 20, 1854.

3. This "age of the bestseller" began properly with Susan Warner's book, *The Wide, Wide World,* published by George Putnam in 1850. See G. M. Goshgarian, *To Kiss the Chastening Rod: Domestic Fiction and Sexual Ideology in the American Renaissance* (Ithaca, N.Y.: Cornell University Press, 1992).

4. Thomas F. Gossett, *Uncle Tom's Cabin and American Culture* (Dallas, Tex.: Southern Methodist University Press, 1985), 164; Stephen A. Hirsch, "Uncle Tomitudes: The Popular Reaction to *Uncle Tom's Cabin,*" in *Studies in the American Renaissance,* ed. Joel Myerson (Boston: Twayne, 1978), 318–20.

5. Gossett, *Uncle Tom's Cabin and American Culture,* 106.

6. For example, Sam, of the Shelby plantation, who dreams of becoming the master's right-hand man with Tom's sale. The same Sam deceives the slave trader (Mr. Haley), despite being ordered by his mistress to aid in the capture of two fugitives. Aunt Chloe argues with her mistress about the proper way to make pie crusts and essentially kicks her out of the kitchen. Topsy, the slave child encountered in New Orleans, represents the possibility of evil within children—she lies, cheats, and steals with no conscience to stop her. Sambo and Quimbo—Simon Legree's henchmen—are trained like bulldogs to be savage.

7. Richard Yarborough, "Strategies of Black Characterization in *Uncle Tom's Cabin* and the Early Afro-American Novel," in *New Essays on Uncle Tom's Cabin,* ed. Eric J. Sundquist (Cambridge: Cambridge University Press, 1986), 45–57.

8. Michael J. Meyer, "Toward a Rhetoric of Equality: Reflective and Refractive Images in Stowe's Language," in *The Stowe Debate: Rhetorical Strategies in Uncle Tom's Cabin,* ed. Mason I. Lowance, Ellen E. Westbrook, and R. C. De Prospo (Amherst: University of Massachusetts Press, 1994), 231–32. This is confirmed in Saidiya V. Hartman, *Scenes of Subjection: Terror, Slavery, and Self-Making in Nineteenth-Century America* (New York: Oxford University Press, 1997), 25–28.

9. James Baldwin, "Everybody's Protest Novel," in *Collected Essays,* The Library of America (New York: Library of America, 1998). Very shortly after the publication of this article in the *Partisan Review* in 1949, critics began reassessing Stowe's work. Some critics claimed that Uncle Tom himself had been victimized by the stage play. See Charles Foster, preface to *The Rungless Ladder: Harriet Beecher Stowe and New England Puritanism* (Durham, N.C.: Duke University Press, 1954), viii–ix.

10. Sentimentalism was not confined to the novel. It permeated all manner of literary forms, such as advice books, pamphlets, sermons, and political speeches. In the argument of one author, it was more than a rhetorical form—it situated the reader in such a way that emotional response consumed the sentimental subject itself. See Shirley Samuels, ed., *The Culture of Sentiment: Race, Gender, and Sentimentality in Nineteenth-Century America* (New York: Oxford University Press, 1992), especially Samuels's introductory chapter.

11. David Grimsted, "Uncle Tom from Page to Stage: Limitations of Nineteenth-Century Drama," *Quarterly Journal of Speech* 56 (October 1970): 135.

12. Gossett, *Uncle Tom's Cabin and American Culture,* 265–67.

13. Harry Birdoff, *The World's Greatest Hit: Uncle Tom's Cabin* (New York: S. F. Vanni, 1947), 88–89.

14. "Uncle Tom's Cabin," *Milwaukee Sentinel,* March 13, 1854.

15. Grimsted, "Uncle Tom from Page to Stage," 238.

16. "Uncle Tom's Cabin," *Milwaukee Sentinel,* March 13, 1854.

17. U.S. Census Office, *The Seventh Census of the United States: 1850* (Washington, D.C.: Robert Armstrong, 1853), 914–36.

18. Zachary Cooper, *Black Settlers in Rural Wisconsin* (Madison: State Historical Society of Wisconsin, 1977). This pamphlet should be used as an initial guide only; its research and conclusions are outdated.

19. Augustin Grignon, "Seventy-two Years' Recollections of Wisconsin," *Wisconsin Historical Collections* (Madison: State Historical Society of Wisconsin, 1857), 3:195–295. Online facsimile available at Wisconsin History, Wisconsin Historical Society, http://www.wisconsinhistory.org/turningpoints/search.asp?id=28.

20. I owe this observation to personal conversations with Jack Holzheuter.

21. In this respect, Wisconsin's free black community resembled others across the North. See James Oliver Horton, *Free People of Color: Inside the African American Community* (Washington, D.C.: Smithsonian Institution Press, 1993), 25–39;

Nikki M. Taylor, *Frontiers of Freedom: Cincinnati's Black Community, 1802–1868* (Athens: Ohio University Press, 2005), 28–49.

22. The census listed them as living in the First Ward. There are numerous references to blacks as barbers, maids, and unskilled laborers, but there is no published study on this subject. The best available resource is John O. Holzheuter's "Black Settlers in Early Wisconsin, 1840–2000," a manuscript collection of research notes and articles collected over the past three decades. One of his files has index cards for all Wisconsin's free black residents in each census. Cross-referencing these names with advertisements in newspapers and city directories would provide a definitive indication of what employment they held in Wisconsin's cities and towns. Unfortunately, such an enterprise is beyond the scope of this study.

23. *Annual Message of Alexander W. Randall, Governor of the State of Wisconsin* (Madison: Atwood and Rublee, 1858).

24. Kathleen N. Conzen, *Immigrant Milwaukee, 1836–1870: Accommodation and Community in a Frontier City* (Cambridge, Mass.: Harvard University Press, 1976), 127–36.

25. The first black church was the Colored Union Baptist Church, established in 1857 in Racine. A formidable collection of research is available in John O. Holzheuter, "Black Settlers in Early Wisconsin, 1840–2000," Wisconsin Historical Society Archives, Madison, Wisconsin.

26. "The Slave's Crusade in Wisconsin," *Milwaukee Sentinel*, December 22, 1901. Online facsimile available at Wisconsin History, Wisconsin Historical Society, http://www.wisconsinhistory.org/turningpoints/search.asp?id=944.

27. In re Booth, 3 Wis. 144, 150 (1854); 3 Wis. 157, 163.

28. The witnesses were residents of St. Louis, Missouri, who were questioned in the form of interrogatories. Garland v. Booth, Case #35, March 1854, U.S. District and Circuit Court, Eastern District of Wisconsin, Milwaukee, 1848–1862, Civil Case Files, RG 21, National Archives, Great Lakes Regional Facility, Chicago. (hereafter NA, Great Lakes Regional Facility.)

29. Joshua Glover, the Fugitive Slave. From the Wisconsin Historical Society Archives, Madison, Wisconsin. I am not sure where the picture comes from. Jack Holzheuter verified that it was drawn in the 1880s based on a picture provided by the family, but nothing else is known about it.

30. "Speeches at the Mass Convention of Freemen, in Young's Hall," *Daily Free Democrat*, April 15, 1854.

31. Cited in Nancy F. Cott, "Marriage and Women's Citizenship in the United States, 1830–1934," *American Historical Review* 103 (December 1998): 1447.

32. *Opinion of Attorney General Edward Bates on Citizenship* (Washington, D.C.: Government Printing Office, 1862). This was part of the executive branch's repudiation of *Dred Scott*.

33. "Citizen Daniel," *Harper's New Monthly Magazine* 8 (May 1854): 842.

34. Joyce Appleby, *Inheriting the Revolution: The First Generation of Americans* (Cambridge, Mass.: Harvard University Press, Belknap Press, 2000), 28.

35. Cott, "Marriage and Women's Citizenship," 1451–59. It did, however, coincide with rising concern for the rights of married women. Legislatures—including Wisconsin's—began considering acts to protect married women's property in the 1850s. These protections afforded to the weak (from a legal standpoint) fared much better in legislatures than did the extension of political rights, like the franchise. See, in general, Hendrik Hartog, *Man and Wife in America: A History* (Cambridge, Mass.: Harvard University Press, 2000).

36. U.S. Constitution, art. IV, § 1.

37. Joseph Story, *Commentaries on the Constitution of the United States; with a Preliminary Review of the Constitutional History of the Colonies and States, before the Adoption of the Constitution* (Boston: Hilliard, Gray, 1833), 673.

38. James Kent, *Commentaries on American Law*, 2d ed., 4 vols. (New York: O. Halsted, 1832).

39. Rogers M. Smith, *Civic Ideals: Conflicting Visions of Citizenship in U.S. History* (New Haven, Conn.: Yale University Press, 1997), 152–53.

40. William J. Novak, *The People's Welfare: Law and Regulation in Nineteenth-Century America* (Chapel Hill: University of North Carolina Press, 1996), 168.

41. Ibid., 208–11.

42. See, e.g., Smith, *Civic Ideals*, 170–73, 186–89, 220–25. The police power's origins in early modern governance cannot be overemphasized, as many of the nineteenth-century powers granted to justices of the peace, town councils, and overseers of the poor—powers that included summary commitments, "warning out" (i.e., expulsion), and arbitrary restrictions on liberty—were derived from a common-law regime that coexisted with newer, more liberal ideas about governance. On this complicated transition, see William J. Novak, "The Legal Transformation of Citizenship in Nineteenth-Century America," in *The Democratic Experiment: New Directions in American Political History*, ed. Meg Jacobs, William J. Novak, and Julian E. Zelizer (Princeton, N.J.: Princeton University Press, 2003), 85–119; Christopher L. Tomlins, *Law, Labor, and Ideology in the Early American Republic* (New York: Cambridge University Press, 1993).

43. An Act Concerning Real Property, § 5, in *Statutes of the Territory of Wisconsin* (Albany: Packard, Van Benthuysen, 1839). Act Concerning Real Property, Wis. Stat. tit. 1 (1849); Of Elections other than for Town Officers, Wis. Stat. tit. 2 (1849). Milwaukee's German-language newspapers kept their communities informed about these differences. In "Naturalisation und Bürgerschaft," *Der See-Bote* January 11, 1855, the German paper explained that states defined citizenship and political participation and that other states were obliged to recognize only certain privileges.

44. Smith, *Civic Ideals*, 215.

45. Ibid., 143. An Act more effectually to provide for the National Defence by establishing an Uniform Militia throughout the United States, 1 Stat. 271 (1792).

46. James H. Kettner, *The Development of American Citizenship, 1608–1870* (Chapel Hill: University of North Carolina Press, 1978), 315–16.

47. In general, see Paul Finkelman, "Prelude to the Fourteenth Amendment: Black Legal Rights in the Antebellum North," *Rutgers Law Journal* 17 (Spring and Summer 1986): 415–82; Leon F. Litwack, *North of Slavery: The Negro in the Free States, 1790–1860* (Chicago: University of Chicago Press, 1961).

48. See generally, Stephen Middleton, *The Black Laws in the Old Northwest: A Documentary History* (Westport, Conn.: Greenwood, 1993).

49. See generally Finkelman, "Prelude to the Fourteenth Amendment." For Ohio, see Stephen Middleton, *The Black Laws: Race and the Legal Process in Early Ohio* (Athens: Ohio University Press, 2005).

50. Michael J. McManus, *Political Abolitionism in Wisconsin, 1840–1861* (Kent, Ohio: Kent State University Press, 1998), 64–65.

51. In re Booth, 3 Wis. 13, 82 [3 Wis. 1, 83] (1854).

52. "High-Handed Outrage!" *Racine Advocate,* March 12, 1854.

53. Gary Collinson, *Shadrach Minkins: From Fugitive Slave to Citizen* (Cambridge, Mass.: Harvard University Press, 1997), 81–84; Leonard W. Levy, "Sims' Case: The Fugitive Slave Law in Boston in 1851," *Journal of Negro History* 35 (January 1950): 51.

54. "Great Excitement!" *Milwaukee Sentinel,* March 13, 1854.

55. See John G. Gregory, *History of Milwaukee, Wisconsin* (Chicago: S. J. Clarke, 1931), 746.

56. *Daily Wisconsin,* January 15, 1855. See *Milwaukee News,* August 16, 1855, for confirmation that Glover was an adulterer, at least in the eyes of the Democratic press.

57. *Daily Free Democrat,* March 13, 1854.

58. Ibid., March 21, 1854.

59. Both these elements are in the other recorded account of a fugitive slave in Wisconsin, the story of Caroline Quarles and her escape to Canada via the Underground Railroad. She was first betrayed by a corrupted black with whom she took shelter and saved at the last moment by a young boy. The lawyers who aided the slave catchers set out with rifles and whiskey. See *History of Milwaukee, Wisconsin* (Chicago: Western Historical Society, 1881). I consider it in more detail in chapter 2.

60. "The Fugitive Slave Law and the Future," *Daily Wisconsin,* January 15, 1855.

61. William L. Van Deburg, *Slavery and Race in American Popular Culture* (Madison: University of Wisconsin Press, 1984), 17–18.

62. Robert C. Toll, *Blacking Up: The Minstrel Show in Nineteenth Century America* (New York: Oxford University Press, 1974), 25.

63. Ibid., 27–36.

64. Ibid., 74–79.

65. This is itself a complicated problem of minstrelsy. The "authenticity" of African dances and songs, the fascination of audiences with the exotic black, and the ridicule involved in donning blackface all worked both to degrade blacks and to draw them together. Eric Lott, *Love and Theft: Blackface Minstrelsy and the American Working Class* (New York: Oxford University Press, 1993), 112–18.

66. James D. Bilotta, *Race and the Rise of the Republican Party, 1848–1865* (New York: Peter Lang, 1992), 238–45; David Roediger, *The Wages of Whiteness* (London: Verso, 1991), 127.

67. The troupe ran ads for its run in Milwaukee at Young's Hall, advertising an exotic dancer and "Fun Without Vulgarity," *Milwaukee Sentinel*, March 25, 1855.

68. "Ethiopian Minstrels at Young's Hall," *Milwaukee Sentinel*, February 10, 1855.

69. "Anti-Slave Catchers' Convention," *Daily Wisconsin*, April 14, 1854.

70. "Negro-Headed," *Daily Wisconsin*, November 18, 1854.

71. *Milwaukee News*, March 22, 1854.

72. *Milwaukee Sentinel*, July 22, 1855.

73. There were a variety of bases for racist belief, not the least of which was the social and political context of the Free Soil movement, which sought to exclude all blacks, slave or free, from the territories. Eric Foner, "Politics and Prejudice: The Free Soil Party and the Negro, 1849–1852," *Journal of Negro History* 50 (October 1965): 239–56. Racial attitudes, however, had been shaped much earlier. The classic work on this is Winthrop D. Jordan, *White over Black: American Attitudes toward the Negro, 1550–1812* (Chapel Hill: University of North Carolina Press, 1968). By the mid-nineteenth century, elite intellectuals were writing racism into scientific enterprises at the same time that competitive individualism gave antebellum Americans a reason to justify the continued repression of an entire race of people. Bilotta, *Race and the Rise of the Republican Party*; George M. Fredrickson, *The Black Image in the White Mind: The Debate on Afro-American Character and Destiny, 1817–1914* (New York: Harper and Row, 1971).

74. *Milwaukee Sentinel*, March 13, 1854.

75. *Daily Free Democrat*, March 13, 1854.

76. "Ein Negerslave in unserer Jail!, Marz 11," *Der See-Bote*, March 15, 1854.

77. "High-Handed Outrage!" *Racine Advocate*, March 12, 1855.

78. "Speech of Byron Paine in the Defense of S. M. Booth," *Milwaukee Sentinel*, January 24, 1854.

79. "Ein Negerslave in unserer Jail!" *Der See-Bote*, March 11, 1854.

80. William L. Andrews, "The Representation of Slavery and the Rise of Afro-American Literary Realism, 1865–1920," in *Slavery and the Literary Imagination*, ed. Deborah McDowell and Arnold Rampersad (Baltimore: Johns Hopkins University Press, 1989).

81. Elizabeth B. Clark, "'The Sacred Rights of the Weak': Pain, Sympathy, and the Culture of Individual Rights in Antebellum America," *Journal of American History* 82 (September 1995): 463–93.

82. "Great Meeting in the Court-House Square!" *Daily Free Democrat*, March 13, 1854.

83. "Ein Negerslave in unserer Jail!" *Der See-Bote*, March 11, 1854.

84. "Anti-Slave Catchers' Convention," *Daily Wisconsin*, April 14, 1854.

85. Research compiled by Kevin Dier-Zimmel for the Fairwater Historical Society, http://www.wlhn.org/topics/abolition/Douglass/index.html.

86. "Barber-ous Treatment," *Madison State Journal,* July 10, 1854. On William H. Noland, see Edward Noyes, "A Negro in Mid-nineteenth Century Wisconsin Life and Politics," *Wisconsin Academy Review* 15 (Fall 1968): 2–6.

87. *Racine Advocate,* reprinted in *Daily Free Democrat,* March 17, 1854.

88. "Anti-Slave Catchers' Convention," *Daily Wisconsin,* April 14, 1854.

CHAPTER 4

1. U.S. v. Timothy D. Morris, Case #31, January Term 1854, U.S. District and Circuit Court, Eastern District of Wisconsin, Milwaukee, 1848–1862, Civil Case Files, RG 21, National Archives, Great Lakes Regional Facility, Chicago.

2. The act of recaption had already been held valid in Weimer v. Sloane, 29 F. Cas. 599 (D.C.D. Ohio 1854) (No. 17, 363). The case, however, had little to do with violence. A similar case arose in Indiana, in which a fugitive charged a marshal with assault and battery. Although the Indiana Supreme Court fully admitted that Congress had the sole power to legislate on the matter, it held that "[t]he assault and battery, and the extorting of money were no part of [the marshal's] official duty, under [the Fugitive Slave Act] or any other act, and were unlawful. We perceive no conflict between any provision of the fugitive slave law, and the common law right to maintain an action for a personal injury." See Freeman v. Robinson, 7 Ind. 255, 256 (1855).

There were, of course, salient differences—Garland was not a marshal, and the case in Racine was a criminal prosecution, not a civil action. But the principle announced by the Indiana Supreme Court suggested that there were limits to the use of violence in the execution of the law that Judge Miller was unwilling to consider. Additionally, Freeman's suit was dismissed (and the dismissal upheld in *Freeman v. Robinson*) because the statute under which Freeman brought the suit was construed to apply only to state officers. Still, the Indiana Supreme Court indicated that a common-law action would lie.

3. "Case of Garland, the Slave-Catcher, before Judge Miller's Court," *Daily Free Democrat,* March 13, 1854.

4. Miller's citation of the Force Act inspired a lively dialogue in the press about its applicability in the present case. The statute, officially titled An Act further to provide for the collection of duties on imports, 7 Stat. 632 (1833), technically protected U.S. officers only in revenue cases. For evidence of Miller's concern for Garland's safety, see J. R. Sharpstein to W. B. Streeter, March 20, 1854, Solicitor of the Treasury Manuscripts, L/R from U.S. District Attorneys, Marshals, Clerks of Court, 1853–1881, Wisconsin, RG 206, NA; see also W. B. Streeter to John Sharpstein, June 14, 1854, Solicitor of the Treasury Manuscripts, Letters Sent, 1820–1934, RG 206, NA.

5. Copy of arrest warrants issued by commissioner, July Term 1854, Papers of the Grand Jury; U.S. District and Circuit Court, Eastern District of Wisconsin, Milwaukee, 1848–1862, Criminal Records, 1848–1862, Criminal Case Files, 1849–1862, RG 21, NA, Great Lakes Regional Facility.

6. Arrest warrant for Sherman M. Booth, Ex parte Booth, 3 Wis. 134, 135 (1854); 3 Wis. 145, 146.

7. William Blackstone, *Commentaries on the Laws of England, in Four Books* (Oxford: Clarendon Press, 1769), 4:222–23. The American statutes concerning riot achieved two changes in the English law. They raised the number of participants from three to twelve, and they also generally softened the penalties of the English law. The punishment directed by English statute was death, although this was mitigated by statute in 1837 and, on some occasions, by English judges. See John Beattie, *Crime and the Courts in England, 1660–1800* (Princeton, N.J.: Princeton University Press, 1986).

It was made clear in early Massachusetts case law that the legal fiction of force and arms could be discarded in an indictment (or at least not repeated), so long as either violence or terror had been inflicted. Commonwealth v. Runnels, 10 Mass. 518 (1813). This was commonplace in the United States. A complete discussion of this subject can be found in Howard Robert Baker II, "The Rescue of Joshua Glover: Lawyers, Popular Constitutionalism, and the Fugitive Slave Law in Wisconsin" (Ph.D. diss., University of California, Los Angeles, 2004), 153–56.

8. Wharton, *Treatise on the Criminal Law of the United States,* 723.

9. *Daily Free Democrat,* March 23, 1854.

10. Alfons J. Beitzinger, "Federal Law Enforcement and the Booth Cases," *Marquette Law Review* 41 (Summer 1957): 11.

11. I take this portion of the narrative from the *Daily Wisconsin,* March 24, 1854. It is in agreement with the reports in the *Milwaukee Sentinel,* the *Daily Free Democrat,* and the *Milwaukee News.*

12. *Daily Free Democrat,* March 24, 1854.

13. "United States v. Sherman M. Booth," ibid.

14. Ibid.

15. "United States v. Sherman M. Booth," *Daily Free Democrat,* March 24, 1854.

16. For initial reports about this, see "Great Meeting in the Court-House Square!" ibid., March 13, 1854. This was confirmed in court testimony by Charles Cotton himself, who admitted being evasive but claimed that he only said he had not taken part in a "kidnapping." See "U.S. v. Sherman Booth," *Daily Wisconsin,* January 11, 1855.

17. "Judge Smith's Decision," *Daily Wisconsin,* June 6, 1854.

18. The German press translated these arguments without any of the Anglo historical references: "[M]an die Sache nicht etwa in Geheimen abmachen, sondern dem armen Manne . . . eine öffentliche Verhandlung gestatten möge," *Der See-Bote,* March 11, 1854. Translation: One should not do these things in secret, but rather this poor man should have a public hearing.

19. "U.S. v. Sherman Booth," *Daily Free Democrat,* March 22–24, 1854. James Paine repeated this complaint throughout his closing statement.

20. *Milwaukee Sentinel,* March 13, 1854. They based this on information from Racine, provided by the district attorney who was preparing Garland's indictment. See "High-Handed Outrage!" *Racine Morning Advocate,* March 12, 1854.

21. "History of Glover's Arrest," *Daily Free Democrat* March 13, 1854.

22. *Milwaukee Sentinel,* March 13, 1854.

23. "Kidnapping Case! Man-Hunters on our Soil!!" *Daily Free Democrat,* March 13, 1854.

24. A particularly suggestive essay on the depiction of violence in the French Revolution can be found at Imaging the French Revolution, Center For History and New Media, George Mason University, http://chnm.gmu.edu/revolution/imaging/essays/cameron1.html as part of an online collaboration organized by Jack Censer and Lynn Hunt. Information regarding this project can be found on the project's homepage, http://chnm.gmu.edu/revolution/imaging, or in Jack Censer and Lynn Hunt, "Imaging the French Revolution: Depictions of the French Revolutionary Crowd," *American Historical Review* 110 (February 2005): 38–45.

25. "Mr. Sharpstein's Argument; United States Commissioner's Court," *Daily Free Democrat,* March 24, 1854.

26. Garland v. Booth, Case #35, March 1854, U.S. District and Circuit Court, Eastern District of Wisconsin, Milwaukee, 1848–1862, Civil Case Files, RG 21, NA, Great Lakes Regional Facility.

27. "Speeches of the Mass Convention of Freemen, in Young's Hall," *Daily Free Democrat,* April 15, 1854. None of Milwaukee's newspapers reported what Kilgore's or Mitchell's first names were.

28. "Anti-Slave Catchers' Convention," *Daily Wisconsin,* April 14, 1854.

29. This was Lysander Spooner's argument. William M. Wiecek, *The Sources of Antislavery Constitutionalism in America, 1760–1848* (Ithaca, N.Y.: Cornell University Press, 1977).

30. "Speeches of the Mass Convention of Freemen, in Young's Hall," *Daily Free Democrat,* April 15, 1854.

31. Ibid.

32. "In the Case of Mr. Booth," June 3, 1854, Caleb Cushing Papers, legal file, Attorney General's Office, box 236, Manuscripts Division, LC; W. B. Streeter to John Sharpstein, June 14, 1854; Solicitor of the Treasury Manuscripts, Letters Sent, 1820–1934, RG 206, NA.

33. See Marilyn Grant, "Judge Levi Hubbell: A Man Impeached," *Wisconsin Magazine of History* 64 (Autumn 1980): 28–39.

34. Generally, see Alfons J. Beitzinger, *Edward G. Ryan: Lion of the Law* (Madison: State Historical Society of Wisconsin, 1960). Beitzinger is far more ebullient than I about Ryan's character. A look at his papers reveals a man not at all conflicted over the issue of slavery and more interested in preserving the status quo than in standing up for democratic liberty and right, as was his claim. He opposed the admission of females to the bar, even if they were qualified, and wrote that the idea of progress simply did not apply to the continent of Africa and its peoples. I do not mean here to condemn Ryan on his prejudices but rather to point out how desperately he clung to them despite his long association with intelligent members of the bar who asserted otherwise. Ryan held a deep fear of progressive change. Sadly, he allowed that characteristic to become a tragic flaw.

His quick anger was legend. A revealing exchange of letters between Ryan and Milwaukee attorney James Jenkins in 1879 demonstrated his wrath. Ryan wrote to ask whether Jenkins had room in his office for Ryan's son, whom he wanted to apprentice to a lawyer. Jenkins wrote back to say that, sadly, he had no room, and suggested several other attorneys who might have space. Ryan curtly dismissed him and shut off communication. After Jenkins made several apologetic entreaties, Ryan wrote back to inform him how hurt he was. In a terribly revealing statement, he said, "[F]or after all, it is always mortifying to be refused a favor, perhaps more than to be denied a right." Edward G. Ryan to James Jenkins, November 18, 1879, Edward G. Ryan Papers, 1815–1880, Wisconsin Historical Society Archives, Madison, Wisconsin.

35. "U.S. v. Sherman M. Booth; U.S. v. John A. Messinger; U.S. v. John Ryecraft," Criminal Docket Book, 1848–1862, pp. 72–82; U.S. District and Circuit Court, Eastern District of Wisconsin, Milwaukee, 1848–1862, Criminal Records, 1848–1862, RG 21, NA, Great Lakes Regional Facility.

36. Ex parte Booth, 3 Wis. 134 [3 Wis. 145] (1854).

37. John Sharpstein to W. B. Streeter, November 19, 1854, Solicitor of the Treasury Manuscripts, L/R from U.S. District Attorneys, Marshals, Clerks of Court, 1853–1881, Wisconsin, RG 206, box 152, NA.

38. See, e.g., "U.S. v. John Ryecraft," *Milwaukee Sentinel,* November 19, 1854.

39. The criminal counts were (1) that Ryecraft unlawfully obstructed Cotton's execution of a lawful warrant issued by the U.S. District Court for the District of Missouri and the U.S. District Court for the District of Wisconsin, and that Ryecraft unlawfully removed Joshua Glover from Cotton's custody; (2) that Ryecraft aided in the escape of one Joshua Glover; and (3) that Ryecraft removed Joshua Glover from the lawful custody of Cotton. The warrant for Glover's arrest was appended to the final count.

40. E. G. Ryan to C. Cushing, December 11, 1854, Cushing Papers, General Correspondence, box 71, Manuscripts Division, LC. Lakin and Steever did file a motion to quash, because the indictment did not prove that Glover owed service as a slave. Ryan referred to this as the "only point of law raised throughout the case." Judge Miller overruled the motion.

41. "Report of the Ryecraft Trial," *Milwaukee Sentinel,* November 21, 1854. The testimony cited is from the first day of trial, November 17.

42. Ibid.

43. This was not explicitly asserted at the trial. See Wharton, *Treatise on the Criminal Laws of the United States,* 723.

44. "Report of the Ryecraft Trial." *Milwaukee Daily Sentinel,* November 21, 1854. The testimony cited is from the first day of trial, November 17.

45. U.S. v. Rycraft, 27 F. Cas. 918(D.C.D. Wis. 1854) (No. 16,211), Judge Miller's charge to the jury. John Ryecraft's name was alternately spelled "Ryecraft" and "Rycraft," both in legal records and in print sources.

46. "Report of the Ryecraft Trial." *Milwaukee Daily Sentinel,* November 21, 1854. The testimony cited is from the first day of trial, November 17.

47. Ibid.

48. Ibid. The testimony cited is from the second day of trial, November 18.

49. U.S. v. Rycraft, 27 F. Cas. 918 (C.D.C. Wis. 1854) (No. 16,211). The case report consists solely of Judge Miller's charge to the jury.

50. Ibid.

51. Ibid.

52. Ibid.

53. "Report of the Ryecraft Trial." *Milwaukee Sentinel,* November 21, 1854. The testimony cited is from the second day of trial, November 18.

54. Ibid.

55. "Judge Hubbell Sends Law and Order Toast," *Daily Wisconsin,* March 21, 1854.

56. "A Rap over the Knuckles," *Daily Free Democrat,* March 21, 1854.

57. *Milwaukee News,* April 13, 1854.

58. "The Boston Slave Case," *Milwaukee News,* June 5, 1854.

59. Sharpstein to Streeter, November 19, 1854, Solicitor of the Treasury Manuscripts, L/R from U.S. District Attorneys, Marshals, Clerks of Court, Wisconsin, RG 206, box 152, NA.

60. Ryan to Cushing, November 20, 1854, Cushing Papers, General Correspondence, box 71, Manuscripts Division, LC.

61. A. Hyatt Smith to Cushing, November 21, 1854, Cushing Papers, General Correspondence, box 71, Manuscripts Division, LC.

62. K. F. Bartlett to Cushing, November 26, 1854, Cushing Papers, General Correspondence, box 71, Manuscripts Division, LC.

63. "S. M. Booth Found Guilty!" *Milwaukee Sentinel,* January 15, 1855.

64. On December 11, Ryan formally submitted his bill, noting rather wryly that he believed K. F. Bartlett had already sent it along. See Ryan to Cushing, December 11, 1854, Cushing Papers, General Correspondence, box 71, Manuscripts Division, LC.

65. K. F. Bartlett to Cushing, November 26, 1854, Cushing Papers, General Correspondence, box 71, Manuscripts Division, LC.

66. Interrogatories, in Garland v. Booth, Case #35, March 1854, U.S. District and Circuit Court, Eastern District of Wisconsin, Milwaukee, 1848–1862, Civil Case Files, RG 21, NA, Great Lakes Regional Facility.

67. United States of America for the use of Benammi S. Garland v. Stephen V. R. Ableman, Jacob A. Hoover, John J. Perkins, and John Plankinton, January Term 1855, Vol. C, Appearance Docket Books, Law Records 1849–1862, U.S. District and Circuit Court, Eastern District of Wisconsin, Milwaukee, 1848–1862, RG 21, NA, Great Lakes Regional Facility.

68. Grand Jury Presentments, January Term, 1855, January 6, 1855, Criminal Records, 1848–1862, Criminal Case Files, 1849–1862, U.S. District and Circuit Court, Eastern District of Wisconsin, Milwaukee, 1848–1862, RG 21, NA, Great Lakes Regional Facility.

69. District Attorney Sharpstein and Judge Miller also faced a charge of false imprisonment from Booth, who had procured a writ of capias from the Milwau-

kee County Court. They were forced to post bail on the eve of Booth's trial. This prompted Miller to write Attorney General Cushing, asking for his support for a congressional bill protecting federal officers. See Beitzinger, "Federal Law Enforcement and the Booth Cases," 32.

70. "The Speech of Byron Paine," *Buffalo Express,* reprinted in the *Milwaukee Sentinel,* February 12, 1855.

71. Acts 12:4–10 (Revised Standard Version).

72. "Speech of Byron Paine in the Defense of S. M. Booth," *Milwaukee Sentinel,* January 24, 1854.

73. Blackstone, *Commentaries on the Laws of England,* 4:222–28.

74. Wharton, *Treatise on the Criminal Law of the United States,* 508–12.

75. "Speech of Byron Paine in the Defense of S. M. Booth," *Milwaukee Sentinel,* January 24, 1854. Writing under the pseudonym "Watchman," Paine claimed after the Ryecraft trial that the judge had denied the "well known rule of law, that in criminal trials, THE JURY ARE JUDGES OF BOTH LAW AND FACT," *Milwaukee Sentinel,* November 28, 1854.

76. For a discussion of the role of juries in revolutionary America as a part of representative government, see J. R. Pole, "Reflections on American Law and the American Revolution," *William and Mary Quarterly* 50 (January 1993): 126–41. For the strong eighteenth-century Atlantic roots of this doctrine, see Peter Charles Hoffer, "Custom as Law: A Comment on J. R. Pole's 'Reflections,'" *William and Mary Quarterly* 50 (January 1993): 160–67. Both Jefferson and John Jay preserved the distinction between juries as finders of fact and judges as finders of law but as late as the 1790s asserted that, in matters concerning public liberty, juries could vote their conscience. See William E. Nelson, "*Marbury v. Madison* and the Rule of Law," *Tennessee Law Review* 71 (Winter 2004): 221.

77. Matthew P. Harrington, "The Law-Finding Function of the American Jury," in "The American Jury," special issue, *Wisconsin Law Review* 1999: 423–31. J. R. Pole notes the move toward predictability in proceedings and, thus, the decline of the jury's law-finding function in "Reflections on American Law and the American Revolution," 158.

78. U.S. v. Wilson, 28 F. Cas. 699, 712 (C.C.E.D. Penn. 1830) (No. 16,730).

79. U.S. v. Shive, 27 F. Cas. 1065, 1066 (C.C.E.D. Penn. 1832) (No. 16,278).

80. U.S. v. Morris, 26 F. Cas. 1323, 1336 (C.C.D. Mass. 1851). (No. 15,815); Robert M. Cover, *Justice Accused: Antislavery and the Judicial Process* (New Haven, Conn.: Yale University Press, 1975), 191.

81. David A. Pepper, "Nullifying History: Modern-Day Misuse of the Right to Decide the Law," *Case Western Reserve Law Review* 50 (Spring 2000): 628–32. This contentious and highly problematic article nevertheless does a great service in laying out many examples of jury nullification. It was an extraordinarily difficult issue, one that practically and theoretically was limited to issues of great import. Although Pepper does not draw the conclusion, "jury review" was an extraordinary power in the antebellum period, just as "judicial review" was. Both spoke to the possibility of nullification on the basis of fundamental law, but with

different implications in terms of apportionment of power and far-reaching effect.

82. "Speech of Byron Paine in the Defense of S. M. Booth," *Milwaukee Sentinel,* January 24, 1855.

83. Incidentally, this reflects the charge given to the jury by Justice Henry Baldwin in U.S. v. Wilson, 28 F. Cas. 699, 712 (C.C.E.D. Pa. 1830) (No. 16,730). Clearly anticipating that some jurors might object to the death penalty, Baldwin instructed them that they might alleviate their conscience by finding only the facts and allowing the court to assess the general verdict.

84. "Speech of Byron Paine in the Defense of S. M. Booth," *Milwaukee Sentinel,* January 24, 1855.

85. Ibid.

86. "The Fugitive Slave Law and the Future," *Daily Wisconsin,* January 15, 1855.

CHAPTER 5

The epigraph is taken from a letter written by John Sharpstein to William Streeter, and can be found in Solicitor of the Treasury Manuscripts, Letters Sent, 1820–1934, RG 206, box 152, National Archives, College Park, Maryland.

1. Vroman Mason, "The Fugitive Slave Law in Wisconsin, with Reference to Nullification Sentiment," *Proceedings of the State Historical Society of Wisconsin* 43 (1895): 136.

2. Byron Paine, *Argument of Byron Paine, Esq. and Opinion of Hon. A. D. Smith on the Unconstitutionality of the Fugitive Slave Act* (Milwaukee, Wis.: Sherman Booth, 1854), 1 (hereafter *Argument of Byron Paine*).

3. Ibid., 4.

4. William M. Wiecek, *The Sources of Antislavery Constitutionalism in America, 1760–1848* (Ithaca, N.Y.: Cornell University Press, 1977), 202–11.

5. *Speech of Salmon P. Chase in the Case of the Colored Woman, Matilda: Who Was Brought before the Court of Common Pleas of Hamilton County, Ohio, by Writ of Habeas Corpus, March 11, 1837* (Cincinnati: Pugh and Dodd, 1837).

6. Birney v. Ohio, 8 Ohio 230 (1837).

7. U.S. v. Wilson, 28 F. Cas. 699 (C.C.E.D. Pa. 1830) (No. 16,730). This engaged the crucial question of comity, dealt with more fully in Finkelman, *An Imperfect Union: Slavery, Federalism, and Comity* (Chapel Hill: University of North Carolina Press, 1981), 162–65.

8. Birney v. Ohio, 8 Ohio at 237.

9. Salmon P. Chase to Gerrit Smith Esq., May 14, 1842, in John Niven, ed., *The Salmon P. Chase Papers* (Kent, Ohio: Kent State University Press, 1994), 2:98.

10. Salmon P. Chase, "An Address to the Cincinnati Liberty Party," in Charles Dexter Cleveland, *Anti-Slavery Addresses of 1844 and 1845 by Salmon Portland Chase and Charles Dexter Cleveland* (Philadelphia: J. A. Bancroft, 1867).

11. Foner, *Free Soil, Free Labor, Free Men: The Ideology of the Republican Party before the Civil War* (1970; repr., with new introduction, New York: Oxford Uni-

versity Press, 1995), 73–102. This same subject is explored in relation to its understanding of constitutionalism in Wiecek, *Sources of Antislavery Constitutionalism in America*, 202–11. The general outlines of this were reconfirmed in G. Edward White, "Reconstructing the Constitutional Jurisprudence of Salmon P. Chase," *Northern Kentucky University Law Review* 21 (Fall 1993): 41–116, although White's "deep conviction jurisprudence" is problematic. See Herman Belz, "Deep-Conviction Jurisprudence and *Texas v. White:* A Comment on G. Edward White's Historicist Interpretation of Chief Justice Chase," *Northern Kentucky University Law Review* 21 (Fall 1993): 117–31.

12. Salmon P. Chase to John P. Hale, May 12, 1847, in Niven, *Salmon P. Chase Papers*, 2:151.

13. William H. Seward to Salmon P. Chase, March 24, 1847, ibid., 2:147.

14. Salmon P. Chase to John P. Hale, May 12, 1847, ibid., 2:151.

15. Salmon P. Chase, *Reclamation of Fugitives from Service: An Argument for the Defendant, Submitted to the Supreme Court of the United States, at the December Term 1846 in the Case of Wharton Jones v. John Vanzandt* (Cincinnati: R. P. Donough, 1847); *The Trial of Thomas Sims, on an Issue of Personal Liberty, on the Claim of James Potter, of Georgia, against Him, as an Alleged Fugitive from Service; Arguments of Robert Rantoul, Jr. and Charles G. Loring, with the Decision of George T. Curtis; Phonographic Report by Dr. James W. Stone. Boston, April 7–12, 1851* (Boston: Wm. S. Damrell, 1851) (hereafter *Trial of Thomas Sims*).

16. *Argument of Byron Paine*, 1. The states rights argument followed from the strict constructionalist views of Chase and others who organized the Liberty Party. See Foner, *Free Soil, Free Labor, Free Men*, 134–36.

17. The historical parallel was problematic. Jefferson and Madison had protested the Alien and Sedition Acts by going to their state legislators, not by asking their state courts to strike down the laws. The Virginia and Kentucky Resolutions produced heated responses from other states. James Madison attempted to smooth out some of these difficulties in his "Report of 1800," the full text of which can be found in William Thomas Hutchinson, William M. E. Rachal, and Robert Allen Rutland, eds., *Papers of James Madison* (Charlottesville: University of Virginia Press, 1991), 17:303–50.

18. *Argument of Byron Paine*, 18.

19. Charles Sumner to Byron Paine, August 8, 1854, Byron Paine Papers, 1845–1869, Wisconsin State Historical Society Archives, Madison, Wisconsin.

20. "The Glover Rescue Case," *Daily Wisconsin*, May 29, 1854.

21. "The Habeas Corpus Case," *Milwaukee Sentinel,* July 3, 1854. This was according to the *Daily Wisconsin*'s Madison correspondent.

22. In re Booth, 3 Wis. 13, 58 [3 Wis. 1, 54] (1854).

23. Rollin Carlos Hurd, *A Treatise on the Right of Personal Liberty and on the Writ of Habeas Corpus and the Practice Connected with It, with a View of the Law of Extradition of Fugitives* (Albany, N.Y.: W. C. Little, 1858), 165–67.

24. Thomas Sims's Case, 61 Mass. 285, 309 (1851).

25. In re Booth, 3 Wis. 13 at 61 [3 Wis. 1 at 57].

26. Ibid., 87 [89].

27. *Argument of Byron Paine,* 2.

28. The state of Rhode Island made a response and claimed in it that the U.S. Supreme Court was the only body qualified to settle constitutional disputes. This is evidence of the attractiveness of judicial supremacy as a doctrine to New England Federalists, but it does not indicate its general prevalence. Many Democratic-Republicans were unwilling to "oppose in a constitutional manner" (as Madison and Jefferson would term it) federal statutes immediately before the election of 1800. That election, many believed, would settle the enormous constitutional questions raised by the Alien and Sedition Acts. See Larry D. Kramer, *The People Themselves: Popular Constitutionalism and Judicial Review* (New York: Oxford University Press, 2004), 130–44.

29. For the full text of the "Report of 1800," see Hutchinson, Rachal, and Rutland, *Papers of James Madison,* 17:303–50. The quote on this page comes from page 310.

30. This is Larry Kramer's provocative thesis in *The People Themselves.* Kramer's book, preceded by several articles and conference presentations, created a stir well before its release. The serious criticism of Kramer's work has generally admitted that his best evidence for popular constitutionalism has come from the founding period through the Civil War. Larry Alexander and Lawrence B. Solum, "Book Review: Popular? Constitutionalism? *The People Themselves: Popular Constitutionalism and Judicial Review,* by Larry D. Kramer," *Harvard Law Review* 118 (March 2005); Daniel J. Hulsebosch, "Book Review: Bringing the People Back In: *The People Themselves: Popular Constitutionalism and Judicial Review,* By Larry D. Kramer," *New York University Law Review* 80 (May 2005): 653–82; Robert J. Kaczorowski, "Popular Constitutionalism versus Justice in Plainclothes: Reflections from History," *Fordham Law Review* 73 (March 2005): 1415–38. One of the best critical assessments of Kramer's work both confirms its excellent treatment of the antebellum era and criticizes its rather hurried treatment of the Civil War to present. L. A. Powe, Jr., "Are 'the People' Missing in Action (and Should Anyone Care)?: *The People Themselves: Popular Constitutionalism and Judicial Review,*" *Texas Law Review* 83 (February 2005).

Kramer's notion of constitutionalism deserves special notice by historians because of its sensitivity to the term's changing meaning from the seventeenth through the eighteenth centuries. For a more detailed exposition, see J. G. A. Pocock, *The Ancient Constitution and the Feudal Law: A Study of English Historical Thought in the Seventeenth Century; A Reissue with a Retrospect* (New York: Cambridge University Press, 1987). Kramer also explains his understanding of the customary Constitution in Kramer, *People Themselves,* 9–14. It is worth mentioning here that seventeenth-century Englishmen understood constitutionalism very differently from eighteenth-century American revolutionaries, a point both Pocock and Kramer understand well. An excellent treatment is Daniel J. Hulsebosch, "The Ancient Constitution and the Expanding Empire: Sir Edward Coke's British Jurisprudence," *Law and History Review* 21 (Fall 2003). The idea that the people would enforce the Constitution was conceived largely as a federal solution, as advanced in the Federalist Papers, numbers 10, 44, 45, and 51. See Jack N. Rakove, *Original Meanings: Politics and Ideas in the Making of the Constitution* (New York: Vintage Books, 1997), 161–202.

31. *Argument of Byron Paine*, 1.

32. Mason, "Fugitive Slave Law in Wisconsin"; Joseph Schafer, "Stormy Days in Court: The Booth Case," *Wisconsin Magazine of History* 20 (September 1936); James L. Sellers, "Republicanism and State Rights in Wisconsin," *Mississippi Valley Historical Review* 17 (September 1930); Charles Warren, *The Supreme Court in United States History*, rev. ed. (Littleton, Colo.: F. B. Rothman, 1987). A comprehensive review can be found in Howard Robert Baker II, "The Rescue of Joshua Glover: Lawyers, Popular Constitutionalism, and the Fugitive Slave Law in Wisconsin" (Ph.D. diss., University of California, Los Angeles, 2004).

33. An excellent treatment of this is John P. Schmidt, "'Rotten Before She Got Ripe'": Wisconsin Resists the Fugitive Slave Act," manuscript on file with the author. John Schmidt is a masters' student at Roosevelt University, and plans to file his masters' thesis under this title.

34. In general, see Richard E. Ellis, *The Union at Risk: Jacksonian Democracy, States' Rights, and the Nullification Crisis* (New York: Oxford University Press, 1987); Forrest McDonald, *States' Rights and the Union:* Imperium in Imperio, *1776–1876*, American Political Thought (Lawrence: University Press of Kansas, 2000).

35. Saul Cornell, *The Other Founders: Anti-Federalism and the Dissenting Tradition in America, 1788–1828* (Chapel Hill: University of North Carolina Press, 1999), 295–98. Cornell perceptively points out the similarities between Calhoun and the Madison who wrote *Federalist # 10* rather than the Madison who wrote the "Report of 1800." Calhoun claimed the legacy of the Anti-Federalists but clearly worked within the intellectual tradition of the Federalists.

36. *Argument of Byron Paine*, 3.

37. In 1800, Madison had explicitly rejected the courts as the final expositors of the Constitution. He outlined a theory of coordinate construction that gave judicial interpretations no greater weight than those of the legislature or the executive. See Hutchinson, Rachal, and Rutland, *Papers of James Madison*, 17:310–12. Madison was responding to the argument that the U.S. Supreme Court was the only institution that could judge on the constitutionality of congressional statutes.

38. *Argument of Byron Paine*, 24. The publisher included Smith's opinion in the pamphlet.

39. Ibid., 25.

40. Ibid., 25.

41. *Trial of Thomas Sims*, 8–9.

42. In re Booth, 3 Wis. 13 at 66 [3 Wis. 1 at 63].

43. Ibid., 69 [67].

44. Ibid., 80 [80].

45. Ibid., 83 [84].

46. Ibid.

47. Ibid., 85 [86].

48. Barry Friedman, "The History of the Countermajoritarian Difficulty, Part One: The Road to Judicial Supremacy," *New York University Law Review* 73 (May 1998): 395–409.

49. Paul Finkelman, "Sorting out *Prigg v. Pennsylvania*," *Rutgers Law Journal* 24 (Spring 1993): 635–36.

50. *Argument of Byron Paine*, 21. Paine did admit that settled precedent was in favor of the Fugitive Slave Act.

51. Barron v. Baltimore, 32 U.S. (7 Pet.) 243, 249 (1833).

52. Ibid.

53. New York v. Miln, 36 U.S. (11 Pet.) 102 (1837). Justice Barbour distinguished this case from *Gibbons v. Ogden,* which Barbour argued had established that the state licensing of vessels upon navigable waters conflicted with U.S. licenses and was hence null and void. See his opinion at 135–37.

54. Ibid., 138.

55. Ibid., 156–57. Justice Smith Thompson filed a concurrence that stated that the New York law was valid, but not if it conflicted with an act of Congress. On this crucial point, Thompson and the Court (speaking through Barbour) disagreed.

56. The Passenger Cases, 48 U.S. (7 How.) 283 (1849). The two original cases were *Smith v. Turner* and *Norris v. Boston.*

57. Ibid., 396.

58. Ibid., 400.

59. Ibid.

60. Ibid., 466. The issues in this case were legion, and the opinion of Justice James Wayne in the matter revealed that the Court had been more divided over *New York v. Miln* than the record indicated. The question of when a police regulation impinged on Congress's exclusive power to regulate interstate and foreign commerce as well as to control immigration was extremely contentious and found no easy resolution.

61. Groves v. Slaughter, 40 U.S. (15 Pet.) 449 (1841). Even Story concurred that the interstate commerce clause of the U.S. Constitution did not interfere with the portion of Mississippi's constitution that regulated the introduction of slaves. Although slaves were clearly an article of interstate commerce, their dual status at law as persons and things prevented the justices, at least in 1841, from removing them from the states' police power.

62. Permoli v. New Orleans, 44 U.S. (5 How.) 589, 609–10 (1845).

63. Prigg v. Pennsylvania, 41 U.S. (16 Pet.) 539, 671 (1842).

64. See chapter 2.

65. Ex parte Booth, 3 Wis. 134, 137–41 [3 Wis. 145, 147–53] (1854).

66. Ibid., 142 [154].

67. Ibid., 143 [155].

68. In re Booth, 3 Wis. 144, 158 [3 Wis. 157, 173] (1854).

69. Ibid., 167 [183]. This was an extraordinarily strict reading of the indictment, as Crawford noted that the arrest warrant for Glover was appended to the

third count. But Crawford did not ignore it, as Jenni Parrish suggested in "The *Booth* Cases: Final Step to the Civil War," *Willamette Law Review* 29 (Spring 1993): 269. Instead, he construed the indictments narrowly within the *limited* and *explicitly granted* jurisdiction of the U.S. district court. It did not matter that Glover was described as a fugitive from labor in the second and third counts—in those counts, the alleged crimes committed by the petitioners did not fall under the purview of a specified federal statute. Crawford also admitted that the drafter of the indictment had probably intended it to fall within the seventh section of the Fugitive Slave Act of 1850. But he would not construe it in favor of that court with a citizen's liberty at stake.

70. In re Booth, 3 Wis. 144 at 171 [3 Wis. 157 at 189]).

71. Ibid., 161 [176].

72. Ibid.

73. Ibid., 175 [193].

74. In this way, the court deftly elided the greatest objection it faced, that petitioners must be remanded if it was shown that they were held "by virtue of process issued by any court or judge of the United States, in a case where such court or judge has exclusive jurisdiction," in the Habeas Corpus Act, Wis. Stat. tit. 26, ch. 124, § 18 (1849). The court's opinion stated that the indictment had not specified an offense over which the U.S. court had *exclusive jurisdiction.* Technically, this also distinguished their refusal to grant Booth's first request for a writ in July of 1854 from their favorable reply to the second petition in 1855. As Smith made clear in his opinion, the first petition contained a bench warrant and no indictment, and so the court could not interrupt proceedings at that point. Now, with the full record, the justices could inquire into the jurisdiction of the federal court. In re Booth, 3 Wis. 144 at 169, 173 [3 Wis. 157 at 186, 191]. There is substantial evidence that this was a normal practice in antebellum America. Part of the reason was that there existed no federal statute providing for an appeal from U.S. district courts for criminal cases.

75. In re Booth, 3 Wis. 144 at 174–76 [3 Wis. 157 at 192–96].

76. Ibid., 182 [201].

77. "Great Meeting at Young's Hall," *Milwaukee Sentinel,* February 12, 1855. The writ of attachment of which Byron Paine spoke was a remedy available to ensure execution of a judicial order. In this case, a writ of attachment directed against the person of the marshal would have ordered the seizure of his property (which the sheriff would have executed) until he obeyed the writ of habeas corpus filed for Booth.

78. Paul Finkelman, "Fugitive Slaves, Midwestern Racial Tolerance, and the Value of 'Justice Delayed,'" *Iowa Law Review* 78 (October 1992): 97–107.

79. Abolitionists' arguments for absolute freedom and wide latitude in writs of habeas corpus, for instance, evaporated when the national government sued out writs to free marshals and other U.S. officers imprisoned under state antikidnapping laws. See Marc M. Arkin, "The Ghost at the Banquet: Slavery, Federalism, and Habeas Corpus for State Prisoners," *Tulane Law Review* 70 (November 1995): 1–71.

80. Karen Orren, "'A War between Officers': The Enforcement of Slavery in the Northern United States, and of the Republic for Which It Stands, before the Civil War," *Studies in American Political Development* 12 (Fall 1998): 372.

81. In re Booth, 3 Wis. 144 at 187 [3 Wis. 157 at 207].

82. Ibid.

83. Rufus King to William Seward, February 11, 1855. Cited in Foner, *Free Soil, Free Labor, Free Men*, 136.

CHAPTER 6

1. "Extra. U. States District Court," *Milwaukee News*, February 5, 1855.

2. Richard N. Current, *History of Wisconsin*, vol. 2, *The Civil War Era, 1848–1873* (Madison: State Historical Society of Wisconsin, 1976), 221–22; Michael J. McManus, *Political Abolitionism in Wisconsin, 1840–1861* (Kent, Ohio: Kent State University Press, 1998), 91.

3. The 1854 elections were really about party politics. Only 47 percent of the electorate voted during this tense year, and many Democrats simply stayed home. Still, it indicated if nothing else a disgust on the part of Democrats with the proslavery position of their party. See McManus, *Political Abolitionism in Wisconsin*, 93.

4. Current, *History of Wisconsin*, 2:224; McManus, *Political Abolitionism in Wisconsin*, 38.

5. E. G. Ryan to Cushing, January 15, 1855, Cushing Papers, General Correspondence, box 71, Manuscripts Division, LC.

6. Booth published his accounts in his *Daily Free Democrat* on January 5 and 15, 1857. An excellent discussion of the coalition politics is McManus, *Political Abolitionism in Wisconsin*, 139.

7. Ibid., 245n27.

8. John Sharpstein to William Streeter, February 6, 1855, Solicitor of the Treasury Manuscripts, Letters Sent, 1820–1934, RG 206, box 152, NA.

9. W. B. Streeter to John Sharpstein, September 20, 1854, Solicitor of the Treasury Manuscripts, Letters Sent, 1853–1880, RG 206, box 152, NA.

10. John Sharpstein to W. B. Streeter, November 8, 1854, Solicitor of the Treasury Manuscripts, Letters Received from U.S. District Attorneys, Marshal, Clerks, 1853–1881, Wisconsin, RG 206, ox 152, NA.

11. Streeter to Sharpstein, March 5, 1855, Solicitor of the Treasury Manuscripts, Letters Sent, 1820–1934, RG 206, NA.

12. See Leslie Friedman Goldstein, "State Resistance to Authority in Federal Unions: The Early United States (1790–1860) and the European Community (1958–94)," *Studies in American Political Development* 11 (Spring 1997): 149–89. Goldstein charts the kinds of resistance engaged in by states. The only period that saw diminished state resistance was the 1840s, which trend, she concluded, was due to the states rights leaning of the Taney Court. Resistance returned in the 1850s with the issue of slavery and the Compromise of 1850.

Goldstein also concluded that, although common, state resistance was often roundly condemned by other states and oftentimes defeated by time. That is, resistance to unfavorable legislation or Supreme Court rulings became more difficult in the face of public disapproval, legislative disavowal, or censure by other states. This process mediated state resistance and allowed constitutional mechanisms to resolve disputes. This notion, that constitutional resistance could be mediated by the different branches and by the coercion of public opinion, was at the heart of the historical argument against judicial supremacy made in Larry D. Kramer, *The People Themselves: Popular Constitutionalism and Judicial Review* (New York: Oxford University Press, 2004).

13. *Milwaukee News*, March 14, 15, 1855.

14. The practice of state courts reviewing federal proceedings was not uncommon in the antebellum era. Rollin C. Hurd, *A Treatise on the Right of Personal Liberty, and on the Writ of Habeas Corpus and the Practice Connected with It, with a View of the Law of Extradition of Fugitives* (Albany N.Y.: W. C. Little, 1858), 164–70.

15. Sharpstein to Streeter, June 4, 1855, Solicitor of the Treasury Manuscripts, Letters Received from U.S. District Attorneys, Marshal, Clerks, 1853–1881, Wisconsin, RG 206, box 152, NA

16. Sharpstein to Streeter, July 25, 1855, Solicitor of the Treasury Manuscripts, Letters Received from U.S. District Attorneys, Marshal, Clerks, 1853–1881, Wisconsin, RG 206, box 152, NA

17. Legal scholars reviewing the Wisconsin Supreme Court have uncritically sided with Sharpstein's public statements on the illegality of resistance, sometimes without considering its appropriate context. See Jenni Parrish, "The *Booth* Cases: Final Step to the Civil War," *Willamette Law Review* 29 (Spring 1993); Louise Weinberg, "Methodological Interventions and the Slavery Cases; Or, Night-Thoughts of a Legal Realist," *Maryland Law Review* 56, no. 4 (1997). For a detailed treatment of this historiography, see Howard Robert Baker II, "The Rescue of Joshua Glover: Lawyers, Popular Constitutionalism, and the Fugitive Slave Law in Wisconsin" (Ph.D. diss., University of California, Los Angeles, 2004).

18. The temperance issue had traditionally been paired with abolitionism. Byron Paine, for instance, gave lectures in support of temperance legislation. So did most of the abolitionists who later espoused Joshua Glover's cause. See "Temperance Meeting," *Milwaukee Sentinel*, October 8, 1853. On the temperance issue generally, see Frank L. Byrne, "Maine Law versus Lager Beer: A Dilemma of Wisconsin's Young Republican Party," *Wisconsin Magazine of History* 42 (Winter 1958–59): 115–23.

19. The temperance issue had been raised very early in Wisconsin politics. Temperance advocates had suggested such a law directly upon statehood and had met with vociferous German opposition. The Whiskey Act, which required liquor dealers to post a $1,000 bond, was highly unpopular and was not widely enforced. See Kathleen N. Conzen, *Immigrant Milwaukee, 1836–1870: Accommodation and Community in a Frontier City* (Cambridge, Mass.: Harvard University

Press, 1976), 210; Robrcri C. Nesbit, *Wisconsin: A History* (Madison: University of Wisconsin Press, 1973). Both the Whigs and Free Soilers found it impossible to attract Germans to their parties while advocating temperance. See La Vern J. Rippley, *The Immigrant Experience in Wisconsin* (Boston: Twayne, 1985), 27–29. Interestingly, the temperance issue attracted the attention of John Stuart Mill in his tract, *On Liberty* (New York: Bantam, 1993), 115.

20. Barstow's first veto cited several defects of the bill—it made provisions for the sale of certain spirits for medical, chemical, and mechanical purposes but not for their manufacture, and the exemption for beer, cider, and wine seemed arbitrary. He also cited constitutional concerns. Noting that the law provided for "the arrest and confinement of any individual" who appeared intoxicated and the further confinement of that individual until he disclosed where and from whom he had received the alcoholic beverages, he considered "the discretion thus given to the magistrate dangerous to individual liberty, and entirely incompatible with the spirit of our system of Government." *Journal of the Wisconsin Assembly 1855,* 7th Assembly, 915–16 (March 24, 1855).

His second veto was even more explicit: "there are in my opinion several plain provisions of our constitution which have been entirely overlooked by the legislature in the consideration which they have given this bill." Barstow then attacked the revised bill's broad powers of search and seizure. It allowed for warrants issued on suspicion and did not require specification of the goods to be seized, a violation of article I, section 12, of the Wisconsin constitution. Under the proposed bill, the "privacy of [the citizen's] home might be violated with impunity." Goods seized were subject to forfeiture without trial, a violation of article I, section 12, of the constitution. Finally, the bill prohibited citizens from any court action designed to restore to them their goods. Feeling these objections "insuperable," Barstow returned his veto on March 31. See *Journal of the Wisconsin Assembly 1855,* 7th Assembly, 1074–75 (March 31, 1855).

Vetoes on stated constitutional grounds were not frequent in Wisconsin legislative history, but not unprecedented either. In 1854, Barstow vetoed a bill "to divide the county of La Crosse, and organize the county of Monroe" because the legislature had moved the seat of a county without a vote of the people, which the Wisconsin constitution required. *Journal of the Wisconsin Assembly 1854,* 6th Assembly, 544–45 (March 14, 1854).

21. "Rejoicings over the Veto," *Madison Journal,* cited in *Milwaukee Sentinel,* March 28, 1855.

22. There were temperance advocates among the foreign born, but the movement was distinctly upper class and largely flaccid. See Steven M. Avella, *In the Richness of the Earth: History of the Archdiocese of Milwaukee, 1843–1958* (Milwaukee: Marquette University Press, 2002), 59–62; Conzen, *Immigrant Milwaukee 1836–1870,* 160, 71.

23. Joseph Schafer, "Know-Nothingism in Wisconsin," *Wisconsin Magazine of History* 8 (September 1924). For a general treatment of Know Nothingism as a political movement, see Tyler Anbinder, *Nativism and Slavery: The Northern Know*

Nothings and the Politics of the 1850's (New York: Oxford University Press, 1992). The Know Nothing Party was a main competitor of the Republicans in 1854 across the North. See William E. Gienapp, *The Origins of the Republican Party, 1852–1856* (New York: Oxford University Press, 1987), 93–99.

24. McManus noted that the influence of Know Nothings was extraordinarily small, if one measured it by the difference in the returns for the native-born governor and foreign-born state treasurer candidates on the Republican ticket, the Know-Nothing vote was about 3,300, "a small number given the time and space devoted to them." The power of this tiny minority party lay in its singular pursuit of nativist policies, its ability to infiltrate other political parties, and the popular perception of its power. See McManus, *Political Abolitionism in Wisconsin,* 234n21.

25. Joseph Schafer, "The Yankee and the Teuton in Wisconsin," *Wisconsin Magazine of History* 7 (December 1923): 164–68.

26. McManus, *Political Abolitionism in Wisconsin,* 105–6.

27. Garland v. Booth, Case #35, March 1854, U.S. District and Circuit Court, Eastern District of Wisconsin, Milwaukee, 1848–1862, Civil Case Files, RG 21, NA, Great Lakes Regional Facility.

28. *Daily Free Democrat,* September 6, 1855.

29. "Republican Platform," *Milwaukee Sentinel,* September 7, 1855.

30. *Milwaukee Sentinel,* November 2 and 5, 1855.

31. McManus, *Political Abolitionism in Wisconsin,* 110–11.

32. "Ode to Lager Beer," *Milwaukee Sentinel,* December 21, 1855. I could not resist including the reference to Roger Sherman, the Connecticut delegate to the 1787 Constitutional Convention who likened returning fugitive slaves across state lines to returning horses (mentioned in chapter 2). He remained a revolutionary hero in the popular imagination in the 1850s, although I have not found anyone citing his remark about the insertion of the fugitive slave clause in the Constitution.

33. As William Gienapp has argued, the Republicans had made a poor showing all over the North in 1855, and in many states the Know Nothings appeared the stronger party. The spring elections of 1856 indicated a party in decline, not one that was about to take control of the country. Gienapp, *Origins of the Republican Party,* 273–94.

34. Current, *History of Wisconsin,* 2:231.

35. *Congressional Globe,* 34th Cong., 1st sess., appendix, 534 (May 19, 1856).

36. Gienapp, *Origins of the Republican Party,* 299–303; James M. McPherson, *Battle Cry of Freedom: The Civil War Era* (New York: Ballantine, 1988), 148–49.

37. "The Carnival in Milwaukee," *Milwaukee Sentinel,* February 25, 1856.

38. Byrne, "Maine Law versus Lager Beer," 122–23.

39. McManus, *Political Abolitionism in Wisconsin,* 122–23.

40. George B. Smith, diary, January 19, 1857, George B. Smith Papers, Wisconsin Historical Society Archives, Madison, Wisconsin.

41. *Milwaukee Sentinel,* January 15, 1857.

42. James L. Sellers, "Republicanism and State Rights in Wisconsin," *Mississippi Valley Historical Review* 17 (September 1930): 218.

43. Ibid., 219–22. Doolittle had expressed this opinion in a private letter. James R. Doolittle to Edward L. Runals, December 25, 1856, Correspondence, 1850–1857, Doolittle Papers, 1831–1935, Wisconsin Historical Society Archives, Madison, Wisconsin.

44. *Journal of the Senate of Wisconsin,* 9th Assembly, 80–88 (January 26, 1857).

45. The political wrangling over the U.S. senator's seat was important because it was a form of constitutional interpretation that did not involve the courts at all. The entire issue turned on the interpretation of the Wisconsin constitution, which declared that judges should hold no other office. One of the overriding questions in the matter was who had the final right to interpret the constitution. In this case, it was a statute that ended the impasse.

The Democratic press delighted in pointing out that the Republican sheets that had argued Doolittle's ineligibility before the selection and had now abruptly done an about-face and come out for his eligibility. See the *Madison Argus and Democrat,* March 21, 1857. The *Milwaukee Sentinel* denied the about-face and instead insisted that it had only softly backpedaled: "we have always maintained that the Constitutional proviso should be a bar to his becoming a candidate and to members of the Legislature voting for him. Of that, however, the members had the exclusive right to judge for themselves," in "The Senator Question," *Milwaukee Sentinel,* February 14, 1857.

The certificate of election signed by the governor's secretary can be found in Correspondence, 1850–1857, James R. Doolittle Papers.

46. "People's Candidate for Chief Justice," *Madison Journal,* February 17, 1857.

47. One such proposed amendment provided that nothing in the act should be construed by the judiciary to supersede the Fugitive Slave Act of 1850. *Journal of the Wisconsin Senate,* 9th Assembly (February 14, 1857), 242.

48. Ibid., 456 (February 18, 1857); Thomas D. Morris, *Free Men All: The Personal Liberty Laws of the North, 1780–1861* (Baltimore: Johns Hopkins University Press, 1974), 176–77.

49. An Act relating to the writ of Habeas Corpus to persons claimed as Fugitive Slaves, the right of trial by jury, and to prevent kidnapping in this State, 1857 Wis. Laws 12.

50. At least one senator said that he would have voted for the bill had it not been for this clause, which he said was an ex post facto law and thus unconstitutional. "Personal Liberty Bill," *Milwaukee Sentinel,* February 18, 1857.

51. Fieri facias (writ of execution), issued by Judge Miller of the U.S. district court on January 21, 1857. In Garland v. Booth, Case #35, March 1854, U.S. District and Circuit Court, Eastern District of Wisconsin, Milwaukee, 1848–1862, Civil Case Files, RG 21, NA, Great Lakes Regional Facility.

52. Morris, *Free Men All,* 182.

53. *Congressional Globe,* 34th Cong., 3d sess., appendix,1 (December 2, 1856).

54. Ibid., 2.

55. Caleb Cushing had provided an opinion that the Missouri Compromise was unconstitutional in that it prohibited certain citizens from taking their prop-

erty into the territories. See Don E. Fehrenbacher, *The Dred Scott Case: Its Significance in American Law and Politics* (New York: Oxford University Press, 1978), 292.

56. Ibid., 417–28. It is almost impossible to overstate the passion with which this decision was denounced and the damage it did to the Supreme Court's authority. See Barry Friedman, "The History of the Countermajoritarian Difficulty, Part One: The Road to Judicial Supremacy," *New York University Law Review* 73 (May 1998): 416–18.

In a provocative work on the *Dred Scott* decision, Marc Graber has compiled evidence demonstrating that some very prominent national politicians—Henry Clay, Stephen Douglas, Jefferson Davis, Henry Polk among them—had stated on numerous occasions that the question was properly a judicial one and that Congress should bow to the decision. See Mark Graber, "*Dred Scott* and the Problem of Constitutional Evil," (2005). Unpublished manuscript on file with the author.

57. "The Convention of Wednesday," *Milwaukee Sentinel,* June 19, 1857.

58. An Act to extend the right of Suffrage, 1857 Wis. Laws 45.

59. "Free Suffrage," *Daily Free Democrat,* September 23, 1857.

60. "Precisely So," *Madison Argus and Democrat,* September 21, 1857. See also "Negro Suffrage—Death Warrant," ibid., September 16, 1857.

61. This was common both before and after Glover's rescue. In 1857, Sherman Booth took note of a "convention of colored men" in Sacramento that had petitioned the government for the removal of legal restrictions on their persons. *Daily Free Democrat,* January 26, 1857. I have not found, yet, a solid indication whether the Glover rescue had any effect on the perception of blacks as *active political agents.*

62. "Free Suffrage," *Daily Free Democrat,* September 23, 1857. His touring was also noted in the *Madison Argus and Democrat,* September 21, 1857

63. *Columbus Republican Journal,* October 20, 1857, cited in McManus, *Political Abolitionism in Wisconsin,* 156. The reference to Byrd as a "bird of African plumage" is from the *Madison Argus and Democrat,* September 21, 1857.

64. Edward Noyes, "A Negro in Mid-nineteenth Century Wisconsin Life and Politics," *Wisconsin Academy Review* 15 (Fall 1968): 2–6.

65. Free Suffrage," *Daily Free Democrat,* September 23, 1857.

66. "For the Extension of Suffrage," *Madison Argus and Democrat,* November 3, 1857.

67. McManus, *Political Abolitionism in Wisconsin,* 156–57. He first introduced these findings in Michael J. McManus, "Wisconsin Republicans and Negro Suffrage," *Civil War History* 25 (March 1979): 36–54. This proves the general experience of western hostility toward black suffrage and toward blacks in general. See Eric Foner, "Politics and Prejudice: The Free Soil Party and the Negro, 1849–1852," *Journal of Negro History* 50 (October 1965): 239–56 However, it also indicates that the Republican Party in the North was solidly in favor of extending to blacks the basic protections and privileges of the Constitution. See Paul Finkelman,

"Prelude to the Fourteenth Amendment: Black Legal Rights in the Antebellum North." *Rutgers Law Journal* 17 (Spring and Summer 1986): 415–82.

68. Current, *History of Wisconsin*, 2:244–45.

69. Ellen D. Langill, *Foley & Lardner: Attorneys at Law, 1842–1992* (Madison: State Historical Society of Wisconsin, 1992), 12–60.

70. William Pitt Lynde to Hon. James D. Westcott, Jr., April 25, 1846, Lynde Family Papers, manuscript 857, Milwaukee County Historical Society, Milwaukee, Wisconsin.

71. "To the Electors of Wisconsin," *Milwaukee Sentinel,* March 9, 1859.

72. Ableman v. Booth, 62 U.S. (21 How.) 506, 515 (1859). The Supreme Court tried *Ableman v. Booth* and *U.S. v. Booth* jointly. Taney did point out that the state's habeas corpus statute ordered remand if it appeared a prisoner was detained by lawful process, and, that being the case, it was the court and not the state that had unconstitutionally asserted its power. The thrust of Taney's argument, however, was that the states did not have the power to give their courts such jurisdiction. In this sense, the decision seemed also to be aimed at the northern states' personal liberty laws.

73. Ibid., 520.

74. Ibid., 526.

75. Ibid., 525.

76. Such was the power of judicial review before the Civil War. In his treatise on habeas corpus, Rollin Hurd could declare that "when [the validity of a congressional act] is questioned, in a suit or proceeding in a state court, over which it has jurisdiction, it becomes, not a privilege but the unavoidable duty of the court to decide the question." This was a principle that had been "repeatedly advanced and enforced by the highest courts, state and federal, and ought to be considered settled." Hurd, *Habeas Corpus,* 166–67.

77. *Journal of the Wisconsin Assembly,* 11th Assembly, 777 (March 12, 1859). Democrats introduced their own version demanding deference to the ruling and calling the Wisconsin Supreme Court decision in *Booth v. Ableman* "monstrous." Ibid., 778.

78. Joint Resolution relative to the decision of the United States supreme court, reversing decision of the supreme court of Wisconsin, 1859 Wis. Laws 247.

John Hurd, in his treatise on slavery, however, noted that "this inclination or practice of deferring to extrajudicial authority in questions of constitutional law far more than is customary in other departments of legal science, must indeed be ascribed in part to the fact that in republican states such questions are always more or less political, as well as legal questions; so much so that, whether they are one or the other, whether they are to be decided by the judiciary or by some other branch of the government—itself a constitutional question—can hardly be decided by either branch alone." On the question of who possessed sovereign power and what authority either the state or federal government could wield, he noted that this had been before the courts: "it is however, essentially, a political question, and one which no judicial tribunal whose authority is dependent upon its answer can, in the nature of the case, determine." John Codman Hurd, preface to *The Law of Freedom and Bondage* (1858; repr. Boston: Little, Brown, 1968), 1:xii.

79. "A Timely Reminder," *Milwaukee Sentinel,* March 15, 1859.

80. "To the People of the State of Wisconsin," *Milwaukee Sentinel,* March 17, 1859.

81. *Madison Argus and Democrat,* reprinted in *Milwaukee Sentinel,* March 31, 1859.

82. *Daily Wisconsin,* March 21, 1859.

83. "Principles, Not Men," *Milwaukee Sentinel,* March 21, 1859.

84. The *Milwaukee Sentinel* noted on three occasions in the week before the election that Carl Schurz was out delivering orations on the subject of states rights and constitutional principles. See March 22 and 24, and April 4.

85. "Large and Enthusiastic Meeting at Albany Hall! State Rights and Byron Paine, Speech of Carl Schurz!" ibid., March 24, 1859.

86. Sellers, "Republicanism and State Rights in Wisconsin," 227.

87. McManus, *Political Abolitionism in Wisconsin,* 177–78.

CHAPTER 7

1. *Congressional Globe,* 36th Cong., 1st sess., 766 (February 14, 1860).

2. Toombs reiterated on the floor that there was a difference between matters of ordinary law and constitutional law. On matters fundamental to the compact, Toombs maintained that only the states could judge in the last instance whether the compact had been violated. In all other matters, federal law was deemed to be supreme by the Constitution. This allowed Toombs to differentiate Georgia's resistance to the Supreme Court in the Cherokee cases of the 1830s from Wisconsin's resistance to the Fugitive Slave Act. Ibid., 767.

More revealing, however, was his understanding that fundamental law was not *necessarily* a matter for the courts. State courts began practicing judicial review with some regularity in the 1850s, and at the same time the question whether the U.S. Supreme Court was a controlling authority remained unclear. The Georgia Supreme Court in the 1850s made many more brash pronouncements about the U.S. Supreme Court's being of "coordinate" and not "superior" authority. See *Padelford v. Savannah,* 14 Ga. 438, 505 (1854). The decision was part of a train of decisions about judicial review that revealed both its delicate nature, its extent, and its limits. The 1850s saw a surge in the activity of judicial review, and the states led the way. I owe this observation to Richard Drew, "The Surge and Consolidation of American Judicial Power: Judicial Review in the States, 1840–1880" (paper presented at the annual meeting of the American Political Science Association, Chicago, Ill., September 2–4, 2004).

3. *Congressional Globe,* 36th Cong., 1st sess., 767 (February 14, 1860).

4. Ibid., 768.

5. Alfons J. Beitzinger, *Edward G. Ryan: Lion of the Law* (Madison: State Historical Society of Wisconsin, 1960), 63–64.

6. Ableman v. Booth, 11 Wis. 517, 521 (1859).

7. Ibid., 523.

8. Ibid., 557.

9. *Journal of the Wisconsin Assembly,* 12th Assembly, 50–51 (January 14, 1860).

10. Ibid., 229–30 (February 1, 1860).

11. Alfons J. Beitzinger, "Federal Law Enforcement and the Booth Cases," *Marquette Law Review* 41 (Summer 1957): 28–30.

12. Criminal Docket Book, 1848–1862, vol. 1, p. 86, Criminal Records, 1848–1862, U.S. District and Circuit Court, Eastern District of Wisconsin, Milwaukee, 1848–1862, RG 21, NA, Great Lakes Regional Facility.

13. Arnold v. Booth, 14 Wis. 180, 185 (1861).

14. An Act relating to the writ of Habeas Corpus to persons claimed as Fugitive Slaves, the right of trial by jury, and to prevent kidnapping in this State, § 11, 1857 Wis. Laws 14.

15. I should also state here that it was initially a matter of jurisdiction that had allowed Samuel Crawford to grant Sherman Booth's writ of habeas corpus in 1855. Crawford, who believed the fugitive slave law constitutional, justified his opinion on the basis of a faulty indictment that unconstitutionally extended the U.S. district court's jurisdiction. Cole, who believed the fugitive slave law unconstitutional, justified his opinion on the basis of the constitutional directive granting jurisdiction in suits between citizens of different states to the federal courts.

16. Arnold v. Booth, 14 Wis. 180 at 189.

17. The situation was in many ways more anxious than I have depicted it here. A motion was brought before the Wisconsin Assembly in January 1860, suggesting war with the United States government. The Union guards said they would refuse any illegal requisition by the governor and worked to raise money for their own arms. Current, *History of Wisconsin,* 2:277–83.

18. *Journal of the Senate of the State of Wisconsin,* 12th Assembly, 29 (January 10, 1861).

19. Ibid., 30.

20. Ibid., 29–31.

21. Ibid., 31–32.

22. He recounted the reasons for this in several letters he wrote Horace Rublee and Carl Schurz in 1859 and 1860. See his correspondence in Timothy Howe Papers, 1846, 1854, 1857–1883, Wisconsin Historical Society Archives, Madison, Wisconsin.

23. Howe wrote his friend Horace Rublee about his conflicted feelings about the election of Byron Paine and Sherman Booth's attacks in the *Daily Free Democrat.*

24. "Judge Howe's Letter," *Madison Daily State Journal,* April 14, 1859.

25. Ibid.

26. "Another Letter from Judge Howe," *Madison Daily State Journal,* April 14, 1859.

27. This served him well in the Senate. On April 4, 1864, he addressed the Senate on the propriety of an amendment to the Constitution abolishing slavery. Speaking in favor of it, he addressed the argument of bad faith in the execution of the fugitive slave law in the North. In the same breath, he said that he believed that the courts held the law constitutional, but that the law was unconstitutional. It violated both the U.S. Constitution and "your constitution and mine." For Howe, the final appeal would be to the people who would support its repeal, which Howe would later vote for. For Howe's speech, see *Congressional Globe,* 38th Cong., 1st sess., appendix, 114 (April 4, 1864).

28. Thomas D. Morris, *Free Men All: The Personal Liberty Laws of the North, 1780–1861* (Baltimore: Johns Hopkins University Press, 1974), 214–15.

29. *Wisconsin Senate Journal, 1861,* 376.

30. The Senate held a short constitutional debate over the repeal. Senator Saulsbury, of Delaware, proposed an amendment that, instead of repealing the fugitive slave law, would have enabled Congress to "pass all necessary and proper laws for the rendition" of fugitive slaves. It was handily defeated, but indicated that the debate about the constitutionality of the law was still open as late as 1864. *Congressional Globe,* 38th Cong., 1st sess., 3191 (April 4, 1864).

31. Moseley v. Chamberlain, 18 Wis. 700 (1861).

32. John O. Holzheuter, "Ezekiel Gillespie, Lost and Found," *Wisconsin Magazine of History* 60 (Spring 1977): 179–84.

33. Joseph A. Ranney, *Trusting Nothing to Providence: A History of Wisconsin's Legal System* (Madison: University of Wisconsin Law School Continuing Education and Outreach, 1999), 538.

34. Holzheuter, "Ezekiel Gillespie, Lost and Found."

35. Knorr v. Home Ins. Co. of New York, 25 Wis. 143, 165 (1869).

36. In re Tarble, 25 Wis. 390 (1870); Whiton v. Chicago & Northwestern R.R. Co., 25 Wis. 424 (1870).

37. Tarble's Case, 80 U.S. 397 (1871).

38. Robert M. Cover, *Justice Accused: Antislavery and the Judicial Process* (New Haven, Conn.: Yale University Press, 1975), 187. He did, however, acknowledge that the question of jurisdiction was subject to appeal, by the twenty-fifth section of the Judiciary Act of 1789, to the U.S. Supreme Court.

39. John Bradley Winslow, *The Story of a Great Court* (Chicago: T. H. Flood, 1912), 155.

40. Memorial of Jonathan E. Arnold, 1869, Milwaukee Bar Association, Milwaukee County Historical Society.

41. Winslow, *Story of a Great Court,* 155.

42. State ex rel. Drake v. Doyle, 40 Wis. 175 (1876). The U.S. finally reversed this decision in *Terral v. Burke Const. Co.,* 257 U.S. 529 (1921). On these cases, and for an excellent summary of the issues in the states' rights controversy in the 1860s and 1870s, see Ranney, *Trusting Nothing to Providence,* 113–19.

43. "The Opinion of Judge Smith," *Daily Wisconsin,* June 6, 1854.

Byron Paine's essay on the radical and the conservative in history can be found among his papers at the Wisconsin History Society.

1. Alfons J. Beitzinger, "Federal Law Enforcement and the Booth Cases," *Marquette Law Review* 41 (1957): 32.

2. I take this account generally, and the account of the Little Rock crisis specifically, from Tony Freyer, *The Little Rock Crisis: A Constitutional Interpretation* (Westport, Conn.: Greenwood, 1984).

3. Melvin I. Urofsky and Paul Finkelman, *Documents of American Constitutional and Legal History* (New York: Oxford University Press, 2002), 2:735–37.

4. Aaron v. Cooper, 143 F. Supp. 855 (E.D. Ark. 1956).

5. Faubus sponsored two amendments as well. The first was a resolution calling for an amendment to the U.S. Constitution to forbid federal meddling in issues (like education) traditionally belonging to the states. The second would have given local school boards the authority to assign pupils to schools and would make their decision final. These two initiatives, even if passed, did nothing to make desegregation illegal. Rather, they made it solely a matter of local choice. They turned the process over to local officials and therefore could be seen to fit within the *Brown II* "all deliberate speed" rule. See Freyer, *Little Rock Crisis,* 78–82.

6. Aaron v. Cooper, 243 F.2d 361 (8th Cir. 1957).

7. Aaron v. Cooper, 163 F. Supp. 13 (E.D. Ark. 1958).

8. Aaron v. Cooper, 257 F.2d 33 (8th Cir. 1958).

9. Cooper v. Aaron, 358 U.S. 1 (1958).

10. The instinct to praise *Ableman v. Booth* as a means of praising national supremacy survives to this day. See Michael J. C. Taylor, "'A More Perfect Union': *Ableman v. Booth* and the Culmination of Federal Sovereignty," *Journal of Supreme Court History* 28 (July 2003): 101–15.

11. Cooper v. Aaron, 358 U.S. 1 at 17.

12. Ableman v. Booth, 62 U.S. (21 How.) 506, 516 (1859).

13. Ibid., 525. The statement directly touched on the surrender of certain areas of sovereignty to the federal government.

14. Taney's demonstration of the constitutionality of the Fugitive Slave Act amounted to an assertion that fugitive slave rendition belonged to Congress, and nothing more.

15. Properly, *Prigg v. Pennsylvania* (1842) did this. As I documented in chapter 2, however, this settlement did not last, and it was clear that Congress would have to provide the definitive settlement, including (if necessary) the overruling of portions of Story's opinion in *Prigg.* As it turned out, the constitutional settlement of 1850 accepted *Prigg* and created a new federal police power with its own law enforcement arm to execute the power.

16. Hartog was commenting upon papers delivered in a symposium on "The Constitution and American Life. Part II: Rights Consciousness in American History." His comments spoke to the utopian nature of rights claims—those of the

abolitionists, for instance, who demanded rights against existing laws usually on principle. In this case, the right of free blacks to protection fell conceptually into a different category since it did not (in theory) impede the right of slaveholders to their fugitive property. See Hendrik Hartog, "The Constitution of Aspiration and 'The Rights That Belong to Us All,'" *Journal of American History* 74 (December 1987): 1020.

17. This is made all the more difficult by the conflation of "state sovereignty" and "states rights" by southern segregationists in the 1950s. The former is a doctrine of power, the latter a doctrine of right. Orval Faubus, for instance, frequently referred to "states' rights" when he meant "state sovereignty." This conflation indicated just how much the relationship between federal and state governments had changed since the antebellum era. See Arthur Bestor, "State Sovereignty and Slavery: A Reinterpretation of Proslavery Constitutional Doctrine, 1846–1860," *Journal of the Illinois State Historical Society* 54 (Summer 1961): 170–81.

It is wrong, however, to dismiss arguments on states rights as having been settled by the Civil War. The strength of states rights arguments in the 1950s (and even today) is in part revealed by the trenchant and unyielding decision in *Cooper v. Aaron*. See Kermit L. Hall, "The Constitutional Lessons of the Little Rock Crisis," in *Understanding the Little Rock Crisis: An Exercise in Remembrance and Reconciliation*, ed. Elizabeth Jacoway and C. Fred Williams (Fayetteville: University of Arkansas Press, 1999), 130–34.

18. Tony Freyer has ably demonstrated that Little Rock's public opinion regarding desegregation was heavily divided in 1957. Although interposition measures had succeeded on the ballot in 1956, Orval Faubus and his moderate race views prevailed over his segregationist opponent. Johnson's proposed amendment to the Arkansas constitution also passed by a margin of 185,374 to 146,064. The amendment was designed to circumvent *Brown* by requiring the legislature to pass laws impeding integration. Faubus sponsored two amendments as well. Faubus's two amendments (see note 5 above) made the process of desegregation a matter of local choice.

In short, one could interpret Faubus's handy defeat of Johnson and the wider majorities that his initiatives received as a consensus for moderate opposition to federal meddling in local affairs rather than a mandate to oppose desegregation at all costs.

Freyer pointed to other evidence, as well. Both white and black leaders in Little Rock agreed that the majority of whites opposed extreme segregationist views. After the token integration of Central High School in the fall semester of 1957, Governor Faubus could have endorsed the school board's plan as the best expression of the sovereign will and thrown the weight of his office behind a moderate, locally run desegregation program. Instead, he sent in troops to prevent desegregation.

Eventually, segregation could be maintained only by resorting to an extreme program, one that closed the schools and ultimately threatened to destroy the public education system and recreate it as a private system. The people of Arkansas rejected this extreme position by reopening the schools and accepting gradual de-segregation. See Tony Freyer, "The Past as Future: The Little Rock Crisis and the Constitution," in *Understanding the Little Rock Crisis: An Exercise in Remembrance and Reconciliation,* ed. Elizabeth Jacoway and C. Fred Williams (Fayetteville: University of Arkansas Press, 1999), 143.

A careful comparison with Wisconsin reveals quite the opposite. In every election in which the issue of compliance with the Fugitive Slave Act was before the voters, the voters solidly rejected it. They did so through 1860. The only elections in which republicans did poorly were those in which they adopted the temperance cause, an issue that itself raised constitutional questions.

SELECTED BIBLIOGRAPHY

ARCHIVAL SOURCES

Milwaukee Area Research Center, UWM Libraries,
University of Wisconsin–Milwaukee, Milwaukee, Wisconsin

Downer, Jason. Papers, 1853–1883. Milwaukee Manuscript Collection O. Wisconsin Historical Society.

Booth, Sherman M. Family papers, 1818–1908. Milwaukee Manuscript Collection BB. Wisconsin Historical Society.

Milwaukee County Historical Society, Milwaukee, Wisconsin

Levi Hubbell Papers. Manuscript 570.

Lynde Family Papers. Manuscript 857.

Milwaukee assessor. Assessment rolls, 1852–1860, 1862. Manuscript 720.

Milwaukee city directories, 1848–1860.

Milwaukee County Circuit Court Records, 1837–1858.

Milwaukee treasurer. Tax Rolls, 1838–1845, except 1842. Manuscript 720.

Young Men's Association of the City of Milwaukee. Manuscript 2804.

Wisconsin State Historical Society Archives, Madison, Wisconsin

Doolittle, James R. Papers, 1831–1935.

Grignon, Augustin. "Seventy-two Years' Recollections of Wisconsin," in *Wisconsin Historical Collections* (Madison: State Historical Society of Wisconsin, 1857), 3:195–295. Online facsimile at http://www.wisconsinhistory.org/turningpoints/search.asp?id=28.

Howe, Timothy O. Papers, 1846, 1854, 1857–1890.

Holzheuter, John O. "Black Settlers in Early Wisconsin, 1840–2000." Research files produced and created by John O. Holzheuter.

Olin, Chauncey C. "A History of the Early Anti-slavery Excitement in the State of Wisconsin from 1842–1860." Microfilm, reel 1, P82-5062.

Paine, Byron. Papers, 1845–1869.

Ryan, Edward G. Papers, 1815–1902.
Smith, George B. Papers, 1837–1890.

Library of Congress, Manuscripts Division, Washington D.C.

Cushing, Caleb. Papers. General correspondence, box 71.
———. Papers. Legal file, Attorney General's Office, box 235.

National Archives, College Park, Maryland

Solicitor of the Treasury Manuscripts, Letters Received from U.S. District Attorneys, Marshals, Clerks of Court, 1853–1881, Wisconsin. RG 206.
Solicitor of the Treasury Manuscripts, Letters Sent, 1820–1934. RG 206.

National Archives, Great Lakes Regional Facility. Chicago, Illinois

Appearance Docket Books, volume C. Law Records, 1849–1862. U.S. District and Circuit Court, Eastern District of Wisconsin, Milwaukee, 1848–1862. RG 21.
Civil Case Files. Law Records, 1849–1862. U.S. District and Circuit Court, Eastern District of Wisconsin, Milwaukee, 1848–1862. RG 21.
Criminal Case Files, 1849–1862. Criminal Records, 1848–1862. U.S. District and Circuit Court, Eastern District of Wisconsin, Milwaukee, 1848–1862. RG 21.
Criminal Docket Book, 1848–1862. Criminal Records, 1848–1862. U.S. District and Circuit Court, Eastern District of Wisconsin, Milwaukee, 1848–1862. RG 21.
General Register (Index), 1848–1862. General Records, 1848–1862. U.S. District and Circuit Court, Eastern District of Wisconsin, Milwaukee, 1848–1862. RG 21.

NEWSPAPERS AND PERIODICALS

American Freeman. Wisconsin State Historical Society Archives. Madison, Wisconsin.
Chapman's Chanticleer. Indianapolis–Marion County Library.
Daily Wisconsin. Wisconsin State Historical Society Archives. Madison, Wisconsin.
Harper's New Monthly Magazine. Young Research Library, UCLA. Los Angeles, California.
Madison Argus and Democrat. Wisconsin State Historical Society Archives. Madison, Wisconsin.
Madison Journal. Wisconsin State Historical Society Archives. Madison, Wisconsin.
Milwaukee Daily Free Democrat. Wisconsin State Historical Society Archives. Madison, Wisconsin.
Milwaukee News. Wisconsin State Historical Society Archives. Madison, Wisconsin.
Der Milwaukee See-Bote. Wisconsin State Historical Society Archives. Madison, Wisconsin.
Milwaukee Sentinel. Milwaukee Library. Milwaukee, Wisconsin.

Oshkosh Democrat. Wisconsin State Historical Society Archives. Madison, Wisconsin.
Racine Advocate. Wisconsin State Historical Society Archives. Madison, Wisconsin.
Wisconsin Daily Patriot. Wisconsin State Historical Society Archives. Madison, Wisconsin.

PUBLISHED PRIMARY SOURCES

Adams, John Quincy. *Memoirs of John Quincy Adams,* edited by Charles Francis Adams. Philadelphia: J. B. Lippincott, 1876.

American and Foreign Anti-Slavery Society. *The Fugitive Slave Bill: Its History and Unconstitutionality.* New York: William Harned, 1850.

Annual Message of Alexander W. Randall, Governor of the State of Wisconsin. Madison: Atwood and Rublee, 1858.

Bacon, Leonard. *The Higher Law: A Sermon Preached on Thanksgiving Day, November 27, 1851.* New Haven, Conn.: B. L. Hamlen, 1851.

Baldwin, James. *Collected Essays.* The Library of America 98. New York: Library of America, 1998.

Bates, Edward. *Opinion of Attorney General Edward Bates on Citizenship.* Washington, D.C.: Government Printing Office, 1862.

Blackstone, William. *Commentaries on the Laws of England, in Four Books.* 4 vols. Oxford: Clarendon Press, 1765–69. Accessed through the Avalon Project, Yale University. http://www.yale.edu/lawweb/avalon/blackstone/bk4ch16.htm.

Bush, Charles P. *The Fugitive Slave Law: A Sermon, Preached in the Fourth Congregational Church, Norwich, Conn., June 25th, 1854.* Norwich, Conn.: Woodworth and Perry, 1854.

Cary, John W. *The Organization and History of the Chicago, Milwaukee & St. Paul Railway Company.* Milwaukee: Cramer, Aikens, and Cramer, 1892.

Chase, Salmon P. *Reclamation of Fugitives from Service: An Argument for the Defendant, Submitted to the Supreme Court of the United States, at the December Term 1846 in the Case of Wharton Jones v. John Vanzandt.* Cincinnati: R. P. Donough, 1847.

Cleveland, Charles Dexter. *Anti-Slavery Addresses of 1844 and 1845 by Salmon Portland Chase and Charles Dexter Cleveland.* Philadelphia: J. A. Bancroft, 1867.

Crounse, L. L. *Annual Statement of the Trade and Commerce, Together with the General Business of the City of Milwaukee, for the Year 1858.* Milwaukee: S. M. Booth, Book and Job Printer, 1859.

Farrand, Max. *The Records of the Federal Convention of 1787.* 4 vols. New Haven, Conn.: Yale University Press, 1911–37.

Finkelman, Paul, ed. *Fugitive Slaves and American Courts: The Pamphlet Literature.* 4 vols. New York: Garland, 1988.

Forman, J. G. *The Christian Martyrs; Or, the Conditions of Obedience to the Civil Government: A Discourse.* Boston: Wm. Crosby and H. P. Nichols, 1851.

Hunt, John Warren. *Wisconsin Gazetteer.* Madison: Beriah Brown, 1853.

Hurd, John Codman. *The Law of Freedom and Bondage*. 2 vols. 1858. Reprint, Boston: Little, Brown, 1969.

Hurd, Rollin Carlos. *A Treatise on the Right of Personal Liberty and on the Writ of Habeas Corpus and the Practice Connected with It, with a View of the Law of Extradition of Fugitives*. Albany, N.Y.: W. C. Little, 1858. Nineteenth Century Legal Treatises Microform. Woodbridge, Conn.: Research Publications, 1984–. Fiche: 46093–46100.

Kent, James. *Commentaries on American Law*. 2d ed. 4 vols. New York: O. Halsted, 1832. Nineteenth Century Legal Treatises Microform. Woodbridge, Conn.: Research Publications, 1984–. Fiche: 198–222.

———. "An Introductory Lecture to a Course of Law Lectures." In *American Political Writing during the Founding Era, 1760–1805*, edited by Charles S. Hyneman and Donald S. Lutz, 900–935. Indianapolis, Ind.: Liberty Press, 1983.

Madison, James. "Report of 1800." In volume 17, *Papers of James Madison*, edited by William Thomas Hutchinson, William M. E. Rachal, and Robert Allen Rutland, 303–50. Charlottesville: University of Virginia Press, 1991.

Middleton, Stephen. *The Black Laws in the Old Northwest: A Documentary History*. Westport, Conn.: Greenwood, 1993.

Mill, John Stuart. *On Liberty and Utilitarianism*. New York: Bantam Classics, 1993.

Milwaukee Chamber of Commerce. *An Exposition of the Business of Milwaukee*. Milwaukee: A. Baylies, 1863.

Niven, John, ed. *The Salmon P. Chase Papers*. 5 vols. Kent, Ohio: Kent State University Press, 1993–98.

Paine, Byron. *Argument of Byron Paine, Esq. and Opinion of Hon. A. D. Smith on the Unconstitutionality of the Fugitive Slave Act*. Milwaukee: Sherman M. Booth, 1854.

Rantoul, Robert. *The Trial of Thomas Sims, on an Issue of Personal Liberty, on the Claim of James Potter, of Georgia, against Him, as an Alleged Fugitive from Service: Arguments of Robert Rantoul, Jr. and Charles G. Loring, with the Decision of George T. Curtis; Phonographic Report by Dr. James W. Stone; Boston, April 7–12, 1851*. Boston: Wm. S. Damrell, 1851. Nineteenth Century Legal Treatises Microform. Woodbridge, Conn.: Research Publications, 1984–. Fiche: 36698.

Report and Collections of the State Historical Society of Wisconsin, 1855–1876.

Story, Joseph. *Commentaries on the Constitution of the United States; With a Preliminary Review of the Constitutional History of the Colonies and States, before the Adoption of the Constitution*. Boston: Hilliard, Gray, 1833. Nineteenth Century Legal Treatises Microform. Woodbridge, Conn.: Research Publications, 1984–. Fiche: 26662–26670.

———. *The Constitutional Class Book: Being a Brief Exposition of the Constitution of the United States, Designed for the Use of the Higher Classes in Common Schools*. Boston: Hilliard, Gray, 1834. Nineteenth Century Legal Treatises Microform. Woodbridge, Conn.: Research Publications, 1984–. Fiche: 30671–30672.

Urofsky, Melvin I., and Paul Finkelman, eds. *Documents of American Constitutional and Legal History.* 2 vols. New York: Oxford University Press, 2002.

Thompson, Joseph P. *The Fugitive Slave Law: Tried by the Old and New Testaments.* New York: William Harned, 1850.

Wharton, Francis. *Treatise on the Criminal Law of the United States: Comprising a Digest of the Penal Statutes of the General Government, and of Massachusetts, New York, Pennsylvania and Virginia: With the Decisions on Cases Arising upon Those Statutes, and a General View of the Criminal Jurisprudence of the Common and Civil Law.* 2d ed. Philadelphia: James Kay, Jun, and Brother, 1852. Nineteenth Century Legal Treatises Microform. Woodbridge, Conn.: Research Publications, 1984–. Fiche: 36845–36855.

BOOKS, ARTICLES, PAPERS, AND DISSERTATIONS

Abzug, Robert H. *Cosmos Crumbling: American Reform and the Religious Imagination.* New York: Oxford University Press, 1994.

Alexander, Larry, and Lawrence B. Solum. "Book Review: Popular? Constitutionalism? *The People Themselves: Popular Constitutionalism and Judicial Review,* by Larry D. Kramer." *Harvard Law Review* 118 (March 2005): 1594–640.

Anbinder, Tyler. *Nativism and Slavery: The Northern Know Nothings and the Politics of the 1850's.* New York: Oxford University Press, 1992.

Andrews, William L. "The Representation of Slavery and the Rise of Afro-American Literary Realism, 1865–1920." In *Slavery and the Literary Imagination,* edited by Deborah McDowell and Arnold Rampersad, 62–80. Baltimore: Johns Hopkins University Press, 1989.

Appleby, Joyce. *Inheriting the Revolution: The First Generation of Americans.* Cambridge, Mass.: Harvard University Press, Belknap Press, 2000.

———. *Liberalism and Republicanism in the Historical Imagination.* Cambridge, Mass.: Harvard University Press, 1992.

Arkin, Marc M. "The Ghost at the Banquet: Slavery, Federalism, and Habeas Corpus for State Prisoners." *Tulane Law Review* 70 (November 1995): 1–71.

Avella, Steven M. *In the Richness of the Earth: History of the Archdiocese of Milwaukee, 1843–1958.* Milwaukee: Marquette University Press, 2002.

Baker, Howard Robert, II. "The Rescue of Joshua Glover: Lawyers, Popular Constitutionalism, and the Fugitive Slave Law in Wisconsin." Ph.D. diss., University of California, Los Angeles, 2004.

Beattie, John. *Crime and the Courts in England, 1660–1800.* Princeton, N.J.: Princeton University Press, 1986.

Beitzinger, Alfons J. *Edward G. Ryan: Lion of the Law.* Madison: State Historical Society of Wisconsin, 1960.

———. "Federal Law Enforcement and the Booth Cases." *Marquette Law Review* 41 (Summer 1957): 7–32.

Belz, Herman. "Deep-Conviction Jurisprudence and *Texas v. White:* A Comment on G. Edward White's Historicist Interpretation of Chief Justice Chase." *Northern Kentucky University Law Review* 21 (Fall 1993): 117–31.

Berlin, Ira. *Generations of Captivity: A History of African-American Slaves.* Cambridge, Mass.: Harvard University Press, Belknap Press 2003.

Bestor, Arthur. "State Sovereignty and Slavery: A Reinterpretation of Proslavery Constitutional Doctrine, 1846–1860." *Journal of the Illinois State Historical Society* 54 (Summer 1961): 170–81

Bilotta, James D. *Race and the Rise of the Republican Party, 1848–1865.* New York: Peter Lang, 1992.

Birdoff, Harry. *The World's Greatest Hit: Uncle Tom's Cabin.* New York,: S. F. Vanni, 1947.

Brown, Richard Maxwell. *Strain of Violence: Historical Studies of American Violence and Vigilantism.* New York: Oxford University Press, 1977.

Burke, Joseph C. "What Did the Prigg Decision Really Decide?" *Pennsylvania Magazine of History and Biography* 93 (January 1969): 73–85.

Butler, Diane S. "The Public Life and Private Affairs of Sherman M. Booth." *Wisconsin Magazine of History* 82 (Spring 1999): 167–97.

Byrne, Frank L. "Maine Law versus Lager Beer: A Dilemma of Wisconsin's Young Republican Party." *Wisconsin Magazine of History* 42 (Winter 1958–59): 115–23.

Camp, Bryan. "Law and Politics and Judicial Reform in the 1846 New York Constitutional Convention." Paper presented at the 25th Annual Conference on New York State History, Skidmore College, Saratoga Springs, N.Y., June 10–12, 2004.

Campbell, Stanley W. *The Slave Catchers: Enforcement of the Fugitive Slave Law, 1850–1860.* New York: W. W. Norton, 1970.

Censer, Jack, and Lynn Hunt. "Imaging the French Revolution: Depictions of the French Revolutionary Crowd." *American Historical Review* 110 (February 2005): 38–45.

Clark, Elizabeth B. "'The Sacred Rights of the Weak': Pain, Sympathy, and the Culture of Individual Rights in Antebellum America." *Journal of American History* 82 (September 1995): 463–93.

Collinson, Gary. "Anti-Slavery, Blacks, and the Boston Elite: Notes on the Reverend Charles Lowell and the West Church." *New England Quarterly* 61 (September 1988): 419–29.

———. *Shadrach Minkins: From Fugitive Slave to Citizen.* Cambridge, Mass.: Harvard University Press, 1997.

———. "'This Flagitious Offense': Daniel Webster and the Shadrach Rescue Cases, 1851–1852." *New England Quarterly* 68 (December 1995): 609–25.

Conzen, Kathleen N. *Immigrant Milwaukee, 1836–1870: Accommodation and Community in a Frontier City.* Cambridge, Mass.: Harvard University Press, 1976.

Cooper, Zachary. *Black Settlers in Rural Wisconsin.* Madison: State Historical Society of Wisconsin, 1977.

Cornell, Saul. *The Other Founders: Anti-Federalism and the Dissenting Tradition in America, 1788–1828.* Chapel Hill: University of North Carolina Press, 1999.

Cott, Nancy F. "Marriage and Women's Citizenship in the United States, 1830–1934." *American Historical Review* 103 (December 1998): 1440–74.

Countryman, Edward. *The American Revolution.* New York: Hill and Wang, 1984.

Cover, Robert M. *Justice Accused: Antislavery and the Judicial Process.* New Haven, Conn.: Yale University Press, 1975.

Cronon, William. *Nature's Metropolis: Chicago and the Great West.* New York: W. W. Norton, 1991.

Cunningham, Noble E. *The Process of Government under Jefferson.* Princeton, N.J.: Princeton University Press, 1978.

Current, Richard N. *History of Wisconsin.* Vol. 2. *The Civil War Era, 1848–1873.* Madison: State Historical Society of Wisconsin, 1976.

Currie, David P. *The Constitution in Congress: The Federalist Period, 1789–1801.* Chicago: University of Chicago Press, 1997.

———. *The Constitution in Congress: The Jeffersonians, 1801–1829.* Chicago: University of Chicago Press, 2001.

Davis, David Brion. "The Emergence of Immediatism in British and American Antislavery Thought." *Mississippi Valley Historical Review* 49 (September 1962): 209–30.

———. *The Problem of Slavery in the Age of Revolution 1770–1823.* Ithaca, N.Y.: Cornell University Press, 1975.

Desan, Suzanne. "Crowds, Community, and Ritual in the Work of E. P. Thompson and Natalie Davis." In *The New Cultural History,* edited by Lynn Hunt, 47–71. Berkeley: University of California Press, 1989.

Deyle, Steven. "The Ironies of Liberty: Origins of the Domestic Slave Trade." *Journal of the Early Republic* 12 (Spring 1992): 37–62.

Drew, Richard. "The Surge and Consolidation of American Judicial Power: Judicial Review in the States, 1840–1880." Paper presented at the annual meeting of the American Political Science Association, Chicago, Ill., September 2–4, 2004.

Ellis, Richard E. *The Union at Risk: Jacksonian Democracy, States' Rights, and the Nullification Crisis.* New York: Oxford University Press, 1987.

Fehrenbacher, Don E. *The Dred Scott Case: Its Significance in American Law and Politics.* New York: Oxford University Press, 1978.

———. *The Slaveholding Republic: An Account of the United States Government's Relations to Slavery.* New York: Oxford University Press, 2001.

Feldberg, Michael. *The Philadelphia Riots of 1844: A Study of Ethnic Conflict.* Westport, Conn.: Greenwood, 1975.

Finkelman, Paul. "Fugitive Slaves, Midwestern Racial Tolerance, and the Value of 'Justice Delayed.'" *Iowa Law Review* 78 (October 1992): 89–141.

———. *An Imperfect Union: Slavery, Federalism, and Comity.* Chapel Hill: University of North Carolina Press, 1981.

———. "The Kidnapping of John Davis and the Adoption of the Fugitive Slave Law of 1793." *Journal of Southern History* 56 (August 1990): 397–422.

———. "Prelude to the Fourteenth Amendment: Black Legal Rights in the Antebellum North." *Rutgers Law Journal* 17 (Spring and Summer 1986): 415–82.

———. "*Prigg v. Pennsylvania* and Northern State Courts: Anti-Slavery Use of a Pro-Slavery Decision." *Civil War History* 25 (March 1979): 5–35.

———. "Slavery and the Constitutional Convention: Making a Covenant with Death." In *Beyond Confederation: Origins of the Constitution and American National Identity,* edited by Richard Beeman, Stephen Botein, and Edward C. Carter II, 188–225. Chapel Hill: University of North Carolina Press, 1987.

———. *Slavery and the Founders: Race and Liberty in the Age of Jefferson.* 2d. ed. Armonk, N.Y.: M. E. Sharpe, 2001.

———. *Slavery in the Courtroom: An Annotated Bibliography of American Cases.* Washington, D.C.: Library of Congress, 1985.

———. "Sorting Out *Prigg v. Pennsylvania.*" *Rutgers Law Journal* 24 (Spring 1993): 605–65.

———. "State Constitutional Protections of Liberty and the Antebellum New Jersey Supreme Court: Chief Justice Hornblower and the Fugitive Slave Law." *Rutgers Law Journal* 23 (Summer 1992): 753–87.

———. "Story Telling on the Supreme Court: *Prigg v. Pennsylvania* and Justice Joseph Story's Judicial Nationalism." *Supreme Court Review* 1994: 247–94.

Foner, Eric. *Free Soil, Free Labor, Free Men: The Ideology of the Republican Party before the Civil War.* 1970. Reprint, with new introduction, New York: Oxford University Press, 1995.

———. "Politics and Prejudice: The Free Soil Party and the Negro, 1849–1852." *Journal of Negro History* 50 (October 1965): 239–56.

Foster, Charles. *The Rungless Ladder: Harriet Beecher Stowe and New England Puritanism.* Durham, N.C.: Duke University Press, 1954.

Fredrickson, George M. *The Black Image in the White Mind: The Debate on Afro-American Character and Destiny, 1817–1914.* New York: Harper and Row, 1971.

Freyer, Tony. *The Little Rock Crisis: A Constitutional Interpretation.* Westport, Conn.: Greenwood, 1984.

———. "The Past as Future: The Little Rock Crisis and the Constitution." In *Understanding the Little Rock Crisis: An Exercise in Remembrance and Reconciliation,* edited by Elizabeth Jacoway and C. Fred Williams, 141–52. Fayetteville: University of Arkansas Press, 1999.

Friedman, Barry. "The History of the Countermajoritarian Difficulty, Part One: The Road to Judicial Supremacy." *New York University Law Review* 73 (May 1998): 333–432.

Gara, Larry. *The Liberty Line: The Legend of the Underground Railroad.* 1961. Reprint, with new preface. Lexington: University of Kentucky Press, 1996.

———. *The Presidency of Franklin Pierce.* Lawrence: University Press of Kansas, 1991.

Gienapp, William E. *The Origins of the Republican Party, 1852–1856.* New York: Oxford University Press, 1987.

Gilje, Paul A. *Rioting in America.* Bloomington: Indiana University Press, 1996.

————. *The Road to Mobocracy: Popular Disorder in New York City, 1763–1834.* Chapel Hill: Published for the Institute of Early American History and Culture by the University of North Carolina Press, 1987.

Ginzberg, Lori D. *Women and the Work of Benevolence: Morality, Politics, and Class in the Nineteenth-Century United States.* New Haven, Conn.: Yale University Press, 1990.

Goldstein, Leslie Friedman. "State Resistance to Authority in Federal Unions: The Early United States (1790–1860) and the European Community (1958–94)." *Studies in American Political Development* 11 (Spring 1997): 149–89.

Goshgarian, G. M. *To Kiss the Chastening Rod: Domestic Fiction and Sexual Ideology in the American Renaissance.* Ithaca, N.Y.: Cornell University Press, 1992.

Gossett, Thomas F. *Uncle Tom's Cabin and American Culture.* Dallas, Tex.: Southern Methodist University Press, 1985.

Grace, Adam S. "From the Lighthouses: How the First Federal Internal Improvement Projects Created Precedent That Broadened the Commerce Clause, Shrunk the Takings Clause, and Affected Early Nineteenth Century Constitutional Debate." *Albany Law Review* 68, no. 1 (2004): 97–153.

Grant, Marilyn. "Judge Levi Hubbell: A Man Impeached." *Wisconsin Magazine of History* 64 (Autumn 1980): 28–39.

Gregory, John G. *History of Milwaukee, Wisconsin.* Chicago: S. J. Clarke, 1931.

Grimsted, David. *American Mobbing, 1828–1861: Toward Civil War.* New York: Oxford University Press, 1998.

————. "Rioting in Its Jacksonian Setting." *American Historical Review* 77 (April 1972): 361–97.

————. "Uncle Tom from Page to Stage: Limitations of Nineteenth-Century Drama." *Quarterly Journal of Speech* 56 (October1970): 235–44.

Hall, Kermit L. "The Constitutional Lessons of the Little Rock Crisis." In *Understanding the Little Rock Crisis: An Exercise in Remembrance and Reconciliation,* edited by Elizabeth Jacoway and C. Fred Williams, 123–40. Fayetteville: University of Arkansas Press, 1999.

Harrington, Matthew P. "The Law-Finding Function of the American Jury." In "The American Jury," special issue, *Wisconsin Law Review* 1999: 377–440.

Hartman, Saidiya V. *Scenes of Subjection: Terror, Slavery, and Self-Making in Nineteenth-Century America.* New York: Oxford University Press, 1997.

Hartnett, Stephen John. *Democratic Dissent and the Cultural Fictions of Antebellum America.* Urbana: University of Illinois Press, 2002.

Hartog, Hendrik. "The Constitution of Aspiration and 'The Rights That Belong to Us All.'" *Journal of American History* 74 (December 1987): 1013–34.

————. *Man and Wife in America: A History.* Cambridge, Mass.: Harvard University Press, 2000.

Haskell, Thomas L. "Capitalism and the Origins of Humanitarian Sensibility, Part 2." *American Historical Review* 90 (June 1985): 547–66.

Hirsch, Stephen A. "Uncle Tomitudes: The Popular Reaction to *Uncle Tom's Cabin.*" In *Studies in the American Renaissance,* edited by Joel Myerson, 303–30. Boston: Twayne, 1978.

History of Milwaukee, Wisconsin. Chicago: Western Historical Company, 1881.

Hodder, Frank H. "The Railroad Background of the Kansas-Nebraska Act." *Mississippi Valley Historical Review* 12 (June 1925): 3–22.

Hoffer, Peter Charles. "Custom as Law: A Comment on J. R. Pole's 'Reflections.'" *William and Mary Quarterly* 50 (January 1993): 160–67.

Holt, Michael F. *The Political Crisis of the 1850s.* New York: W. W. Norton, 1978.

Holzheuter, John O. "Ezekiel Gillespie, Lost and Found." *Wisconsin Magazine of History* 60 (Spring 1977): 179–84.

Horton, James Oliver. *Free People of Color: Inside the African American Community.* Washington, D.C.: Smithsonian Institution Press, 1993.

Horton, Lois E. "Kidnapping and Resistance: Antislavery Direct Action in the 1850s." In *Passages to Freedom: The Underground Railroad in History and Memory,* edited by David W. Blight, 149–73. Washington, D.C.: Smithsonian Books, 2004.

Hulsebosch, Daniel J. "The Ancient Constitution and the Expanding Empire: Sir Edward Coke's British Jurisprudence." *Law and History Review* 21 (Fall 2003): 439–82.

———. "Book Review: Bringing the People Back In: *The People Themselves: Popular Constitutionalism and Judicial Review,* by Larry D. Kramer." *New York University Law Review* 80 (May 2005): 653–92.

Hurst, James Willard. *Law and the Conditions of Freedom in the Nineteenth-Century United States.* Madison: University of Wisconsin Press, 1956.

Jessup, Dwight Wiley. *Reaction and Accommodation: The United States Supreme Court and Political Conflict, 1809–1835.* New York: Garland, 1987.

Jordan, Winthrop D. *White over Black: American Attitudes toward the Negro, 1550–1812.* Chapel Hill: University of North Carolina Press, 1968.

Kaczorowski, Robert J. "The Inverted Constitution: Enforcing Constitutional Rights in the Nineteenth Century." In *Constitutionalism and American Culture: Writing the New Constitutional History,* edited by Sandra F. VanBurkleo, Kermit L. Hall, and Robert J. Kaczorowski, 29–63. Lawrence: University Press of Kansas, 2002.

———. "Popular Constitutionalism versus Justice in Plainclothes: Reflections from History." *Fordham Law Review* 73 (March 2005): 1415–38.

Kettner, James H. *The Development of American Citizenship, 1608–1870.* Chapel Hill: University of North Carolina Press, 1978.

Klafter, Craig Evan. *Reason over Precedents: Origins of American Legal Thought.* Westport, Conn.: Greenwood, 1993.

Kramer, Larry D. "But When Exactly Was Judicially-Enforced Federalism 'Born' in the First Place?" *Harvard Journal of Law and Public Policy* 22 (1998): 123–37.

———. *The People Themselves: Popular Constitutionalism and Judicial Review.* New York: Oxford University Press, 2004.

Langill, Ellen D. *Foley & Lardner: Attorneys at Law, 1842–1992.* Madison: State Historical Society of Wisconsin, 1992.

Levy, Leonard W. "Sims' Case: The Fugitive Slave Law in Boston in 1851." *Journal of Negro History* 35 (January 1950): 39–74.

Litwack, Leon F. *North of Slavery: The Negro in the Free States, 1790–1860.* Chicago: University of Chicago Press, 1961.

Lott, Eric. *Love and Theft: Blackface Minstrelsy and the American Working Class.* New York: Oxford University Press, 1993.

Maier, Pauline. "Popular Uprisings and Civil Authority in Eighteenth-Century America." *William and Mary Quarterly* 27 (January 1970): 3–35.

Maltz, Earl M. "The Idea of the Proslavery Constitution." *Journal of the Early Republic* 17 (Spring 1997): 37–59.

———. "Slavery, Federalism, and the Structure of the Constitution." *American Journal of Legal History* 36 (October 1992): 466–98.

Marcus, Maeva. "Judicial Review in the Early Republic." In *Launching the "Extended Republic": The Federalist Era,* edited by Ronald Hoffman and Peter J. Albert, 25–53. Charlottesville: Published for the United States Capitol Historical Society by the University Press of Virginia, 1996.

Mason, Vroman. "The Fugitive Slave Law in Wisconsin, with Reference to Nullification Sentiment." *Proceedings of the State Historical Society of Wisconsin* 43 (1895): 117–44.

McDonald, Forrest. *States' Rights and the Union:* Imperium in Imperio, *1776–1876.* American Political Thought. Lawrence: University Press of Kansas, 2000.

McInerney, Daniel John. *The Fortunate Heirs of Freedom: Abolition and Republican Thought.* Lincoln: University of Nebraska Press, 1994.

McManus, Michael J. "'Freedom and Liberty First, and the Union Afterwards': State Rights and the Wisconsin Republican Party, 1854–1861." In *Union and Emancipation: Essays on Politics and Race in the Civil War Era,* edited by David W. Blight and Brooks D. Simpson, 29–56. Kent, Ohio: Kent State University Press, 1997.

———. *Political Abolitionism in Wisconsin, 1840–1861.* Kent, Ohio: Kent State University Press, 1998.

———. "Wisconsin Republicans and Negro Suffrage." *Civil War History* 25 (March 1979): 36–54.

McPherson, James M. *Battle Cry of Freedom: The Civil War Era.* New York: Ballantine Books, 1988.

Melhorn, Donald F. *"Lest We Be Marshall'd": Judicial Powers and Politics in Ohio, 1806–1812.* Akron, Ohio: University of Akron Press, 2003.

Meyer, Michael J. "Toward a Rhetoric of Equality: Reflective and Refractive Images in Stowe's Language." In *The Stowe Debate: Rhetorical Strategies in Uncle Tom's Cabin,* edited by Mason I. Lowance, Ellen E. Westbrook, and R. C. De Prospo, 236–54. Amherst: University of Massachusetts Press, 1994.

Middleton, Stephen. *The Black Laws: Race and the Legal Process in Early Ohio.* Athens: Ohio University Press, 2005.

Morris, Thomas D. *Free Men All: The Personal Liberty Laws of the North, 1780–1861.* Baltimore: Johns Hopkins University Press, 1974.

————. *Southern Slavery and the Law, 1619–1860*. Chapel Hill: University of North Carolina Press, 1996.

Nash, Gary B. *Race and Revolution*. Madison, Wis.: Madison House, 1990.

Nelson, William E. "*Marbury v. Madison* and the Rule of Law." *Tennessee Law Review* 71 (Winter 2004): 217–39.

Nesbit, Robrcri C. *Wisconsin: A History*. Madison: University of Wisconsin Press, 1973.

Newmyer, R. Kent. *John Marshall and the Heroic Age of the Supreme Court*. Baton Rouge: Louisiana State University Press, 2001.

————. *Supreme Court Justice Joseph Story: Statesman of the Old Republic*. Chapel Hill: University of North Carolina Press, 1985.

Nichols, Roy F. "The Kansas-Nebraska Act: A Century of Historiography." *Mississippi Valley Historical Review* 43 (June 1956): 187–212.

Novak, William J. "The Legal Transformation of Citizenship in Nineteenth-Century America." In *The Democratic Experiment: New Directions in American Political History*, edited by Meg Jacobs, William J. Novak, and Julian E. Zelizer, 85–119. Princeton, N.J.: Princeton University Press, 2003.

————. *The People's Welfare: Law and Regulation in Nineteenth-Century America*. Chapel Hill: University of North Carolina Press, 1996.

Noyes, Edward. "A Negro in Mid-nineteenth Century Wisconsin Life and Politics." *Wisconsin Academy Review* 15 (Fall 1968): 2–6.

Orren, Karen. "'A War between Officers': The Enforcement of Slavery in the Northern United States, and of the Republic for Which It Stands, before the Civil War." *Studies in American Political Development* 12 (Fall 1998): 343–82.

Padgett, Chris. "Comeouterism and Antislavery Violence in Ohio's Western Reserve." In *Antislavery Violence: Sectional, Racial, and Cultural Conflict in Antebellum America*, edited by John R. McKivigan and Stanley Harrold, 193–214. Knoxville: University of Tennessee Press, 1999.

Parrish, Jenni. "The *Booth* Cases: Final Step to the Civil War." *Willamette Law Review* 29 (Spring 1993): 237–78.

Pepper, David A. "Nullifying History: Modern-Day Misuse of the Right to Decide the Law." *Case Western Reserve Law Review* 50 (Spring 2000): 599–643.

Pocock, J. G. A. *The Ancient Constitution and the Feudal Law: A Study of English Historical Thought in the Seventeenth Century; A Reissue with a Retrospect*. New York: Cambridge University Press, 1987.

Pole, J. R. "Reflections on American Law and the American Revolution." *William and Mary Quarterly* 50 (January 1993): 123–59.

Powe, L. A., Jr. "Are 'the People' Missing in Action (and Should Anyone Care)?: *The People Themselves: Popular Constitutionalism and Judicial Review*." *Texas Law Review* 83 (February 2005): 855–95.

Rakove, Jack N. *Original Meanings: Politics and Ideas in the Making of the Constitution*. New York: Vintage Books, 1997.

————. "The Origins of Judicial Review: A Plea for New Contexts." *Stanford Law Review* 49 (May 1997): 1031–64.

Ranney, Joseph A. *Trusting Nothing to Providence: A History of Wisconsin's Legal System*. Madison: University of Wisconsin Law School Continuing Education and Outreach, 1999.

Reed, Parker McCobb. *The Bench and Bar of Wisconsin: History and Biography, with Portrait Illustrations*. Milwaukee, Wis.: Reed, 1882.

Reid, John Phillip. *The Constitutional History of the American Revolution*. Vol. 2, *The Authority of Rights*. Madison: University of Wisconsin Press, 1986.

———. *The Constitutional History of the American Revolution*. Vol. 3, *The Authority to Legislate*. Madison: University of Wisconsin Press, 1991.

———. *In a Rebellious Spirit: The Argument of Facts, the Liberty Riot, and the Coming of the American Revolution*. University Park: Pennsylvania State University Press, 1979.

Rippley, La Vern J. *The Immigrant Experience in Wisconsin*. Boston: Twayne, 1985.

Roediger, David. *The Wages of Whiteness*. London: Verso, 1991.

Rohrbough, Malcolm J. *The Trans-Appalachian Frontier: People, Societies, and Institutions, 1775–1850*. New York: Oxford University Press, 1978.

Ross, Dorothy. "Historical Consciousness in Nineteenth-Century America." *American Historical Review* 89 (October 1984): 909–28.

Rudé, George F. E. *The Crowd in History: A Study of Popular Disturbances in France and England, 1730–1848*. New York: Wiley, 1964.

Ruger, Theodore W. "'A Question Which Convulses a Nation': The Early Republic's Greatest Debate about the Judicial Review Power." *Harvard Law Review* 117 (January 2004): 826–97.

Russel, Robert R. "The Issues in the Congressional Struggle over the Kansas-Nebraska Bill, 1854." *Journal of Southern History* 29 (May 1963): 187–210.

Samuels, Shirley, ed. *The Culture of Sentiment: Race, Gender, and Sentimentality in Nineteenth-Century America*. New York: Oxford University Press, 1992.

Schafer, Joseph. "Know-Nothingism in Wisconsin." *Wisconsin Magazine of History* 8 (September 1924): 3–21.

———. "Stormy Days in Court: The Booth Case." *Wisconsin Magazine of History* 20 (September 1936): 89–110.

———. "The Yankee and the Teuton in Wisconsin." *Wisconsin Magazine of History* 7 (December 1923): 148–71.

Sebok, Anthony J. "Judging the Fugitive Slave Acts." *Yale Law Journal* 100 (April 1991): 1835–54.

Sellers, James L. "Republicanism and State Rights in Wisconsin." *Mississippi Valley Historical Review* 17 (September 1930): 213–29.

Smith, Kimberly K. *The Dominion of Voice: Riot, Reason, and Romance in Antebellum Politics*. Lawrence: University Press of Kansas, 1999.

Smith, Rogers M. *Civic Ideals: Conflicting Visions of Citizenship in U.S. History*. New Haven, Conn.: Yale University Press, 1997.

Snowiss, Sylvia. *Judicial Review and the Law of the Constitution*. New Haven, Conn.: Yale University Press, 1990.

Sosin, Jack M. *The Aristocracy of the Long Robe: The Origins of Judicial Review in America.* New York: Greenwood, 1989.

Stachiw, Myron O. "'For the Sake of Commerce': Slavery, Antislavery, and Northern Industry." In *The Meaning of Slavery in the North,* edited by David Roediger and Martin H. Blatt, 33–44. New York: Garland, 1998.

Stegmaier, Mark J. *Texas, New Mexico, and the Compromise of 1850: Boundary Dispute and Sectional Crisis.* Kent, Ohio: Kent State University Press, 1996.

Stewart, James Brewer. "From Moral Suasion to Political Confrontation: American Abolitionists and the Problem of Resistance, 1831–1861." In *Passages to Freedom: The Underground Railroad in History and Memory,* edited by David W. Blight, 67–92. Washington, D.C.: Smithsonian Books, 2004.

Stickles, Arndt M. *The Critical Court Struggle in Kentucky, 1819–1829.* Bloomington: Indiana University, 1929.

Streichler, Stuart. *Justice Curtis in the Civil War Era: At the Crossroads of American Constitutionalism.* Charlottesville: University of Virginia Press, 2005.

Taylor, Michael J. C. "'A More Perfect Union': *Ableman v. Booth* and the Culmination of Federal Sovereignty." *Journal of Supreme Court History* 28 (July 2003): 101–15.

Taylor, Nikki M. *Frontiers of Freedom: Cincinnati's Black Community, 1802–1868.* Athens: Ohio University Press, 2005.

Thompson, Edward P. "The Moral Economy of the English Crowd in the Eighteenth Century." Chapter 4 in *Customs in Common.* New York: New Press, 1993.

Thompson, John P. *The Fugitive Slave Bill: Its History and Unconstitutionality; With an Account of the Seizure and Enslavement of James Hamlet, and His Subsequent Restoration to Liberty.* New York: William Harned, 1850.

Toll, Robert C. *Blacking Up: The Minstrel Show in Nineteenth Century America.* New York: Oxford University Press, 1974.

Tomlins, Christopher L. *Law, Labor, and Ideology in the Early American Republic.* New York: Cambridge University Press, 1993.

Utter, William T. "Judicial Review in Early Ohio." *Mississippi Valley Historical Review* 14 (June 1927): 3–24.

Van Deburg, William L. *Slavery and Race in American Popular Culture.* Madison: University of Wisconsin Press, 1984.

Volpe, Vernon L. *Forlorn Hope of Freedom: The Liberty Party in the Old Northwest, 1838–1848.* Kent, Ohio: Kent State University Press, 1990.

Von Frank, Albert J. *The Trials of Anthony Burns: Freedom and Slavery in Emerson's Boston.* Cambridge, Mass.: Harvard University Press, 1998.

Waldstreicher, David. *In the Midst of Perpetual Fetes: The Making of American Nationalism, 1776–1820.* Chapel Hill: University of North Carolina Press, 1997.

Warren, Charles. *The Supreme Court in United States History.* Rev. ed. Littleton, Colo.: F. B. Rothman, 1987.

———. *The Supreme Court of the United States History.* Rev. ed. 2 vols. Boston: Little, Brown, 1937.

Weinberg, Louise. "Methodological Interventions and the Slavery Cases; Or, Night-Thoughts of a Legal Realist." *Maryland Law Review* 56, no. 4 (1997): 1316–70.

White, G. Edward. *The History of the Supreme Court of the United States: Volumes III–IV, the Marshall Court and Cultural Change, 1815–1835.* New York: Macmillan, 1988.

———. "Reconstructing the Constitutional Jurisprudence of Salmon P. Chase." *Northern Kentucky University Law Review* 21 (Fall 1993): 41–116.

Wiecek, William M. "'Old Times There Are Not Forgotten': The Distinctiveness of the Southern Constitutional Experience." In *An Uncertain Tradition: Constitutionalism and the History of the South,* edited by Kermit L. Hall and James W. Ely, 159–97. Athens: University of Georgia Press, 1989.

———. "Slavery and Abolition before the United States Supreme Court, 1820–1860." *Journal of American History* 65 (June 1978): 34–59.

———. *The Sources of Antislavery Constitutionalism in America, 1760–1848.* Ithaca, N.Y.: Cornell University Press, 1977.

———. "The Witch at the Christening: Slavery and the Constitution's Origins." In *The Framing and Ratification of the Constitution,* edited by Leonard W. Levy and Dennis J. Mahoney, 167–84. New York: Macmillan, 1987.

Wilson, Carol. *Freedom at Risk: The Kidnapping of Free Blacks in America, 1780–1865.* Lexington: University Press of Kentucky, 1994.

Winslow, John Bradley. *The Story of a Great Court.* Chicago: T. H. Flood, 1912.

Wolfe, Christopher. *The Rise of Modern Judicial Review: From Constitutional Interpretation to Judge-Made Law.* Rev. ed. Lanham, Md.: Rowman and Littlefield, 1994.

Wood, Gordon S. *The Creation of the American Republic, 1776–1787.* 2d ed. Chapel Hill: University of North Carolina Press, 1998.

———. "The Origins of Judicial Review Revisited, or How the Marshall Court Made More out of Less." *Washington and Lee Law Review* 56 (Summer 1999): 787–809.

———. *The Radicalism of the American Revolution.* New York: Vintage Books, 1991.

Wright, Conrad Edick. *The Transformation of Charity in Postrevolutionary New England.* Boston: Northeastern University Press, 1992.

Yarborough, Richard. "Strategies of Black Characterization in *Uncle Tom's Cabin* and the Early Afro-American Novel." In *New Essays on Uncle Tom's Cabin,* edited by Eric J. Sundquist, 45–84. Cambridge: Cambridge University Press, 1986.

INDEX

Page numbers in italics refer to illustrations.

kidnapping
  congressional consideration of, 32, 33,
    34, 35, 56
  of free blacks, 31–32, 199n33
  slave catchers accused of, 66, 77, 83,
    99, 151, 213n16
  states' duty to prevent, 36, 38, 40, 43,
    46, 57, 128–29, 148
  versus legitimate reclamation, 41, 44,
    92–94, 99, 185
  See also personal liberty laws; *Prigg v.*
    Pennsylvania
King, Rufus, 12, 19, 20, 74, 92, 101, 134,
    135, 142, 145, 152–56, 194n54
Knoop, Piqua Branch of the State Bank of
    Ohio v., 204n91
Knorr v. Home Insurance Company of New
    York, 162
Know Nothing Party, 139–42, 144,
    226–7nn23–24, 227n33. *See also* na-
    tivism
Kramer, Larry, 200n41, 220n30, 225n12
Ku Klux Klan (KKK), 180, 185

Lakin, George, 97–98, 215n40
legislature, Wisconsin, 153, 170, 232n17
  and black suffrage, 59, 69, 151–53, 173,
    229n67
  and civil rights, 68, 171, 209n35
  elections for, 136–37, 142, 145
  and personal liberty law, 148–49, 169,
    171
  Resolves of '59, 155–56
  states' rights, retreat from, 167, 172
  and temperance. *See* Maine Law
Lemley, Harry J., 181–82
Liberty Party, 8, 114, 116, 136
Livingston, Edward, 32
Livingston v. Van Ingen, 201n55
Lynde, William Pitt, 48, 154, 157, 159, 164

Madison, James, 28, 33, 118, 121, 131,
    158–59, 174, 219n17, 220n28, 221n35,
    221n37. *See also* popular constitution-
    alism; "Report of 1800"; Virginia
    and Kentucky Resolutions
Maine Law, 139–40, 142. *See also* anti-
    slavery movement
Marshall, John, 46, 126, 127
Martin, In re, 42–43, 201n57
Martin, Jack v., 41, 42, 43, 201n57
Maryland, McCulloch v., 126
Mason, James, 50–51

mass meetings. *See under* crowd action
McCulloch v. Maryland, 126
McLean, John, 127, 128–29
McManus, Michael J., 153, 224n6,
    227n24, 229n67
Messinger, John, 23, 96, 195n67
Miller, Andrew Galbraith, *84*, 112, 129,
    195n58
  and arrest of Joshua Glover, 2–10,
    18–22, 89, 94, 189n1
  Fugitive Slave Act, opinion on, 98–100,
    135–36, 141
  habeas corpus, opinion on, 83–85, 94,
    135–36, 212n2, 212n4
  and trials of John Ryecraft and Sher-
    man Booth, 96–110, 215n40,
    216–17n69
Miln, New York v., 126, 222n53, 222n55,
    222n60
Mingus, Charles, 178–81, 186, 188
Minkins, Shadrach. *See* Shadrach
minstrelsy
  advertisements for, 58, 211n67
  description of, 59, 72–73, 210n65
  influence of, on popular perceptions of
    blacks, 72–74, 78, 152–53, 211n73
Missouri Compromise, 4, 150, 128–29n55
mobs. *See* crowd action
Moore v. Illinois, 47
Morris, Timothy D., 3, 83
Murphy, Newton S., 155

nativism, 15–16, 140–41, 142–43, 191n24.
    See also Know Nothing Party
Nelson, Samuel, 19, 41–42, 43, 44, 195n58
New York v. Miln, 126, 222n53, 222n55,
    222n60
Noland, William H., 77, 152
Northwest Ordinance, 29, 115
nullification, doctrine of, 122, 138, 139,
    146, 147, 161, 171, 172, 217–18n81

Ogden, Gibbons v., 126, 222n53
Ohio, Birney v., 114–16
Olin, Chauncey C., 64
Original American Harmoneon
    Ethiopian Opera Troupe. *See* min-
    strelsy
Orren, Karen, 203n78

Padelford v. Savannah, 231n2
Page, Herman L., 13, 17, 18, 21, 24, 80,
    112, 149

Thompson, Edward P., 192nn32–33
Thompson, Smith, 42–43, 201n57, 222n55
Tompkins, Johnson v., 41
Toombs, Robert, 163–64, 231n2
Toucey, Isaac, 54
trial by jury
    constitutional right to, 19–21, 35, 70, 76, 92–94, 119, 163–64
    history of, 9–10
    and jury nullification, 82, 97, 102, 106–7, 109, 122, 139, 217nn75–77, 217–18n81, 218n83
    suspension by Fugitive Slave Act, 37, 39, 40, 48, 52, 56–57, 115, 117, 118–20, 125, 155
    See also antislavery movement; Booth cases; citizenship; personal liberty laws
Uncle Tom's Cabin (Stowe), 59–63
    criticism of, 61–62, 63, 207n9
    depictions of blacks in, 61–62, 206n6
    dramatic adaptations of, 59, 62, 73
    influence of, 60, 64, 66, 71, 78
    See also sentimentalism
Underground Railroad, 23, 48–49, 58, 63, 65. *See also* antislavery movement
United States v. cases. *See name of opposing party*

Van Buren, Martin, 18, 84
Van Ingen, Livingston v., 201n55
Van Zandt, Jones v., 48, 117, 203n85

violence, 12–17, 177, 180, 187, 214n24
    absence in Glover rescue, 23, 86, 186, 195n69
    in antislavery movement, 41, 49, 53–56, 91, 101, 132, 144, 168, 186
    and recaption of fugitive slaves, 28, 85, 189–90n4, 212n2
    in riots, 12–17, 191–92n31, 192n33, 213n7
    and slavery, connection in antislavery rhetoric, 62, 75, 82, 90–91, 97–98, 104, 106–8, 144, 165, 170–71, 184
    See also crowd action; Glover, Joshua
Virginia and Kentucky Resolutions, 118, 120–21, 132, 138, 146, 158, 219n17

Walworth, Reuben, 43, 44, 46
Washington, George, 31, 54
Washington, Lewis, 64
Watkins, Charles, 22, 73, 83, 85, 92, 93, 94, 103, 114
Webster, Daniel, 50, 53, 205n106
Weimer v. Sloane, 212n2
Weinberg, Louise, 225n17
Wells, Daniel,   136
Whiton, Edward, 119, 120, 123, 124, 129, 130, 131, 134, 148, 160, 166
Whiton v. Chicago & Northwestern Railroad Company, 174
Wilson, U.S. v., 218n83 (chap. 4), 218n7
Wolcott, Edward B., 17, 18, 21, 92, 103
Woodbury, Levi, 48, 203
Wright v. Deacon, 38